I HATE PIÑATAS

Surviving Life's Unexpected Surprises

HEATHER MALOY

I Hate Piñatas
Copyright © 2015 by Heather Maloy

First edition, published January, 2015

Edited by Sarah Nawrocki
Cover art by Brook Rosser
Interior layout by Author's HQ

This book is true and correct based on my memory of the events and how they transpired. The names of people and certain institutions have been changed to protect the wicked. (Don't get your undies in a twist. I'm referring to myself.)

For my boys.

Introduction

I'm a planner. I like to be in control. I think the fates or God or whatever entity rules the universe know this about me. That's why I ended up with an amazing husband, a nutty mother-in-law and a son who was born with only half a heart. You could say I've had a few wrenches thrown into my life plan. The Powers That Be must have thought it was hilarious.

Kevin and I were married fifteen years ago on the Big Island of Hawaii on the Friday after Thanksgiving. November 26, to be exact. Kevin only remembers that we were married the Friday after Thanksgiving, no matter when that holiday falls. I had no idea the floating holiday concept would be such a difficult one for him to grasp.

As a result, some years he's early in wishing me happy anniversary and others he's late. I think he's been right on the mark twice in the past fifteen years. I find the whole thing pretty amusing, actually. I just feel bad for Kevin. I can see that missing our anniversary induces some sort of panic that I'll be angry with him, but I am one of the biggest scatterbrains I know as far as that kind of stuff goes. Like, just now, I couldn't remember how long we'd been married. I had to do the math. So I wouldn't dare be mad at him for something silly like that.

The main reason I wanted to get married in Hawaii is it's beautiful there. Like I really need to clarify that. But flowers are one of the most expensive items at weddings, and they are everywhere you look in Hawaii. Above all else, I'm practical: Combine the wedding and the honeymoon in a two-week vacation and have someone else do all the planning.

The other huge plus about having a wedding so far away is I was fairly certain no one would come. Don't get me wrong—I love my family. But Kevin and I had a courtship that lasted close to four years, and I just wanted everybody to butt out of my relationship status. I was tired of the "When are y'all going to get married?" question. And I was super tired of hearing my dad say, "Well, why should he buy the cow when he's getting the milk for free?"

Rule number one: Comparing your daughter to a cow is never okay. Besides, what I do with my milk is nobody's business. What I should have said was, "Really? Why should I buy the whole pig for a little piece of sausage?" But I would never compare Kevin to a pig. Or even remotely imply that he has a little sausage. That's just rude and untrue.

My dad's an asshole, plain and simple—a self-proclaimed perfect asshole. (This was verified later by the gastroenterologist who performed his colonoscopy.) When I was in junior high my dad quizzed me about my report card. I had a B in conduct, and he wanted to know why I didn't have an A. Dad always said he didn't care about our grades as long as we had an A in conduct, because that grade showed him we were trying our hardest. (I tested this theory in high school, and it wasn't entirely true, by the way. I had an A in conduct but a 43 in Physical Science, and Dad was pretty steamed.) I told him that my P.E. coach had informed me that she didn't give anyone an A in conduct ever. My dad said, "Well, you tell her you need an A in conduct because your dad is an asshole. A for Asshole." Um, okay, I'll get right on that. It was fucking P.E., for crying out loud. That's not even a real subject.

My father is one of the funniest people I know, and he instilled a great sense of humor in all three of his children—although my humor tends more toward the irreverent. I have him to thank (or blame) for shaping me into the strong woman I've become. I never would have survived what I've been through without the crucial training I underwent as a child.

All of my family is from South Texas—like, the last six generations—and all of Kevin's family lives in northwest Missouri. Because our families are geographically so far apart, I guess everyone figured they would have to travel for our wedding no matter what. We ended up with twenty-six guests, which I thought was quite large considering the distance. I suppose that's what happens when you send out invitations.

I truly wanted our wedding to be just the two of us, but Kevin thought I would eventually regret not having our families in attendance. He's fourteen years older than I am, so I used to defer to him in matters like these. Please notice the use of the past tense. Fifteen years later I am still positive I would have been perfectly satisfied with an elopement.

Kevin is wicked smart and super funny—not life-of-the-party funny, but witty and dry—and it's always when you least expect it. But when he reads that last sentence, he's going to say, "What do you mean I'm not the life of the party?" and get all broody. He's incredibly sensitive. Maybe I'll just tell him this is a chick book. That should ensure he never opens the cover.

I could go on about what a wonderful guy Kevin is, but I'll just hit the high points. He's a criminal defense lawyer, double board certified in criminal and juvenile law. What that means to me is I am married to a lawyer who's really good at what he does and it sucks to get into an argument with him. He has his own practice and loves running his own business. He jokes that he has to work for himself because he is basically unemployable. I would have to agree with that statement as the God's honest truth. Most important, Kevin is a good husband to me and a loving father to our three boys, always quick to encourage them and help them in everything they do.

There are times when he provokes my dark side, though. He probably doesn't even know he does it. Or maybe he does and delights in the sick pleasure of it all. Like when he uses my pink Daisy razor in the shower. It's mine, and it's pink. What kind of person uses someone else's razor? Or when he slurps his soup at supper. For the love of God, stop it! I want to plant my fork right in his Adam's apple. Did I mention that sometimes I feel a tad hostile?

There must be times when I infuriate him—like when I chew my fingernails while we're watching a movie or leave hair in the shower drain and it gets curled around his toes—and he fantasizes about killing me and our kids and going off to Brazil to live with some hot babe who only speaks Portuguese and wears bathing suit bottoms that are completely obscured by her big, bronze buns. And I can't blame him. She sounds like a lot of fun.

I think it's perfectly normal for all married couples to feel this way about each other at some point. I have it on good authority that a lot of women do. In fact, I'm pretty sure my own mother has felt this way about my father several times a week in their forty-some-odd years of wedded bliss. It's your mind's way of blowing off steam. I mean, we can't be ridiculously happy all the time.

If you still doubt me, attend a mom's night out with a bunch of professional thirty-somethings who have infants or toddlers or both. The mothers are positively murderous. It's a wonder any man makes it out of their child's toddler years alive. (Just for the record, if something awful happens to Kevin at the dinner table or in the kitchen, I am innocent.)

Seriously, though, how can anyone eat cereal as loudly as he does? Or slam kitchen cabinets and drawers any louder when the baby is sleeping?

It's not his fault. He can't help it any more than any other human being with a Y chromosome. Don't get me wrong. I adore men. I find that I identify more with males than females. My psychologist, Dr. Z, once said, "Don't take this the wrong way, Heather, because you seem to be very confident and comfortable in your femininity, but I think this might be your first time around on this earth as a woman." I took that as a compliment.

Back to the point I was trying to make. I had a lunch meeting a couple of years ago where a doctor was speaking about stem cell research. It's fascinating, all of the things they can do and will be able to do once they have a better understanding of stem cells. I found it particularly interesting that in order to grow new tissue from stem cells, they can only use female stem cells. The male stem cells just bump into each other and nothing gets accomplished. When they put female stem cells together—presto—new heart valve tissue or whatever it is they're trying to grow.

If you ever need evidence that women are the superior beings, there it is at the cellular level. Sorry I can't give you the science behind it. I'm a court reporter, not a doctor.

Because of that scientific evidence, I give Kevin a break. I don't say anything when he uses my razor, slurps his soup or acts like a bull in a china shop, slamming all the doors and cabinets and banging things that he feels need to be banged in order to work right. Wait. That sounds weird. And he would probably put me in the category of things that need to be banged to act right, but we're not going to talk about that because it's my milk. Remember?

So I'm positive that he can't help it. He would if he could. He doesn't like me to be annoyed with him any more than I like to be annoyed with him. I have three boys. I know what I'm talking about—we've got to give the guys a break every now and then.

And in case you're wondering, I quit serving soup at dinner and I haven't bought cereal in years. Another thing you just discovered about me: I'm a great problem-solver.

CHAPTER 1

We welcomed our first son, Kevin Liam, on June 26, 2002. I wanted to make him Junior, but Kevin thought he needed his own identity. So instead of Kevin Lloyd, he's Kevin Liam.

I'm glad I listened to my husband on that one. I've never been that crazy about "Lloyd" anyway. I loved the name Liam, but I just wasn't feeling it. Every time I thought about that name, I would picture a blond-haired, blue-eyed little boy, and it didn't fit the brown-haired, brown-eyed child who existed in my mind.

I can't tell you the number of times I dreamed I had given birth to a monkey instead of a human baby. Sometimes it was a litter of puppies. Mostly, though, it was a baby monkey. Only once did I dream I had a human baby. He had come early, and I wasn't prepared. I had forgotten to buy diapers. I was holding the infant under the arms, and his little legs were dangling over the bathtub because of the diaper situation. His huge head of coarse, dark hair was parted perfectly down the middle. I kept pleading with Kevin to go to the store, and he kept replying vaguely, "In a minute. I'm in the middle of something."

I was looking at this baby, who kind of reminded me of a Chucky doll, and thinking, This is not at all what I envisioned. He's not even remotely cute. He's actually pretty ugly. I don't even like this baby. That's got to be a bad sign.

I awoke from my nightmare completely exasperated and a little pissed off. I made Kevin promise that if I ever needed him to get diapers, he would drop whatever he was doing and head to the store right away.

When we went for the sonogram at twenty weeks, I was positive that I was having a girl. So when the sonographer said, "Oh, look, there's the penis," I was thinking, Why does my baby girl have a penis? Then it hit me: A boy. A woman's intuition isn't all it's cracked up to be.

It's weird being pregnant for the first time—or maybe it was just weird for me. I don't know. I didn't find it enjoyable at all. I was never miserable or sick, and I never felt hugely fat, but I wouldn't say it was amazing. When women say, "Oh, I just love being pregnant!" I have to make an effort not to roll my eyes. It's a knee-jerk reaction. I'd like to think I'm not that odd. Maybe, just maybe, I'm in the majority on this one.

Kevin and I both have dark hair and eyes, so I was excited to meet our brown-haired, brown-eyed little boy. When both parents have dominant genes, those genes almost always win. Just a little something I remember from high school biology. That's why I insisted on leaving Kevin as our baby's first name—I thought that would fit him better. Also, at that time I didn't know anyone by the name of Liam. Even though Kevin and I are both proud of our Irish heritage, Liam seemed a little ethnic, and I didn't want him to be saddled with an odd name.

The day before I delivered our son, I went in to see my doctor. For the first time during my whole pregnancy, I complained to her that I was uncomfortable. I had complained plenty to Kevin, my mom and my sister, Holly, the people who love me the most. But, until that day, I figured the last thing my doctor wanted to hear were complaints from yet another whiny, pregnant woman.

My doctor scheduled me for an induction the next morning at 7 a.m. I was already dilated to two centimeters, and my blood pressure was higher than the normal 100/65, so she thought it was time. I just thought, Crap! Why did I have to go and open my big mouth? This is June. I was going to be ready in July. Now I'm going to have to birth this baby. Like there was ever any other way of getting out of that particular predicament.

My due date was July 11. Being an expert in procrastination, I thought I still had time to pick out birth announcements, pack my bag and several other things I needed to do before the baby arrived. The nursery closet was full of diapers of all sizes after my Chucky-baby nightmare, so no worries there. Even though I'd been told to go home and take it easy—whatever that means—I ran about a thousand errands. First I called Kevin with the news. He'd need to cancel his Lasik surgery for the next morning. (Because scheduling eye surgery is a fantastic idea when you might have to rush your wife to the hospital at any moment. What in the hell were we thinking?)

I called my parents. They wanted to come to San Antonio right away, but I convinced them to meet us at the hospital in the morning. They live in Victoria, about two hours southeast of San Antonio. I know they were excited, and I probably wouldn't have minded having my mom there early. But I wanted it to be just Kevin and me going to the hospital. I wanted to enjoy our last few moments as a couple before becoming a family.

Then Kevin tried to call his parents, but they didn't answer their home phone, and they didn't have cell phones. He left several messages at their house, with his brother, Kent, and with his sister, Kendra. No luck—his parents were incommunicado. It was like going back in time to 1985. I was starting to feel really bad for him.

We had gotten into a terrible argument a couple of weeks earlier over whose parents would stay to help when the baby was born. I said, "My mom should come because I'm the one who has to push this baby out of my vagina." The woman should be able to choose who is in her house after she has a baby. Nonnegotiable. She should be able to get to know her baby in the privacy—and I stress that word—of her own home without any distractions or annoyances.

If Kevin's parents wanted to come right away, they needed to get a hotel. Or they could wait a couple of weeks.

It was like World War III. By Kevin's reaction to the words "get a hotel," you would have thought I had suggested that his parents pitch a tent in our backyard. (That's actually not a bad idea.)

Kevin thought his parents should stay because they live so far away. He said my parents could stay, too, or come and go the same day. (Thanks for that concession.)

I felt awful that Kevin couldn't reach his parents, but it wasn't my fault. Who doesn't have a cell phone in 2002? Against my better judgment, I called my sister-in-law to see if she knew how to get in touch with them. She had a few ideas. She called every casino within a 100-mile radius of their small town in Missouri and managed to find them gambling in Omaha, Nebraska. I'll let y'all draw your own conclusions.

When we left for the hospital the next morning, it was still dark out. That's not a time of day I'm all that familiar with. Usually I'm still in bed asleep. Kevin somehow managed to hit every single bump and pothole on the way there. And that takes talent, my friends. It's not something I would normally notice, but it grates on your nerves when your bladder has been flattened to the size of a pancake.

Then Kevin drove right past the Taco Cabana we were going to stop at. I silently thanked the sweet baby Jesus that this was a planned trip to the hospital because I don't think I could handle the amount of distraction he would exhibit in an emergency situation. Of course, with Kevin there is no such thing as backtracking, and he assured me there would be another one because, hey, it's San Antonio, and there's a Taco

Cabana on every block. Right? Wrong. The next one was only about a block from the hospital. I tried to eat my taco in the car, but Kevin was rushing me. "Let's eat later," he said.

My nurse came in to the labor and delivery room as I was getting settled. When she saw the bag of tacos, she folded her arms and pursed her lips. "You can't have anything to eat now," she said.

To my dismay, Kevin gave her my taco. Then he ate his taco, and I gave him my best dirty look. I knew I should have eaten a piece of toast.

After the nurse finished eating my taco, she began taking a history from me. She turned to Kevin halfway through and said, "Sir, you need to leave the room."

"Why?" Kevin said.

"I need to ask your wife some questions, and you cannot be in here while I do."

I could tell Kevin was pissed. After all, he'd just given her my taco. He looked at me, rolled his eyes and walked out of the room in a huff. Then the nurse asked me if my husband beat me. I started to giggle. Then I received a lecture about how domestic abuse is not a laughing matter.

No shit.

In my defense, I was laughing because the questions caught me off guard and Kevin had just stalked out of the room like I imagine a wife-beater would. I didn't say that, though. I just tried to straighten up and put on my serious face. The nurse continued through her list of domestic abuse questions, and I had to stifle another fit of giggles as I imagined how Kevin might answer the questions, since I can be kind of a bully sometimes.

After that was over, the nurse told Kevin he could come back. Then she asked if I would like an enema. Right in front of Kevin. Why on earth wouldn't she ask me that in private?

"No," I answered, my voice firm.

"Are you sure?" Kevin said.

"Yeah, I'm sure."

At that point, they both started cross-examining me on when I'd last had a bowel movement. I had no freaking idea. I didn't realize I needed to keep records.

There are two kinds of people in this world: those who are obsessed with taking a shit, and those who are not. I fall into the second category. I would have to say my husband falls into the first, along with the nurse, for obvious reasons.

Anyway, I felt like I had failed a huge test and this enema was my only chance at extra credit. I could feel my resolve slipping away.

"Have you ever had one?" I said to Kevin.

"Yeah," he said. "It's no big deal. You'll probably feel a lot better." The nurse was nodding her head.

Liars.

I relented and let the nurse give me an enema. Then I went to the restroom. Nothing. I'd probably crapped that morning and just couldn't remember. This baby was sapping all my brain cells.

After I sat there for a while with nothing happening, I started to feel nauseous and then I vomited. I wasn't really barfing anything, though, because my stomach was empty. To make matters worse, I wanted to wash my mouth out, but the nurse wouldn't let me have any water, even though I promised I wouldn't drink it.

I wanted to do the domestic abuse questionnaire again.

Dr. Voigt, my obstetrician, came in to start the induction, but when she checked me I was already six centimeters dilated. She looked at me in surprise and said, "You're in labor. Why didn't you come in before now?"

"I asked you that very question last month. How will I know if I'm in labor? And you said if I have to ask, then I'm probably not in labor."

Dr. Voigt responded in her usual prissy manner, "Well, you're at six centimeters, so you're definitely in labor."

Thanks, Doctor, for that incredibly useless piece of advice.

"Would you like an epidural?" Dr. Voigt said.

Yeah, I'd wanted one since my seventh month. Instead, I said, "Well, yeah. I was thinking I would get one, but I'm not in any pain yet."

"Well, you don't want to be, do you?"

I noticed the nurse—the one who ate my taco and made me vomit—standing behind Dr. Voigt. She was emphatically nodding her head on the epidural question. After the enema debacle, I felt like such a failure. I couldn't even take a shit, so how was I going to birth this baby? I quickly agreed to the epidural. The anesthesiologist came in immediately. He must have been lurking in the hall. He sat me up on the edge of the bed, and his nurse grabbed me and placed my arms around her neck so my face was resting right in between her giant boobs. When I went to take my first breath, I almost gagged. She reeked of cigarettes. She had me lean into her, and I tried to breathe only minimal amounts of the smoke-tinged oxygen my body required so I wouldn't pass out or puke down her shirt. I was beginning to wonder why I'd bothered to shower.

My parents came in just a few minutes after the epidural, and I put my dad to work getting rid of a pesky fly that kept buzzing around me. I know. Gross. I felt like Pigpen from Charlie Brown. Dad managed to catch the fly and let it loose in the hall outside my door. To this day, I don't know why he didn't just kill it.

Our baby probably would've been born around 9:30 a.m., but the nurse forgot to check on me for a couple of hours. My mom kept saying, "Don't you think you're probably at ten already?" and I would say, "I don't know. Probably," with as little enthusiasm as possible. She was dying to get the nurse, and I kept telling her, "Would you just cool it? I'm sure she'll be in here soon enough."

The nurse finally came in, and it was just as my mother suspected. I was at ten. The nurse asked me to push, and I refused. I motioned for her to come closer so I could tell her, in confidence, to get my parents out of the room. I wasn't going to do anything as long as I had an audience.

After the nurse cleared everybody out, she called my doctor to come over. Our baby boy was born shortly thereafter. I remember him taking a huge breath and screaming loudly, and I thought, Oh, wow—he works! I know that's not very maternal, but it's the truth.

They handed him to me after they had weighed him and cleaned him up. He looked like a red, wrinkled man with the slightest of white peach fuzz and blue eyes. I should say "eye" in the singular. He only opened one at a time and promptly closed it if he caught me looking at him. I guess I was overwhelming him. He looked exactly like a Liam.

Kevin and I relaxed for a while with our new baby. Liam was then taken to the nursery for an observation period and his first bath. On the way up to my room, we stopped by the nursery. I had just spent an hour with my baby, and I couldn't have picked him out of a baby lineup to save my life. Finally, my dad said, "He's right there. Yours is the only one that doesn't have any hair." I was thankful that I had paid attention when they gave Liam a hospital band that matched mine because if they brought me someone else's baby, I'm not sure I would've known. I noticed right after delivery that he had a funny purple mark on the front of his head, and I made a mental note to check for it when they brought him to me later, you know, just in case.

Kevin had upgraded to a suite in the top floor of Mercy Hospital. It was actually two rooms, and you could pull a divider in between them. One room had a bed and a chair, like a regular hospital room, and the other had a seating area with a coffee table and a small, well-stocked refrigerator. Each room was equipped with its own bathroom.

By the time I made it to the room, it was close to two o'clock and I had missed lunch, so I filled out my menu for dinner. I was famished. My brother, Hunter, and my sister, Holly, arrived around that time, and everyone kept going to the nursery to check on Liam.

Kevin's parents showed up around 3 p.m., after driving all night from Omaha. I was happy they made it, and I could tell from Kevin's face that he was relieved to have his family there. While I visited with my family, he took his parents to meet Liam and get a bite to eat.

The hospital staff finally brought Liam to my room about seven hours after he had been born. Kevin went down to the nursery and said he wouldn't leave until they brought the baby up to me. Nothing like an irate new father to get them hopping.

They brought Liam to me in a hospital bassinet. I pulled back his hat and checked for the purple mark. I had the right baby. I asked my mom to shut the divider so I could have some privacy while nursing him.

After Liam was finished nursing, I handed him to Kevin since Kevin had only held him briefly in the delivery room.

"Oh, this is what I've been waiting for," his mother said, "to see Kevin hold the baby. You know, he's just terrible with babies." She and Kevin's dad laughed. "Look, everybody," she continued. "He's just so unnatural. Kevin, that's not how you hold a baby!"

My family traded questioning looks and laughed uncomfortably.

This was more uncomfortable than my dad's joke about the fancy circumcision versus the plain circumcision. The fancy they do with pinking shears. Awful, I know. No way in hell was I letting a doctor anywhere near my baby boy's penis with a medieval apple corer. No circumcision. My father still thinks I am ruining Liam's life.

I digress.

I could see doubt replace the happiness that had been on Kevin's face moments before. "I think he's doing a great job," I said. "How else are you supposed to hold a baby?"

Kevin looked a little relieved but still skeptical. His mother didn't take the hint because it was subtle. "Oh, Heather," she said. "He's so awkward. He's not holding the baby right!" She continued in a loud voice, "He may be good at a bunch of other things, but he's terrible at this. I knew he would be. I can't wait to tell his brother and sister because they just couldn't imagine Kevin with a baby either."

I smiled and said, "I don't know what on earth you're talking about. He's doing a fantastic job, and I'm sure Liam thinks so as well."

At that moment I was sorry I'd contacted my sister-in-law, Alicia, the night before to try to find them. With a mother and father like that, who needs enemies?

Here was this woman, my husband's mother, a teacher for over thirty years, with a master's degree in education, who obviously thought she could parent a child better than he would be able to. Why did she need to denigrate her first-born son holding his first-born son in a room full of people?

I realized she wanted him to fail. They both did. For the first time I wondered if Kevin had gotten where he is today in spite of his family, not because of them.

It broke my heart.

Everybody got ready to leave. My mom gave me a hug. "We're going to get on the road to Victoria tonight since y'all have other company," she said. "I'll come back when your in-laws leave."

There it was. I had hunted down Kevin's parents, and now mine were leaving because they didn't want to impose. I wanted to cry. As the saying goes, no good deed goes unpunished.

My mom came as soon as Kevin's parents left, and I began to get into a routine with Liam.

My mom had only been there a day when she received a call that scared the daylights out of me. She was sitting across from me, and I could hear her saying, "Oh, no. That's terrible. I just can't believe it." She went on and on. She's kind of got a flare for the dramatic.

I looked at her and mouthed, "What?"

"Rowdy died," she whispered.

That was my brother's dog. Relief washed over me, and I began to laugh. "Geez. The way you were going on I thought it was Nana," I said, and she tried not to laugh as she got all the gruesome details of Rowdy's tangle with an 18-wheeler on IH-35 outside San Marcos.

I was wishing it had been my dog, Lucy. She was the worst dog ever. She was a Brittany, and she was a complete idiot. Kevin gave her to me as a Christmas present six months before Liam was born because he thought it would be great practice for the baby.

That's just stupid.

All in all, I was pretty happy that my Nana was not dead and my mother would be sticking around for the rest of the week to help out with Liam. My mom was great with Liam. She seemed surprised that I was good with him, since I was kind of a tomboy and never really played with dolls growing up. Because how good you are with dolls is a pretty good indicator of how you'll be as a mother.

Whatever.

My mom was really sweet with Liam, though. She would lean over him and say things like, "I love you so much."

I would look at my little lump of flesh lying in the bassinet and wonder what was wrong with me. I didn't have that huge rush of love at first sight when he was born. Instead, I felt like we kind of needed to get to know each other, and he wasn't really contributing much to that effort.

I fed and changed him. Mostly I sat on the sofa, feet up and knees bent, with Liam propped up on my lap. We stared at each other for hours. We went on long walks, and I told him the names of things, although I don't think he was really paying attention. I would catch myself thinking, Wow, this has been fun, but I wonder when his real parents are coming to pick him up? Oh, yeah—that would be me.

One morning when Liam was about six weeks old, I felt him moving around beside me in our bed, and I said, "Good morning, baby." He looked directly at me and smiled a huge smile. He recognized me. And I felt it, a huge rush of love.

I was his mommy.

CHAPTER 2

The first year of Liam's life flew by, even though the days and nights seemed unspeakably long. Finally, after a year, Liam could be counted on to sleep through the night, which equated to pure bliss in my mind. (I love to sleep. I've been tempted to list it as a hobby, but what would people think?)

Our little family had settled into a good routine with the help of our wonderful nanny, Esme, who took care of Liam while Kevin and I were working. Having a child is definitely an adjustment. Kevin called it "baby jail." I cannot think of a more apt term to describe it.

I knew Kevin would be a great dad, but I was a little surprised at how he jumped right in. Often I would come home from work to find Kevin puttering in the yard or cleaning the pool with Liam along for the ride in the Baby Bjorn. Kevin would let the nanny go home early after she helped him get Liam strapped in. Getting the baby situated in the carrier is kind of a two-person job, and Kevin, who has no grasp of spatial concepts, only managed to complicate matters, I'm sure. Esme was such a good sport.

Kevin was always ready to change diapers, build train tracks, read books and handle the occasional feeding during the day when I wasn't available. He didn't always do things the way I would, but I figured there's a mommy way and a daddy way and a kid has to learn to cope. Kevin reminded me that in the baby class we took at the hospital, we'd learned that we were supposed to wipe the baby's bottom from front to back. I found it hilarious that of all the information given, the instructions he remembered were specifically for a baby girl. At least, if we ever did have a girl, he would be in front-to-back mode.

Kevin never woke up to take a feeding during the night, which seemed patently unfair to me at the time. Who am I kidding? It still seems unfair. I did nurse Liam for the entire first year, however, so I guess it wasn't practical for Kevin to warm a bottle of breast milk when I had it ready to go. Even so, it took me a while to get over feeding the baby several times a night while he slept.

After leaving the baby with Kevin a few times to run errands on the weekends, I realized that I needed to make Liam's bottles beforehand. Kevin would ruin a day's supply in under an hour by dumping all the breast milk from the refrigerator into one bottle. He was incapable of comprehending the words "limited supply" and "the baby only drinks four ounces at a time" and "I'm not a dairy cow."

I'll never forget the day I learned I was pregnant with our second child. It was a Friday in July, and I had just gone for a three-mile run in the late afternoon. (Call me crazy, but I love to run in the heat.) I was standing in the kitchen dripping sweat and drinking a cold bottle of water when Kevin walked in the door. He'd taken off early and spent the afternoon with some friends watching the Missions play baseball.

Kevin smiled when he saw me standing there. "Hey, babe, did you just run in this heat?" he asked.

"Yep." I knew he wanted to lecture me about heatstroke and how only a complete nut job would run in 100-degree weather, which is probably all true. I turned my attention to the sippy cups in the sink that needed washing. That's when Kevin came up behind me, hugged me tight and planted a kiss on my neck.

"Ugh. Don't do that! I'm all sweaty, and I'm sure I stink," I said.

"You are sweaty, but you don't really stink." He planted another kiss on my neck and took a big whiff, which made me cringe. "You smell— well, you smell pregnant," he said with a laugh.

"What? What's that supposed to mean?" I wasn't laughing. It was such a weird thing to say. He'd never mentioned that I smelled different when I was pregnant with Liam. I turned around so that we were facing each other.

"Don't get mad," he said. "It's not a bad smell. It's just different. I just now realized it when I kissed you."

He smelled like cologne, sunshine and beer, which left me wondering if he was just a little drunk. I quickly dismissed that thought because he didn't look drunk at all. "I'm not pregnant, Kevin," I said.

"Okay. You're not pregnant. Whatever you say. I'm probably wrong."

My mind was racing. How could I be pregnant? I'd been taking the birth control pill Micronor, which is safe to use while breastfeeding, in theory.

I thought back to a conversation I had with Dr. Voigt about the drug's efficacy. I also read the packaging insert. (Yes, I'm one of those people.)

It didn't sound like it worked that well. From what I could understand, not including all the chemistry symbols, it didn't actually keep you from ovulating. It's supposed to—and these are my own words—gunk up the passageway so the sperm cannot make their way through. Dr. Voigt had assured me I wouldn't have any problems. I would count pregnancy as a problem.

I grabbed my wallet and keys and headed out the door. Kevin yelled after me, "Where are you going?"

"Eckerd, to buy a pregnancy test. I'm going to prove you wrong," I shouted back.

I freaked out all the way to the store, which was only about a half mile away, and all the way back, and chugged another twenty ounces of bottled water. I needed to pee on the stick as soon as I got back to the house.

I went straight to the restroom. I could hear Kevin upstairs in the nursery. Liam must have woken from his nap. I opened the box, tore off the foil packaging and promptly peed on the stick for the required five seconds. This wasn't my first rodeo.

I replaced the cap on the end of the stick and put it on the back of the toilet to wait. I was pulling my shorts back up when I happened to glance at the test. In a matter of seconds it was already showing two lines.

Pregnant.

I sat on the edge of the toilet and watched the two lines grow darker. This was a totally different experience. With Liam, I waited the full five minutes. Even then, Kevin and I had to consult each other as to whether there really was a second line.

This pregnancy sucked for a multitude of reasons. First, I wasn't sure I wanted to have another baby, but I did know I didn't want one so soon. I had planned to wait until Liam was four years old before I even thought about having another child—which would give me three years of much-needed rest. Yet there I sat.

I was worried about my body. And I mean that in the vainest of ways. I finally felt like I was getting back in shape after pregnancy, birth, sleepless nights and nursing for the past year. Well, mostly in shape. I wasn't sure my boobs would ever be the same. They looked like a couple of golf balls dangling in the bottom of old sweat socks. But I continued to hold out hope that they would regain some of their shape. And I hadn't ruled out plastic surgery either.

Unexpected pregnancies don't happen to women like me. In the past, whenever I heard about somebody getting pregnant on the pill, I thought it such bullshit. They must not have taken it correctly, or they skipped a day, or maybe they lied. Maybe they were just stupid. Whatever.

I was completely blindsided. How could Kevin know something like this before I did? I probably wouldn't have gone running in the heat that day or the several days preceding. I would have been better about taking my prenatal vitamins.

Was Kevin going to be happy about another baby? Or overwhelmed or angry?

I didn't have to wonder for long. The next thing I knew, Kevin was standing at the door holding Liam. I held the pregnancy stick out for him to see and burst into tears. Kevin had a huge smile on his face. He set Liam down and gave me a hug. "Why are you crying? This is great news. We're having a baby!"

I did not share his enthusiasm, but I was relieved that he was happy. At least that made one of us. "I wasn't expecting this," I said. "I'm not ready to have another baby while Liam is still a baby."

"This is going to be awesome. They'll be so close in age, and they'll play together. I wish you weren't sad. I can't wait to tell everybody we're having another baby."

That stopped my crying for a second. "You can't tell anyone."

"Why not?" Kevin said, his voice incredulous. "You're not thinking you would have an abortion, are you?"

"I was actually thinking of suicide, but abortion is a much better option. I knew you could cheer me up," I said.

When I saw his horrified expression, I added, "No, I wasn't thinking about getting an abortion. Kevin, I am still trying to process this. I don't want everybody knowing about it before I'm ready, or before we're out of the first trimester, whenever that is. I don't even know how far along we are."

Kevin and I were pregnant before we had Liam, and it ended in a miscarriage. I learned my lesson the hard way. Don't tell anyone you're pregnant that you don't want to have to untell later. That's the worst.

"Plus," I went on, "it's a little embarrassing that I'm pregnant already. I feel like we're rabbits or something, having babies every five minutes."

"Well," Kevin said, "let's go out to dinner and celebrate our cautionary good news then. I'm excited! This is going to be fun."

I tried to let his excitement infect me, but it just wouldn't. I had this crazy idea that we were tempting fate. I couldn't quite put my finger on it, but I was worried.

"Kevin," I said, "what if there's something really wrong with this baby?"

"What do you mean?"

"Like, what if it's really screwed up?"

"Don't say that. It's not going to be. I was worried that something would be wrong with Liam, and he's perfect. Don't worry. Nothing's going to be wrong with the baby. Don't even think like that. Okay?"

"Okay."

I didn't feel okay, though. I looked down at Liam. He was standing beside me, patting me on the knee with a concerned look. He'd never seen me cry before. I picked him up, dried my tears and kissed him on the cheek. "It's okay, my little man. Mommy's okay." I handed Liam to Kevin and decided to take a shower so I would be ready to go to dinner.

The shower made me feel better, and I was able to renew my outlook on this unexpected bit of news. I decided I should focus on the positive. My first order of business was to call Dr. Voigt's office Monday for an appointment, so I could find out how pregnant I was and start planning for a new baby brother or sister for Liam.

Over the next weeks, I stayed busy with work and taking care of my family, and I tried not to think too much about what I was feeling. I remembered the times I had been wrong about things, and I told myself this bad feeling was just the shock of finding out I was pregnant. The more I thought about this new addition to our family, the happier I felt. But the feeling that something wasn't quite right was still bubbling below the surface.

Now I live with that feeling every day. Sometimes I can ignore it for days and weeks at a time, but it's always there. It never leaves me. An overwhelming feeling of dread.

CHAPTER 3

My due date was April 15, 2004. According to the sonogram that Dr. Voigt ordered, I was exactly ten weeks pregnant, which meant my children would be twenty-one months apart in age. Two babies at completely different stages, under the age of two, both in diapers. All I could think was, What a nightmare.

"On the bright side," Kevin said, "we'll have all the baby stuff done at one time." We were already accustomed to baby jail, so there wouldn't be a huge adjustment like we had with Liam. I knew Kevin was right, but it was difficult to see the light at the end of another long sleepless tunnel. Just thinking about another infant made me feel exhausted and the baby wasn't even here yet.

I was in a terrible mood sitting in Dr. Voigt's waiting room. Liam had awakened early that morning, screaming for his breakfast. I stepped in a huge pile of steaming dog shit in my bare feet on the way to the kitchen. There's nothing like the combination of pregnancy hormones and the feeling of warm dog shit oozing between my toes to make me start screaming like a banshee at Kevin, who replied calmly, "You told me to be careful before you even hopped out of bed because you thought you smelled dog shit. You're the one with the super-sniffer. How could you step in it?"

"Feed the baby and clean that up," I said in a voice channeled straight from *The Exorcist*.

I glanced at the magazines in Dr. Voigt's office—*Veranda* and Martha Stewart's *Living*—and picked up a pregnancy brochure instead. If I looked through one of those magazines, I might just go home and torch our house with our stupid dog locked inside. *Veranda* is so beautiful, grown-up and completely out of my league. As for Martha, she bugs the living shit out of me, mainly because I love just about everything she does and am so fundamentally inept when it comes to creativity. Yeah, I'm jealous. Just not of the time she spent in federal prison.

The brochure was full of information, most of which I knew. There was a list of pregnancy symptoms and something like, "If you're experiencing any of these symptoms, you should tell your doctor at once." At the end of the list, after stuff like hemorrhaging, extreme nausea and intense cramping, was ". . . if you have a terrible feeling something is wrong with you or your baby."

That's just stupid, but, hey, it was in the brochure. During my appointment I told Dr. Voigt about my bad feeling. I'll give her credit for not laughing, but of course she said she was sure everything was fine. What else could she say? I'm not sure why they even list something so intangible.

The nine weeks that followed flew by. I blame it on denial. The next thing I knew, Kevin and I were going to the radiologist's office for our twenty-week sonogram—a little early because both of our work schedules were nuts and I didn't want to wait. I was actually at nineteen weeks.

I lay down on the exam table and the sonogram started. The sonographer made some quick measurements of the baby's head, spine, leg and arm bones. Then she moved on to the genitalia and announced we were having a boy. Kevin and I looked at each other and laughed. We were both thinking how crazy things were going to be with two little boys running around.

Just when I was happily resigning myself to living in the land of twigs and berries for the rest of my life, I noticed that the sonographer had grown really quiet. She was taking measurements and pictures of our baby boy's heart, measuring the same places again and again.

"Does his heart have four chambers?" I asked.

"Yeah. Yeah, his heart has four chambers," she answered, and then she grew quiet again. I had just exhausted my knowledge of the human heart.

An hour later she was still measuring and taking pictures. Kevin had lost interest after he heard we were having a boy and was playing a game on his cell phone. We made eye contact and he mouthed, "What is taking so long?"

I mouthed back, "It's his heart."

Kevin sighed and rolled his eyes.

About this time, the sonographer said she needed to make sure her pictures had uploaded and left the room. Kevin said, "I don't remember it taking this long with Liam."

"No," I said. "Something is wrong with the baby's heart. She's been measuring for the last hour and a half."

"How can you know that?" Kevin demanded. He was annoyed with me for saying it, but it was the truth. If he had cared to look up from his game, he would have seen for himself.

"They didn't look at Liam's heart near that long. We were out of here in under an hour. If she brings a doctor back in here, we're screwed," I told him.

"Don't be ridiculous," Kevin said, with a look of exasperation.

Right about that time the door opened and the sonographer walked in, followed by one of the radiologists. He introduced himself and stood behind the sonographer as she started putting red and blue color on the baby's heart, which I correctly guessed was blood flow. Then he started measuring and taking pictures, and I asked my one question again: "Does his heart have four chambers?"

"Yes, his heart definitely has four chambers," the doctor said. "Let me take a few more measurements, and I'll talk to you guys in a minute."

He finally got up and turned on the lights. "I know you're wondering why I came in here," he said. "The sonographer noticed something and wanted me to check it. Your baby's heart has an asymmetry to it, but I can't tell how it's asymmetrical at this point. At nineteen weeks, it's so small that it's hard to know if the left side is smaller or if the right side is bigger. I suggest you come back in four weeks so we can check it again."

Okay. Now I had a shit-ton of questions, but Kevin beat me to most of them. He was asking things like, "What could it mean? In what sorts of diagnoses do you see this particular asymmetry? Will he be able to play soccer? Will he have any specific limitations? What's the worst possible scenario?"

Duh—death, I thought, but I let Kevin do the talking. He was in cross-examination mode, and the radiologist was a stubborn witness. He wouldn't say anything more.

"All I can tell you is there is an asymmetry in your baby's heart, but I can't say, at this point, which side is causing the asymmetry. It could be that the right side is too big, or it could be that the left side is too small. Both are completely different problems. Right now the heart is too small to tell."

"Should we go to a pediatric cardiologist to see if they can make a diagnosis?" I asked.

"I don't think a pediatric cardiologist could tell you any more than what I just did," the radiologist said. "My recommendation is to come back in four weeks and we'll look again. I'll send a letter to your doctor explaining our findings, and she may be able to tell you a little bit more. Another concern I have is that the baby's head is measuring in the one hundredth percentile. His body is only in the tenth percentile."

"Do you think he has hydrocephalus or something?"

"No, I didn't see any evidence of that. It's just a concern."

"Our older son is seventeen months old and has a one-hundredth-percentile head. He's also tenth in height and fifteenth in weight. Maybe this baby is going to be a bobblehead like his brother. Do you think it's possible that that's just the way our kids turn out?"

My attempt at humor didn't really work. Kevin glared at me. Everybody was so freaking serious.

"Yeah," the doctor said, "it's possible."

Kevin shook hands with him, and we thanked him for his time. He left the room.

I wiped the goo off my belly and got dressed in silence. Even though the feeling of dread had never left me, I felt weirdly numb. This was it. This was what I had been feeling, but I didn't know what it meant. I just knew it was bad.

I made a follow-up appointment for December 31, 2003. As Kevin and I were walking out of the office, the sonographer came running after us. "Wait! Wait, Mr. and Mrs. Connelly! I forgot to give you the pictures of your baby." She handed me a small stack of grainy images.

"Thank you," I said. I shoved the slips of paper into my purse.

Kevin and I made our way to the elevator. He punched the button and said, "I can't believe you called Liam a bobblehead."

Oh, for the love of God!

"Honey," I said, "I was trying to illustrate a point—that our older child, who is perfectly healthy, has the same type of head and body measurements as this baby."

"Well, you made him sound like a freak, and he's not."

"I know that. You wouldn't look at Liam and think, Wow, that kid's noggin is huge. But his percentiles are the same. I was just letting the doctor know that Liam's measurements were similar."

"I think all those percentiles are a bunch of shit," Kevin said.

Here we go. Now we're going to argue with science. I had to give in at this point because this kind of conversation with Kevin can go nowhere real fast. "I'm sure you're right," I said.

"Please don't say that about Liam again."

"Okay! Geez, I won't. I'll never call Liam a bobblehead again." I tried to stifle a fit of the giggles and decided to change the subject. "I think we need to see a pediatric cardiologist. If this is something where the baby's going to need a bunch of surgeries or not survive, that's something we need to find out sooner rather than later."

"You don't think it's that serious, do you?" Kevin asked.

"I don't know. What I do know is that I have a really bad feeling about this pregnancy. What if this baby isn't going to survive? What if he requires a bunch of open-heart surgeries? I don't feel good about putting an infant through something like that."

"I doubt it's anything that bad. We need to think of a name for him."

That was the absolute last thing I wanted to do. I didn't want to name him. I didn't want to do anything until I knew what we were dealing with. "Why don't we call him Nemo?" I suggested. "Liam's favorite movie is *Finding Nemo* right now, and Nemo has a little fin. And his fins are asymmetrical. It's the perfect nickname until we can think of a real name."

"Okay," Kevin said.

I saw Dr. Voigt the following week and voiced my concerns about the radiologist's findings. I also told her that my bad feeling had never gone away.

Dr. Voigt said she had never seen a radiology report that was so completely vague. She wasn't sure what kind of heart problem it could be or what it could mean, but she was positive that my baby was fine. Based on the report, there was no reason she could imagine for me to see a pediatric cardiologist. She explained that a fetal heart is very complicated and constantly changing, and all kinds of things happen over the course of a pregnancy that can affect the heart. "I don't know what to think of this report," she said. "It's nonsense, and I think this radiologist is crazy. It doesn't make any sense."

What she said sounded reasonable, but I was skeptical. I had a hard time seeing the radiologist as a bogeyman going around scaring pregnant women. When I boiled it down, I had two doctors—my trusted OB/GYN and the "crazy radiologist," as she termed him—both of the same opinion, which was to see what the heart showed in four weeks.

"I'd feel better if I had a pediatric cardiologist check this out," I said to Dr. Voigt. "If something is really wrong with this baby's heart and he's going to die after birth or require extensive surgeries, it would be better to have that information now so we can decide what we're going to do."

"Heather," she said, "there is no way this could be anything that serious. The baby's heart has all four chambers. I think you are looking at having a baby who is ninety-five percent okay. I can see this being the type of thing where he might have to visit a pediatric cardiologist once a year, and that's talking worst-case scenario."

I'd started to feel a little better until Dr. Voigt added, "Look at the Cisneros boy. He only has a three-chambered heart, and he's fine."

In an instant I was back to feeling worried. How could a doctor say that anybody was fine with a three-chambered heart? The Cisneros boy, as she called him, was the son of Henry Cisneros, onetime mayor of San Antonio and U.S. secretary of housing and urban development under Bill Clinton. My brain was fuzzy on the details, but I thought the boy was probably around age sixteen and had undergone at least a couple of heart surgeries. I clung to the fact that my baby did indeed have a four-chambered heart, and maybe this wasn't going to be such a big problem after all.

If you ever want to make a pregnancy go really fast, just dread the whole thing. It works like a charm. Kevin and I had plans to go to dinner the evening of the follow-up sonogram with my parents and his parents, who were visiting from Missouri, for New Year's.

When I walked into the radiologist's office, I felt like I'd just left. Kevin was meeting me there, so I sat down to wait. I wish I could say I wasn't annoyed when I saw him walk in with his parents in tow. I'd become more worried about what the sonographer and radiologist might find, and I didn't want to have to face my in-laws during this appointment or make small talk with them. I just wanted to be with Kevin and focus on our baby. I needed that twenty-minute drive home to mentally prepare myself, but I wasn't going to get it.

I put on my game face fast. When Kevin hugged me, I whispered in his ear, "They are not going back in the room with us."

Kevin gave me a look and said quietly, "Oh, I figured that would be the nice thing to do, but you're so weird about stuff like that."

You mean boundaries, or their obvious lack thereof? I smiled and leaned in so he could hear me. "If you call weird not wanting your parents to witness my pregnant state in various states of undress, then, yeah, I'm weird, and don't you forget it." I squeezed his hand, and he laughed.

Kevin and I went into the sonogram room. The same sonographer as before made quick measurements of Nemo's little body and took some measurements of his head. Then she spent the better part of an hour taking measurements and running more blue and red color through his heart at different intervals to check the direction of blood flow.

Nobody said a word. The only noise was the clicking of the mouse button and keyboard. The sonographer finally said she had all the measurements she needed and left the room to check on a couple of things. I knew where this was going. The radiologist followed her back into the room and took a few more measurements before he turned on the light to talk to us.

"I'm glad you guys came back," he said. "There is a definite asymmetry in your baby's heart. Now that it's a little bigger, I can tell that the left side is smaller than the right."

"What does that mean?" I asked.

"Well, I can't really tell you exactly. You need to talk to your doctor about that. But it would be a good idea to have a pediatric cardiologist on standby for the birth to check him right away," he said.

"Why not have a pediatric cardiologist look now so we know what we're dealing with?" I asked.

"You could do that, too, but I don't know if it's necessary. The fetal heart will change even more. All kinds of things change and take place in a baby's heart the first few days after birth. I think you would be fine having a pediatric cardiologist check him out after he's born."

"Does the heart have all four chambers?" I asked again.

"Yes," he said, "the heart has four chambers."

We talked for a while longer, but I knew from our previous experience that he wouldn't tell us anything except his findings, which were completely unhelpful to me. I'd have to be a doctor to figure out the exact ramifications. He also reiterated his concern about the baby's head in proportion to his body, but this time I kept my mouth shut.

Kevin and I left the office with another set of sonogram pictures, and Kevin took his parents home in his car. I called Dr. Voigt's office, as she'd instructed me to do after the sonogram, and left a message for her to call me.

I also called Frank Stone. Dr. Stone is Liam's pediatrician and a good friend of ours. He's married to one of my best friends, Sarah, who is also the judge I work for. Sarah and Kevin were each other's first trial partners in the Bexar County District Attorney's Office. I met Sarah when I was the court reporter assigned to an aggravated sexual assault trial in which she was prosecuting some disgusting pervert, whom the jury sent to prison for a very long time.

I told Frank what the radiologist had said, and we sort of thought out loud about the whole heart thing. I'd also called him after the first sonogram to ask what he thought about the asymmetry business. In the meantime he'd run into his friend and colleague Dr. Jerome Roberts and told him what was going on.

Dr. Roberts asked Frank several questions that I don't think we had the answers to, but in the end he said the left side of the heart is always smaller than the right, so he wasn't exactly sure what the asymmetry meant. Was the left side just smaller than the right? That might be a normal heart. Was the left side measuring small for a left side? Was the right side measuring large for a right side? Those could be problems.

All of this was completely over my head, and I told Frank that. He wanted to see the radiologist's report and said he would call Dr. Voigt and talk to her about it. Then he'd call Dr. Roberts and discuss what we should do.

I felt a little better. Frank is just with it and completely thorough. If he doesn't know the answer to something, he'll find somebody who does. He told me that the nurse who used to work for him had something almost exactly like this happen and it turned out that the baby was fine.

I asked what he thought the worst-case scenario would be.

"You know," he said, "there's something called hypoplastic left heart syndrome, but that's so rare. I just can't believe it could be that."

I finished the call as I pulled into the driveway. I grabbed my purse and saw the second set of pictures from the sonogram in there. I decided I should compare the baby's head and body measurements from the nineteen-week sonogram against the measurements I had on the pictures of Liam from his twenty-week sonogram to see if they were close.

I went straight to our bathroom and pulled out the drawer where I had placed the pictures from Liam's sonogram and those of the new baby. Both babies' measurements were identical, which was reassuring. I was indeed going to have another bobblehead.

I thumbed through the rest of the grainy images and stopped cold when I saw the last picture from the sonogram four weeks before. The sonographer had typed, "I love you, Mommy and Daddy."

The horrible thought crept into my head that she'd typed it because she thought our baby might never get the chance to say it.

CHAPTER 4

The only New Year's resolution I made for 2004 was to not worry so much. I decided not to let my worrywart tendencies take over on the asymmetrical heart business because this is the type of thing that can drive you bananas when you're heading into your third trimester. Worrying ranks right up there with guilt as far as being a wasted emotion.

As a child, I worried about nuclear war because I grew up in the Cold War era and Russia was a constant threat. It seemed like every time I got a grip on my fear I would hear something about war on the news or my music teacher would bring it up. Why was she talking about nuclear war with a bunch of third-graders anyway?

When I wasn't worrying about being blown to smithereens, I worried that my mom would die in a car wreck and leave us kids alone with our dad. Sometimes I'd worry, when my mom set out for the grocery store, that she'd decide to keep on driving. She'd never come home again because Holly, Hunter and I fought all the time. This usually resulted in a call to H-E-B, the grocery store, to have her paged. This was way before cell phones. I'm sure she thought we were a bunch of assholes.

If my mom died or took off, I'd have to tell my father, Wendall, when I started my period. Even as an adult, I can't think of anything worse than asking him to pick up a box of Kotex at the store. Just the idea is enough to make me break into a sweat.

I hate that childhood prayer, Now I lay me down to sleep / I pray the Lord my soul to keep / If I should die before I wake / I pray the Lord my soul to take.

I wondered why I would ever die in my sleep. It had obviously happened before; the prayer was proof. Was it a common occurrence?

I mean, what the fuck? Why is this a good prayer for children? Why not reserve the scary shit for old people? I realize it's supposed to be comforting; if you did die in your sleep, you'd go to heaven to be with Jesus. Don't get me wrong. That's all fine and dandy. But I never heard anyone say, "Wow! I just can't wait to die. It's going to be so great." The preacher at our church in Victoria would sometimes say, "Heaven is going to be so great!" but he was about the only person I'd met who seemed ready to hurl himself into a grave. I often wondered if our preacher would forego cancer treatment, if he got sick, in favor of meeting Jesus.

When you're eight years old, staying alive and being with your parents and your annoying siblings trumps dying in bed and spending eternity with Jesus.

After I said my prayers, I would lie in bed and force myself to breathe in and out just in case my body wanted to stop for some reason. When I'd finally settled down I'd turn on my side, and that's when I heard what I thought was someone digging with a shovel. I imagined it was the devil digging up from hell to steal my soul.

Hello, dipshit! That digging sound is actually your own pulse when your ear is to the pillow.

I think that's what happens when you take your children to church too often. I grew up in the Methodist church. It wasn't a strict church, but I internalized every cotton-picking moment and completely exasperated my Sunday school teacher, Ms. Jones. She was so sweet and kind as I asked my gazillion questions. She always answered, "Heather, you have to have faith" and something about a mustard seed.

Ugh! Are you kidding me? The answer to my questions about invisible things was invisible as well.

Now you know that I was a neurotic and anxiety-filled child. That's fine. I tell you all of this so you can feel confident that I've got this worrying shit down to a science. As I grew older, I made the decision to enjoy my life. Maybe I just came up with better coping mechanisms, but it was a real turning point.

As I entered the third trimester, I asked Dr. Voigt loads of questions about the radiologist's reports and about seeing a pediatric cardiologist. Knowledge is power.

Dr. Voigt said that Kevin and I were looking at having a baby who was 95 percent okay. I've never really heard one doctor trash talk another—it seems to be against their ethics code—but she came pretty close. She went so far as to say, "I think sonograms pick up things that we otherwise would never have known about. A lot of times I find that sonograms make mischief where there shouldn't be any. This is probably one of those things that maybe your parent or grandparent had and still lived a full life, never even realizing they had it."

As I was working on the referral to a pediatric cardiologist, so was Frank, our pediatrician. He'd talked to Dr. Voigt about the radiologist's report, and she'd proven to be just as stubborn as she had been with me. Frank's opinion (and mine) was, if it's nothing, that's great, but let's find out so we can move on. Thank God for Frank Stone!

At my thirty-week appointment, Dr. Voigt finally said she thought it'd be a good idea to get the baby checked out. There were two names—Bradley and Roberts—that everyone kept throwing around as the best children's heart doctors in San Antonio. Since Frank had already spoken to Dr. Roberts, we thought we should probably see him, and Dr. Voigt agreed.

I took the first available appointment with Dr. Roberts, a little over two weeks away. I breathed a huge sigh of relief. I trusted Dr. Voigt to shoot me straight, and I felt like she was probably right. I just wanted to know for sure.

When I told her about the appointment, she said, "I'm so happy you're getting that taken care of. You'll feel so much better after the doctor tells you the baby is fine and that radiologist is crazy."

"Yeah, I hope so," I said, and kind of laughed.

Kevin and I went to the Heart Center for Children in the South Texas Medical Center for our appointment with Dr. Roberts, which consisted of a fetal echocardiogram. We were feeling upbeat with just a little nervousness thrown in. We were pretty secure in the knowledge that our baby was fairly healthy. Dr. Roberts would confirm this once and for all.

The echo room was really warm even in February, and super tiny. The giant echo machine gives off a lot of heat. I'd been in there no more than thirty seconds when I was ready to strip off every last piece of clothing. I'm sure it had nothing to do with the fact that I was thirty-two weeks pregnant and wearing wool pants and a sweater.

Dr. Roberts entered the room with a resident in tow and introduced himself. He was soft-spoken, and I judged him to be in his mid- to late fifties. They both sat down to watch while the fetal echo was performed, so counting the sonographer we had five people in that unbearably hot room.

Dr. Roberts watched the fetal echo for a while and then excused the sonographer. While he was taking measurements of the tiny beating heart on the screen, he was speaking in a low voice to the resident. I strained to hear what he was saying, but I could only catch a phrase or two and it never seemed to be in context. Dr. Roberts could have been speaking in Greek for all the good it did me.

I caught a glimpse of Kevin on my left, and he gave me a thumbs-up and a little grin. I smiled back.

I asked Dr. Roberts, "So is this something that my parents or grandparents could have had and never known it?"

Dr. Roberts looked directly at me and pursed his lips like he'd tasted something bitter. "No," he said. "I'll be done in just a few more minutes and then we can talk about what's going on with your little boy."

I felt like I was falling. I turned back to look at Kevin, whose eyes were wide, and gave him the thumbs-down sign.

Kevin mouthed to me, "Don't think the worst," and squeezed my hand.

"Do either of you have a family history of congenital heart defects or heart problems?" Dr. Roberts said.

Kevin and I both answered no.

"You have an older child?"

"Yes," I said.

"Does he have any sort of heart defect?"

"No, not that I know of." What the hell?

"How old is your son?" Dr. Roberts asked.

"Liam is eighteen months old," I answered.

Dr. Roberts finished up the fetal echo himself and took us to one of the exam rooms, which was, thankfully, much cooler. We all took a seat, and Dr. Roberts said, "Does your baby boy have a name yet?"

Kevin and I glanced at each other and said "no" at the same time. It didn't seem like a good time to tell Dr. Roberts that we'd been calling our baby Nemo after a cartoon fish with asymmetrical fins.

"Okay. Your baby boy has something called hypoplastic left heart syndrome. Now let me tell you guys how we manage this type of illness."

I startled Kevin by interrupting. "I'm sorry. Manage? Did you just say manage?"

"Yes."

"Yeah, I don't want to manage anything. I need for you to tell me how we're going to fix this." I struggled to keep my voice even.

"This is not something we can fix."

Don't kill the messenger. I took a deep breath to pull myself together. I tried to focus, but I felt like I had been hit in the stomach with a piñata stick.

Dr. Roberts explained that hypoplastic left heart syndrome is a rare combination of congenital heart defects that occurs in about one in four thousand babies. We had three options.

The first option was three open-heart surgeries staged in the first three years of life. The first surgery, the Norwood procedure, would be performed shortly after birth, followed by the Glenn between six months and one year of age and the Fontan at around age three. The second option was a heart transplant, but because of the shortage of neonate hearts our baby would probably die waiting. The third option was compassionate care, or palliative care.

"Palliative care?" I asked.

"Yes," Dr. Roberts said. "That means we do nothing and you take him home."

"Take him home," I repeated.

"Yes, and he'll probably die within a week."

"That's one of our options," I repeated. I was starting to feel like a parrot, but I was having a difficult time processing what he was saying. "Dr. Voigt said we were looking at having a baby who was ninety-five percent okay, but you're telling us this baby is one hundred percent not okay?"

"Yes, that's what I'm telling you. Without the surgeries or a heart transplant, HLHS is one hundred percent fatal. The left side of your baby's heart is actually a little bit bigger than what this diagram shows." Dr. Roberts made a sketch on the back of the patient folder to show how our baby's heart differed from the diagram.

"So since the left side of his heart is a little bit bigger, is that an advantage for him?" I asked hopefully.

"No. It's still too small to be of any use to him."

I looked at the diagrams side by side, and I couldn't make heads or tails of them. It was so unbelievably complicated that I wondered how it was possible for a heart to develop normally.

I looked over at Kevin, who had been holding my hand this whole time. His eyes were brimming with tears. I felt tears prick my eyes and quickly looked down at my lap. The lump in my throat was getting bigger and bigger, but I just kept trying to breathe it down. I didn't want to cry in front of Dr. Roberts. I kept taking deep breaths and tried not to look at Kevin. The devastation on his face was too much for me.

"It seems like the heart transplant would be the better way to go since it would only be one surgery," Kevin ventured.

"Yes," Dr. Roberts agreed, "but the problem is the shortage of neonate hearts. Most infants with HLHS die waiting. Then, if you can get a heart, the antirejection drugs can cause cancer and coronary artery disease. The body is always trying to reject that organ. It's not a cure."

"So, really, we're back to the three-step surgical approach?" Kevin asked.

"Yes."

"Where would those surgeries be done if we went that route?" I asked.

"There are only a handful of surgeons who can successfully do a Norwood procedure. We have one surgeon here in San Antonio, Dr. Jack Callaway, who is very good. And we do all of these babies at South Texas Medical Hospital."

"South Texas Medical Hospital? Why not Mercy?" I said.

"You wouldn't want to do this type of surgery at Mercy Hospital."

"That's funny because all their billboards say 'heart hospital' on them," I said.

"Yeah, not for this type of heart surgery."

"What is the prognosis for this?" I asked.

"There's no prognosis."

"No prognosis," I repeated. (I'm obviously half parrot when dealing with a stressful situation.)

Dr. Roberts explained what he meant. "The oldest kid with hypoplastic left heart syndrome is probably in their mid- to late teens now." At that point they had been doing Norwood procedures for about twenty years, but they used the wrong size shunt for the first several years and all the babies died. Since it was still a fairly new approach, the doctors wouldn't give a prognosis because they simply didn't know.

We talked for a while longer and found out that the first surgery had about a 70 percent chance of survival, which was pretty much across the board at most hospitals performing the Norwood procedure in 2004. The second surgery, the Glenn, had a higher chance of survival, closer to 90 percent. The Fontan, the third and final surgery, had an 80 to 85 percent chance of survival.

In a normal heart, the oxygen-poor blood flows into the right side of the heart and through the pulmonary arteries to the lungs, and then the left side of the heart pumps the oxygenated blood out to the body. The right side is the receiving side and is generally much weaker than the left. These surgeries would essentially reroute the baby's heart so that the oxygen-poor blood would return to the right atrium and the oxygenated blood would pump out the right ventricle—something a right ventricle was never meant to do—and this would make a functioning two-chambered heart.

Our baby would never have good oxygen saturations. He would always be cyanotic or blue. Most people have oxygen saturations between 98 and 100 percent. This baby's oxygen saturations would probably always be somewhere in the 80s, if we were lucky.

Dr. Roberts said that most babies with HLHS have to take a baby aspirin and usually some sort of blood pressure medication daily for their entire lives. Our baby would definitely have limitations. No team sports at all. He might be able to play tennis, but golf was a much better choice.

Dr. Roberts told us to make another appointment in two weeks, as we would probably have more questions.

"You asked whether our older son had any heart problems. Why?" I said.

"Usually, when we see something this severe, there is a family history of congenital heart defects or the siblings have some other lesser type of heart defect. The fact that he's over a year old and has never been diagnosed with anything means it's unlikely that he has anything wrong."

"Do you think we should get Liam checked out?" I asked.

"He's probably fine, but I would be happy to examine him," he said kindly.

"Liam's fine. There's nothing wrong with his heart," Kevin declared.

"I know, but I'd like to know for sure," I said. "I keep thinking about how Liam runs through the living room, dining room and kitchen in a big circle and never gets tired. It won't be the same for this baby, will it?"

"No," Dr. Roberts answered. "He will probably tire very easily. Do you have any other questions?"

"Yes. Could you be wrong about this diagnosis?" I asked.

Dr. Roberts looked me straight in the eye. "No. I'm not wrong. I'm sorry."

As we stood to leave I turned and said, "Could I ask a huge favor?" My eyes started to fill with tears.

"Sure."

"Would you call Frank Stone and tell him what's going on? He knew we were coming to see you today, but I don't think I could get through that conversation right now. Plus, you'll explain it much better than I ever could."

"Of course. I'll call Frank right now," Dr. Roberts said.

I made appointments to come back in two weeks and to bring Liam in for an echocardiogram. We got the number for Dr. Callaway's office so we could make an appointment to discuss surgical options. Before we left, I asked Dr. Roberts to write the exact diagnosis so I wouldn't forget the name (like that could ever happen).

Kevin and I walked to the elevators in silence. I finally felt like I could look at him without bursting into tears. He pressed the elevator button and said, "What do you know about the heart?"

"I know that the heart has four chambers and that the two on top are called the atrium, or atria plural, and the two on the bottom are the ventricles."

"How do you know that?"

"I had to label a heart in anatomy and physiology for a test. The way I remembered it is that A comes before V in the alphabet."

"We're so fucked," Kevin said. His face was contorted in anguish, which I'm sure was a mirror image of my own.

Yes, I thought. Yes, we are.

CHAPTER 5

When we finally reached the house, we went inside and gave Esme a quick rundown of the situation—which, of course, completely freaked her out.

Awesome.

After Esme left, Kevin asked me, "Do you think she's going to quit?"

"Shit if I know," I said.

"Well, this baby may be too sick to stay with a nanny, if he even survives. You might have to quit work and take care of him."

"Screw you" was on the tip of my tongue, but I managed to swallow the words through the enormous lump in my throat. This was our child. How did he go from being our problem to mine? I wanted the best thing for our little boy, but what was that?

We'd been given three terrible choices. I'd been tempted to say, "option D, none of the above," but denial would do nothing to help our baby. We needed to educate ourselves about HLHS as quickly as we could to make the best decisions possible.

In my eighteen months of motherhood, I felt like I'd struck a pretty good balance between work and home. I didn't really need to work, but I liked it. I worked hard to become a court reporter, and I was proud of my status as an official in district court. And if I'm being honest with myself, I'm a much better mama when I've had a break. I'm not cut out for one-on-one or one-on-two with infants and small children twenty-four hours a day, seven days a week. My patience runs thin, and I turn into a real bitch.

On Fridays everybody is always, TGIF! I'm the opposite. On Monday mornings I get into my car and jam out to rock-and-roll the whole way to work while chanting to myself, TGIM! Thank God, it's Monday!

In short, I love my career, and I'm good at it. Kevin's implication that my job was less important was galling, to say the least. I'm glad I didn't tell him to buzz off, though, because in the next breath, he said, "Shit! You can't quit your job because you carry our health insurance."

I looked at him with wide eyes and said, "Maybe you'll have to close your law practice and stay home with the baby."

"I can't do that. That's absolutely ridiculous!"

No shit, I thought. But what's good for the goose . . .

"We probably need to call our parents," Kevin said.

"I'll call in a little while. I can't face it right now." The knot that had set up residence in my throat and chest expanded a little more. I didn't even know where to begin with my parents.

Liam started to cry, which meant his nap was over. I ran upstairs to get him. When I opened the door to his room, his sweet face lit up with a huge smile and he said, "Mama!" I felt like the wind had been knocked out of me, like I might cry. For a moment I couldn't separate the bad news from Liam. I had to remind myself that Liam's heart was healthy—or so we thought—and that no matter what happened to the baby, Liam would be okay.

I scooped him out of his bed, and we snuggled in the rocking chair for a few minutes. I breathed in his sweet scent and cuddled him close. Then I changed his diaper and took him downstairs. Kevin and I weren't hungry, so I made Liam a plate of shredded turkey, crackers and a small pile of blueberries I'd cut in half.

After Liam finished devouring his food, he was getting sleepy again. Esme normally had a full day of activities and kept him going full steam. They usually hit the park or the zoo and then ran by the grocery store for a gallon of milk or whatever we were running low on. By midafternoon Liam was pretty exhausted. He'd nap until six, eat his dinner and go back to bed at seven-thirty.

That evening, after Liam was in bed, Kevin and I could finally discuss what we'd learned at Dr. Roberts' office. Kevin had already been on the Internet researching HLHS and children's hospitals around the country.

"What happened when you typed in HLHS?" I asked.

Kevin hung his head and rubbed his eyes like he always does when he's exhausted. "Dead babies. Lots of web pages dedicated to dead babies, along with some medical information on HLHS. Pretty much what Dr. Roberts said as far as HLHS being 100 percent fatal without surgical intervention or a heart transplant and the palliative care option. It doesn't look good. Even if everything goes perfectly, the baby will never really be okay. He'll always just have half of a heart."

Note to self: Stay off the Internet.

"Okay." I checked my phone and saw that my mom and sister had called. "I better tell my mom what's going on," I said.

"Yeah. I'm going to call my parents in just a minute," Kevin said.

I took a deep breath and dialed. My mother answered after the first couple of rings.

"Hey, Mom," I said. I walked into our bedroom and began pacing.

"What's going on with you? I haven't talked to you all day," she said.

"We went to the appointment with the pediatric cardiologist."

"Oh, gosh. I forgot that was today. What did he say?"

"It's not good." My voice was going to crack, so I took another deep breath. "The baby has some major structural problems with his heart. He did have some options for us, but they're all terrible."

"Oh, my gosh. Honey, I'm so sorry."

"Kevin's doing some research on the Internet, but he's having to wade through tons of web pages dedicated to dead babies. It's awful. Thank goodness he can do this—I don't think I can deal with dead babies right now."

I explained everything Kevin and I had learned. My mother was clearly devastated for me, for us, for the baby. "What about getting a second opinion?" she said.

"I thought about that, but the thing is, Dr. Roberts is not wrong. I know he's not. I really liked him. He's the first person who's been honest about what's going on with this baby. I'm not ruling out a second opinion, but he's not wrong."

"What about Dr. Voigt?" Mom asked. "Didn't she say you were looking at having a baby who was 95 percent okay?"

"That's what she told me, but he's 100 percent not okay. I left a message with her answering service, but I haven't heard anything."

We talked for a little while longer, and my mom said, "I just want you to know that whatever you decide to do, we're here for you and we support you."

"Thanks, Mom. That really means a lot. Can you call Holly and Hunter? I want them to know, but Kevin and I need to talk and I don't want to go through it with them right now."

"Sure, sweetie."

"Hey, Mom? Do you know of anyone in our close family who has a child with heart problems or a baby who died shortly after birth? Dr. Roberts said that when they see something this severe, there's almost always a family history of heart defects."

"Not that I know of. I mean, Mammaw used to complain about heart palpitations, but that's the only thing I can think of." (Mammaw was my paternal grandmother, who died when I was twelve.)

When I walked out of our bedroom, Kevin was leaving a message for his parents to call him.

We began sifting through the information he'd printed off the Internet, including details about the congenital heart programs at Texas Children's Hospital in Houston, Children's Hospital of Philadelphia, and Boston Children's Hospital, the standout for congenital heart surgery and the Norwood procedure. Kevin had also emailed an inquiry to the offices of Bill Norwood, who invented the Norwood procedure, at the Nemours/Alfred I. DuPont Hospital for Children.

These hospitals had great reputations for staged palliative surgeries, but at that point in time, as Dr. Roberts told us, hospitals that were good at the Norwood were not necessarily the best for neonatal heart transplantation. Conversely, the leading centers at that time for neonatal heart transplantation, in Denver, Colorado, and Loma Linda, California, were not necessarily the best for the staged surgical palliation.

There was no one-stop shop, no St. Jude's equivalent, for babies and children who needed heart surgery.

I wondered about the surgeon in San Antonio, but I didn't say anything. I was impressed with the progress Kevin had made in a little under an hour—especially since all I wanted was to climb into bed, curl up under the covers and stare at the wall for the next eight weeks.

We had a lot of hard questions to ask ourselves. We started a list of pros and cons on a legal pad. Heart transplant was one surgery and would give our baby a four-chambered, fully functional heart. But the shortage of donor hearts meant our baby would likely die waiting. If he did receive a new heart, he would be on antirejection medications his entire life because his body would always try to reject that foreign organ. The antirejection medications suppress the immune system and make the person more susceptible to illnesses; plus, they can cause cancer. Some transplant patients also get coronary artery disease, which is another form of rejection that can be difficult to detect, and they're either listed for retransplant or die from a massive heart attack. Patients need constant, close monitoring and heart catheterizations to check for rejection.

The third major drawback is that the heart usually lasts ten to fifteen years before you're looking at another transplant or death. Heart transplant was described to us as trading one critical illness for another. It's not a cure.

We were in a pick-your-poison situation. If we decided to list the baby for transplant, we'd have to choose the facility pretty quickly, and then I would go to Denver or Loma Linda so he could be placed on the transplant list as soon as he was born.

We were both leaning toward the three palliative surgeries, with the Norwood being performed shortly after birth. It had a 70 percent survival rate, which didn't sound too bad until I realized there was a 30 percent mortality rate. Three out of ten babies don't make it.

The other two surgeries had better survival odds, but our baby would always have cyanosis due to low oxygen saturations. He would have strict limitations on physical activity. He would tire easily. What would his quality of life be like? Would he be able to run and play? With no prognosis, was it worth putting him through three open-heart surgeries in the first three years of his life, all so he could die the horrible death of heart failure in five, ten, fifteen or twenty years?

This brought me to our third choice: compassionate, or palliative care. Kevin had a hard time seeing this as a valid possibility, but I felt that we needed to weigh all of the options carefully and equally.

The Norwood was, and still is, an extremely difficult surgery for an infant to undergo. With survival odds at just 70 percent, a lot of cardiologists and heart surgeons believed it wasn't worth putting an infant through.

I kind of agreed. We were on the edge of what medical science could do, with no clear path to the future. I couldn't imagine doing nothing, but the thought of surgeons slicing through skin and bone to cut into his heart just a few days into his life made my knees buckle. I wouldn't allow Liam to be circumcised because I didn't want him to be in unnecessary pain. How could I put this baby through so much worse? I wanted to fight for him, but this was his fight—and I didn't know if he'd even want to fight it. How could I subject an innocent baby to what amounted to pure torture, in my mind, for the selfish purpose of keeping him here with me?

If he died in the hospital days or weeks after undergoing the Norwood procedure, then his world would've consisted of hospitals and pain. That's it. If we brought him home to die, we'd be able to hold him; he'd know he was loved. The quality of his days mattered, not the quantity. And when he stopped breathing, I guess we'd call hospice instead of 911?

All the scenarios were unimaginable. Kevin and I talked through every angle and came to the conclusion that there were no right decisions. We were going to make mistakes no matter what, and we'd have to live with them.

Frank called about then. I had a fleeting hope when I saw his number on my phone that maybe we were being irrational and things were not as bad as they seemed. Maybe Frank would be able to shed some light on the situation. So I took the call.

"Hey, Heather," he said. "I just spoke to Jerry. I'm so sorry."

My eyes filled with tears. I knew this was bad, but Frank's words confirmed it.

As promised, Dr. Roberts had given Frank a verbal report. Frank and I talked about HLHS, and I asked if he'd ever had a patient with it.

"Yes," Frank said, "but it was a long time ago."

"So he died?"

"Yes."

"From talking with Dr. Roberts, do you think it's worth it to do the three surgeries?" I asked.

"Well, I think even if you get six months out of it, wouldn't it be worth it?"

"Um, yeah, I don't know," I mumbled.

I'd gone through life like a normal person and imagined that my child and future children would outlive me, not the other way around. I couldn't bear the thought of loving this baby for six months and then putting him in the dirt. I couldn't even fathom it. The new reality hit me like a ton of bricks. No matter what I did, barring some sort of accident or illness happening to me, I *would* bury this child.

I had to stop thinking about the big picture. This was going to be an hour-by-hour, minute-by-minute situation. It was the only way I would make it through. I handed Kevin the phone. He wanted to ask Frank some questions of his own.

"I just don't understand why this happened to us," Kevin said to me after he hung up.

"I've sort of been asking myself the opposite question: Why not us? Why would we be immune from something like this?"

"Do you think it's something you did, like that horrible medicine you used to clear up your skin?"

"You mean the Accutane I took almost four years ago? No. It leaves your bloodstream in thirty days or less, and we had a seemingly perfect child between then and now. So I don't think this is because of some medication," I said, biting back my anger.

I took a deep breath. I had to nip this in the bud. "Look, I know you always feel the need to assess blame, but this is nothing I did or you did. We could speculate about all sorts of reasons, but it doesn't change the facts. Maybe it's because you're an older dad, but I doubt it. Do you see how that line of thinking is not helpful?"

"Yeah, you're right."

"Dr. Roberts said that left-sided defects are usually genetic. I don't know of anything like this in my family, but there could be someone with a lesser defect that we don't know about. If we can find out about our family histories, that might be a good thing for Dr. Roberts to know."

"Yeah, I'm sorry," Kevin said. "This is just so messed up."

"I know." I stood and stretched. Exhaustion washed over me. I headed to our bedroom to throw on some pajamas. Kevin followed me.

"You know, my uncle had a little girl die when she was just a couple of weeks old. I wonder if she had anything wrong with her heart," he ventured.

"I don't know. Have you talked to your parents yet?"

"I left them a message."

"We need to ask them about that. And we definitely need to make an appointment with Jack Callaway, the local surgeon. If he's the one I'm thinking of, I read a newspaper article years ago about him, and he has an excellent reputation."

"I'll check his credentials," Kevin said.

"It would be a lot easier to do the three surgeries here in San Antonio, if we go that route. And we have to think of Liam. He's not even two. I don't want to have to go to some other city to have this baby. Your law practice is here. If the recovery takes a long time, you'll eventually have to come back with Liam, which leaves me on my own in a strange city with a really sick baby."

Kevin and I climbed into bed. I was completely drained. And I was a little worried I'd have weird dreams about babies, surgeries and death. I couldn't imagine how this would play out in my brain while I slept.

I turned my back to Kevin, and he wrapped his arms around me and held me for a long time. I thought maybe I should pray, but what for, exactly? I wanted to pray that the baby would survive, but would the cost to him be too high? I could pray for God's will, but what if His will didn't necessarily jibe with mine?

"Heather, we have to name him," Kevin murmured into the back of my neck.

"You name him," I replied.

"Why don't you want to name him? He needs a name."

"I want his middle name to be Maloy, my maiden name, but I don't care what his first name is. You pick it."

"Sweetie, we need to choose his name together. I think he needs a strong name."

"I can't do it right now. I keep picturing what it will look like on a tiny tombstone," I said, distraught.

Kevin held me for a long time and sobbed.

My eyes stayed dry. Not because I couldn't cry but because if I started I might not be able to stop.

CHAPTER 6

Kevin named the baby Colman. In our past discussions I'd said I liked the names Henry and Colman. Kevin made a great choice, but I still couldn't say the baby's name without feeling awfully sad. Calling him "Nemo" or simply "the baby" didn't have the same crushing effect on me.

I was looking forward to work on Monday, even though my emotions were raw and I felt more than a bit fragile. Many times during that horrible weekend, I selfishly thought about how I would handle this situation better if I were on my own. Every time I looked at Kevin, the man I loved and adored, and saw the grief apparent in every line of his face, I felt cut to the quick.

Kevin and I are both pretty private people, but he wanted to talk to our friends and colleagues about what was going on; I didn't. We didn't have enough information, and I was still trying to come to terms with Colman's health problems. We decided to tell our families and our closest friends—about four people outside blood relations. That was it.

As Colman's birth date drew near, Kevin would have to inform a few judges whom we both knew because of the timing of some of his case settings, but I hoped I'd feel stronger by then. I worked in the Juvenile Justice Center and most of Kevin's cases were in the Bexar County Justice Center and Federal Court, but the news would spread like wildfire in the legal community, which puts most small-town gossip grapevines to shame. I didn't want to talk about it at work. I was already annoyed at random people who wanted to touch my belly or talk to me about normal pregnancy stuff. I wanted to avoid, for as long as possible, people saying things like, "My brother's friend's sister's cousin had a friend who was going to have a baby with heart problems, and the doctors were wrong. It was born healthy."

How do you respond to that? Somehow "Well, halle-fucking-lujah!" seemed inappropriate. I knew people meant well and only wanted to make me feel better, but they didn't know what I knew, what I sensed even before a doctor told me—that something was very wrong.

Dr. Voigt finally called on Monday when I was between court hearings.

"I got your message," she said, "and I see Dr. Roberts left me a message as well on Friday. What did he say?"

"Well, it wasn't good news. He said the baby has hypoplastic left heart syndrome."

"Yeah." She sighed. "I was afraid of that."

I felt the blood drain from my face, and I turned my chair so that my back was to the window of my office. "You mean, you thought this baby had HLHS all along?"

"Well, I couldn't be sure until you saw a pediatric cardiologist, but I was worried that it could be."

She'd lied to me. "Why didn't you tell me that before?" I said.

"I didn't want you to worry."

"Look, I appreciate that to a certain extent, but I have a mother. I need you to be my doctor." And be honest with me.

"It's not like you would have done anything differently, would you? I mean, you'd be in this exact situation whether you knew earlier or not."

"I don't know what I would have done if I'd received this information sooner," I said.

"I doubt you would have terminated the pregnancy because you're such a nice person."

What? What did that have to do with anything?

"I might not have terminated," I replied, "but there might have been more options than what we're left with now. Kevin and I have been doing some research, and Boston Children's Hospital has an in utero surgery program that as early as 2002 boasts having fixed a baby who was going to be born with HLHS. It's a slim possibility that our baby would have been a candidate for that surgery, but it had to be done between twenty-four and twenty-eight weeks. We're way past that window."

"In utero surgery is very risky. I don't think you would have done that. And don't you think you're getting a little designer baby?" Dr. Voigt said.

I could hear the blood pounding in my ears. I was livid. "No, I don't. I'm not saying this baby has to have blond hair and blue eyes like his brother or be six feet tall like my grandfathers. But I'd like him to have a fair shot at life. They told us we could take him home to die because heart transplant or three open-heart surgeries are so much for a baby to undergo. So I don't think in utero surgery is too risky. But we need to move forward now. It's kind of a moot point, don't you think?"

"Yeah. Now that we know what kind of heart problem the baby has, we can move forward with a few interventions," she said.

"What interventions?" I asked testily.

"You probably need to see a perinatologist so they can monitor the baby for the last several weeks. You need to look into having your baby at South Texas Medical Hospital. And you're probably going to need a C-section."

"Do you have privileges at South Texas Medical Hospital?"

"No. You'll need to get into the clinic there, and whoever the resident is on call will probably deliver the baby."

She was trying to get rid of me. I wasn't going to let her off the hook so easily. "Dr. Roberts said most babies with HLHS tolerate a vaginal delivery. He said I could have the baby at Mercy."

"How do you expect the baby to get from Mercy to South Texas Medical Hospital?" Her voice was thick with condescension.

"Dr. Roberts will arrange for South Texas Medical Hospital to send a transport team for the baby. My understanding is HLHS babies usually present healthy at birth. In fact, a lot of them get sent home before anyone realizes they're sick. The opening in the heart that allows the blood to mix—the patent ductus arteriosus—closes a couple of days after birth, and that's when they go into heart failure. Worst-case scenario, I could probably carry him over there in my arms. It's only a couple of blocks."

"We'll see what Dr. Roberts has to say. I'll give him a call sometime today."

"I think that's a good idea," I said, and hung up the phone.

I was furious. I must have called her every bad name, every curse, in the English language. I'll spare you the details.

I stood and caught a glance of my reflection in the mirror. My face was flushed like I'd been running sprints. I closed the door and smoothed my skin with my fingers, raked my hands through my hair, applied some gloss. I took a few deep breaths and tried to calm down.

Dr. Voigt had crossed a major line with the designer baby comment. No one is guaranteed a perfect baby, I get that—but she had a duty as my doctor not to hide the fact that our baby might be facing major health issues and the high likelihood of death. She never should have sent me to Dr. Roberts so unprepared for a devastating diagnosis.

I called Dr. Callaway's office to make an appointment to discuss surgery and got one for the following week, the day after I was scheduled to take Liam to see Dr. Roberts for the echo of his heart.

I still had to work in a perinatologist at some point, and Kevin and I probably needed to see a counselor or psychologist. We'd both seen the statistics on how having a sick child wreaks havoc on a marriage. Kevin and I have always had great communication, and I didn't want that breaking down when we needed it the most. Especially since we were beginning to piss each other off, and Colman wasn't even here yet.

Kevin's optimism is one of the things I adore about him. That being said, I felt like he wasn't fully comprehending what we were up against. It was going to be hard, really hard. I didn't want to kick him in the balls with reality all the time. I just wanted us both to be prepared.

Kevin thought I was too pessimistic about Colman's chances. I don't think I'm a pessimist, but I am a realist, which is somewhere in the middle. I wanted Colman to have the best outcome possible, and I would do everything in my power to make that happen, but this was not going to be an easy road.

Kevin had also contacted the pastor of the church we sporadically attended to discuss possible baptism and/or funeral arrangements. Kevin wanted Colman to be baptized in the NICU before the surgery, and I thought that was probably a good idea. I'm sure the pastor was like, Who are these people? You probably have to go to church more than twice a year (early April and late December) to leave an impression.

Kevin and I had drawn up our wills right after Liam was born, but it's not like we'd bought burial plots. I should say burial plot, since I'm going to be cremated. Kevin wanted to know what I would like done with my ashes. I don't give a rat's ass. I'm not the sentimental sort. Bury them, save them, spread them or throw them in the ocean. I don't care.

We wouldn't be able to put our baby in the ground and walk away. It just felt too awful. "Maybe we need to buy two plots together so when I die I can be buried with him," Kevin said. That sounded marginally better to me, but I still wasn't feeling it. I'd still have to put him in the dirt and walk away. No matter how many times I visualized that scenario, it was always as horrific as the first time.

Then Kevin said, "I'm not even sure where I want to be buried."

"What do you mean?" I asked.

"Well, do I want to be buried in Missouri or Texas?"

Now he had my full attention. "Have you lost your mind? Missouri? Do you want anybody to actually visit your grave? Because I'm sure as hell not traveling to Missouri to put flowers on your grave, and I can guarantee you that by the time you're dead, there will be nobody still alive in Missouri to put flowers on your grave either. As long as you're married to me when you die, I'm burying you in Texas."

Kevin laughed. "Well, I guess that solves it. Texas it is, then."

"I get that all of your family is from Missouri and you feel nostalgic about it sometimes, but my family is from here. You got out of Missouri and away from your family as fast as you could. I never imagined you'd want that to be your final resting place."

Kevin embraced me, and I said, "Seriously, I'm sorry. You surprised me. I never thought you'd want to be buried in Missouri."

"No. You're right. I never really thought about where I'd like to be buried."

"Well, other than you, I have no connection to Missouri. Colman belongs in Texas."

"So do we look for something in one of the cemeteries here?"

"I don't know. I think we should have him cremated. Then when you die, I can put him in with you."

"What do we do with him until then?"

"I'm not sure. Cemeteries creep me out, though. I just feel like we need to keep him close," I said.

Kevin hugged me to him again. "Hopefully, we won't have to worry about it for a really long time, he said.

Kevin told me that he couldn't sit through Liam's echocardiogram, so I made our nanny, Esme, come. It was too much for Kevin. I completely understood; we both have our strengths. I'd been unable to get on the Internet and do my own HLHS research. I wasn't ready yet, and I was thankful I had Kevin's research to rely on.

Liam's echo lasted less than forty-five minutes. Helen, the X-ray technician, said she didn't see anything to worry about.

Dr. Roberts called that evening to say that Liam's heart was perfect. There were no holes or structural abnormalities. I breathed a huge sigh of relief.

He continued, "I did want to let you know that in reviewing the baby's echo again, it looks like he has a mild tricuspid valve regurgitation."

"What does that mean?" I asked.

"It complicates things."

"It's already complicated. How could it get any more complicated?" I blurted out. Then it began to dawn on me.

"If the leak is anything more than mild, he won't be a candidate for surgery."

"Do we need to have another fetal echo?"

"No. I won't be able to tell how bad the leak is until he's born. Then we'll be able to hold him still and get a good look. I just wanted you to know."

"Thank you."

I hung up the phone and saw Kevin watching me. "What's wrong?" he said.

"Liam is fine, but the baby has a leak in his tricuspid valve that could complicate things."

"It's already complicated."

"Yeah. But if the leak is bad, they won't be able to do the surgery."

"So we'll be back to the heart transplant?"

"Except we won't know until he's born and we'll lose time during the transfer, if he's even stable enough to transfer."

"This is so screwed up."

"I know. The little guy can't catch a break, and he hasn't even been born."

There was no way out of this predicament that didn't include loads of heartache, literally and figuratively. I'd never felt more trapped in my life. I was hugely pregnant with a baby I hadn't planned, and I didn't want to be pregnant one second more than I had to. On the other hand, as long as Colman stayed inside of me, he was safe.

Liam was six weeks old before I felt the connection that happens at birth for most women. That seems like an eternity when your baby is born equipped with a heart that will last only a couple of weeks.

I mentioned my experience with Liam and my worry about not bonding right away to Dr. Z, our psychologist.

Kevin looked at me like I was a mama cat that could eat her own young and said, "I loved him the moment I laid eyes on him." Of course he did.

Dr. Z didn't think it was anything to really worry about, that I probably bonded with Liam and didn't realize it. But here's the thing: I know I didn't. I wondered if I was somehow emotionally broken, which only added to my anxiety. This baby's heart might be beyond repair, and it was my body that grew him that way. Colman deserved to have a mama who wasn't broken.

Kevin and I had an appointment with the pastor on the same day we were meeting with Dr. Callaway. We both had court that morning, so we drove separately and met at the Methodist church we attended on the north side of San Antonio. I let Kevin do all the talking.

We discussed having Colman baptized in the NICU at Mercy Hospital. The pastor said he'd done that many times before and it wouldn't be a problem. Kevin talked to him about the possibility of making other arrangements. The pastor kept glancing nervously at me, but I sat there dry-eyed and mute.

Then, in what must have been an attempt to comfort me, he said, "If your baby does pass away, I want you to know that he will have a free pass into heaven because an infant is without sin. This is something that we, as humans, cannot understand here on Earth, but when we pass away and go to heaven, I think everything will make sense. This is all part of God's plan."

He meant to provide us with guidance or relief, but it didn't make me feel better that any child suffering could be part of a bigger plan. It didn't make sense at all.

I feel like when I die, I'm dead. That's it. Eternal life is living on through my children in a literal sense. If there is a God, I doubt anything will make sense to me when I pass away, since I'll be burning in Hell after I tell God what I think of His stupid plans.

I had to get out of that church before the Eye of Sauron, God or Jesus—or whatever—could screw with me a little further. The whole God element made me feel sad and disappointed, and I wanted to focus all my energy positively toward helping this baby get better.

Kevin and I left the church to grab a sandwich at home and then head to Dr. Callaway's office in one car. Much to my relief, we didn't talk about the pastor. I could do without that kind of comfort for the remainder of my life. At that moment, I wanted the comfort of something a bit more tangible, like science and modern medicine.

Kevin and I arrived at South Texas Medical Hospital a few minutes early. I instructed him on where to park and led the way into the building. I'd been there several times before to take depositions as a freelance court reporter, so for once I had a pretty good idea of where we were going.

I was about half a step in front of Kevin, holding his hand, when we both spotted a wild-eyed little man walking hurriedly in our direction with a mess of books and papers. He was mostly bald, but the hair he did have was long and gray and shot out in a tangled mess. He had a crazy mustache and silver-rimmed spectacles held together on the side with a piece of tape that went perfectly with his rumpled khakis, bow tie and tweed jacket. I stopped and turned to face Kevin. We both said, "Absolutely not!" in low voices and started laughing. We were pretty sure that wasn't Dr. Callaway, but it was a relief to know we were both on the same page as far as having a mad professor perform heart surgery.

We checked in at the clinic and were shown to an exam room. I was nervous. A lot was riding on this visit.

Kevin had asked his investigator to pull everything he could find on Jack Callaway. The investigator's report and the research Kevin had compiled was almost a half an inch thick.

"Are we going to talk to Dr. Callaway, or are you going to cross-examine him?" I asked, smiling and gesturing to the file Kevin was holding.

Kevin laughed. "We're just going to talk. It's always good to have as much information as possible. He looks really good on paper."

"I just wanted to be prepared in case of fireworks," I teased.

Kevin squeezed my hand and gave me a quick smile and wink. "No worries."

Jack Callaway did look good on paper. He'd been chief resident at Boston Children's Hospital and had trained under Bill Norwood, who invented the Norwood procedure. But I was afraid to get my hopes up.

Dr. Callaway came into the exam room, and Kevin and I stood to introduce ourselves. Dr. Callaway was probably in his mid- to late forties. He was tall and more athletic than I'd imagined, though I'm not sure why I'd expected him to be paunchy. He was very serious, with green eyes and wavy reddish-blond hair trimmed short. We all sat down, and Dr. Callaway said he'd gotten the report from Dr. Roberts regarding the fetal echo findings. "I see you've been doing a little bit of research," he said, pointing to the file in Kevin's hands.

If he only knew.

"Does your little fella have a name yet?" he said.

Why was everybody so hung up on his name? I looked at Kevin, who answered, "Colman."

I stared down at the shiny tiled floor—the industrial tiles you always see in hospitals and classrooms. They don't have any grout. The kind of floor that makes mopping up blood and vomit easy.

Dr. Callaway was talking about HLHS from a surgeon's standpoint. He was incredibly soft-spoken. I almost snapped "Speak up" but thankfully stopped myself. I'd spent almost ten years bossing around lawyers who didn't enunciate in the courtroom, and it was a hard habit to break. I caught myself leaning in several times to catch Dr. Callaway's words.

"I want you both to know that I believe palliative care is a very real option for these children," he said. "People get mad when I say that sometimes, but the Norwood procedure is brutal. I often wonder if I'm doing more harm than good. I've seen firsthand how this disease destroys families."

My stomach did a flip, and I glanced down at Kevin's hand holding on to mine.

"If you're interested in hearing more, I'd be happy to discuss palliative care with you."

"I think we've decided to go with the surgical repair, but thank you," Kevin said.

I nodded, but I did want to hear more about palliative care. I still wasn't convinced the three surgeries were the way to go, and Dr. Callaway had just said that the Norwood was brutal. However, I wasn't sure I wanted to engage in a conversation about our baby's death right then.

Dr. Callaway explained the procedure using diagrams and pictures. He would make a vertical incision in the chest and separate the sternum. The surgery's main objectives were to divide the pulmonary artery and reconnect part of it to the aorta, then to enlarge Colman's aorta by sewing in a patch of homograft tissue and placing a Sano shunt, made out of Gore-Tex, that would connect the ventricle to the pulmonary artery.

The repair of the aortic arch sounded the trickiest. During that process Dr. Callaway usually placed his patients under circulatory arrest, which requires bringing the body temperature down to 18 degrees Celsius. My understanding of circulatory arrest is that there is no breathing, heartbeat or brain activity, and the blood is drained from the body to eliminate blood pressure. It's used in cardiothoracic surgery and neurosurgery for short periods so the surgeon can make a difficult repair. Colman would be considered clinically dead while he was under circulatory arrest. And I'd thought bypass was scary.

We asked Dr. Callaway how long he might have Colman under circulatory arrest. He promised he'd work fast, which kind of made me laugh. No longer than fifty minutes was his more precise answer— the upper limit of what's considered safe—but he thought it would be significantly shorter than that.

The surgery would probably take between four and six hours, and Dr. Callaway would not, in all probability, close Colman's chest immediately. He would seal it with a small plastic membrane until the swelling had subsided and then attempt the chest closure a few days later.

"Reasons he might not be a candidate for the surgery," Dr. Callaway said, "are if he had a tricuspid valve leak, chromosomal abnormalities—"

"Did you say a tricuspid valve leak?" I interrupted.

"Yes."

"I think he has one of those."

"Dr. Roberts doesn't mention it in his report," he said, skimming the pages. He knitted his eyebrows together. "Are you sure?"

"I just spoke with Dr. Roberts yesterday," I said. "He explained that in reviewing the echo he noticed a tricuspid valve leak that looked mild, but he couldn't be sure until the baby was here and he could echo him."

"Well, he didn't say anything to me about that." Dr. Callaway scribbled something on the chart. "I'll ask him about it, though."

"Why wouldn't you do the surgery if there's a leak? Couldn't we try to fix that, too?" I asked, feeling a little naïve.

"That's the only valve we have between the two chambers, and if it's leaking it won't be a good outcome. Sometimes these little hearts are just too screwed up, and the only thing you can do is give them back to God."

Yuck. As far as I was concerned, there was no better place for Colman than in my arms. I kept my mouth shut, but I wished Dr. Callaway would stick to science.

"I don't think that's what Dr. Roberts said last night. I thought you told me something different," Kevin offered.

"Yeah, maybe I'm mistaken. I'm sorry—I didn't mean to interrupt." Dr. Callaway finished telling us about the surgery.

Kevin asked, "So if you had a child with HLHS, what would you do?"

"That's one of the questions that Bill Norwood, about four other heart surgeons and I have asked each other over dinner. Three of us said we'd take the palliative care route, the other three said they'd proceed with the surgeries and we all argue about it. Then after a couple of scotches," Dr. Callaway said with a chuckle, "the three who said they'd let the baby die said they wanted to do the surgeries, and the three that wanted to do the surgeries were wanting to go the palliative care route." He hesitated a beat. "I think I would take the palliative care route, but it's a really tough question. I feel very strongly that palliative care is a viable option for these babies. The surgery is a lot to put a baby through."

I was thankful for his honesty. His opinion on palliative care, as hard as it was to hear, made me realize that Jack Callaway took his Hippocratic oath seriously. It reminded me again of how we were on a medical precipice, and it made me queasy. Sitting before me was a man who had the skill and talent to possibly repair our baby's heart, telling us letting the baby go might be a better option.

"I understand this surgery is very difficult," I said. "Will you let us know if he's not responding like he's supposed to? I don't want to torture him if it looks like the end result will be the same."

"I will," he promised. "You know, these children can be very vigorous. My advice is to treat him like a normal child. Don't treat him like he's got a heart problem. Just treat him like you would any normal baby."

Normal? I could do normal.

Linda Cabrera, Dr. Callaway's nurse, came in and introduced herself. Dr. Callaway was explaining a Norwood surgery he'd just performed on a baby who was barely four pounds and didn't make it. They couldn't bring the baby off the heart pump. I didn't want to listen as he talked about repairing the baby's aorta, which was only one millimeter in size.

I looked at Linda expectantly. She handed me two books on HLHS and offered to take me on a quick tour of the pediatric intensive care unit where Colman would be after his surgery. As we walked by a room with a sliding glass door, I saw an infant in a bed with an exhausted-looking mother seated by his side. Something struck me as odd, but I kept moving so I wouldn't be caught staring.

On our way past several of the other rooms, I realized what it was. Most of the babies were lying in cribs, but the rails were down. There was nothing to stop them from rolling off. With all of the painkillers and paralytics pumped into their systems, they didn't need rails.

Linda and I met up with Kevin, who was still chatting with Dr. Callaway. I said, "Dr. Roberts mentioned that the congenital heart surgery program is moving to St. John's Children's Hospital on April 1. Will Colman's surgery definitely be here?"

"Yes," Dr. Callaway said quietly. "We are moving the program, but this is a complicated surgery. We don't want Colman to be our first case at St. John's, and neither do you. We have everybody in place here, so he'll probably be our last difficult case before the move is complete. We should have everything running smoothly at St. John's in time for his second surgery."

"Okay."

Kevin and I said our good-byes to Dr. Callaway and Linda.

"What did you think?" I asked Kevin when we got into the elevator.

"I liked him. And if anybody can save Colman, he can. It's nice that he's right here in San Antonio. How about you?"

"He's fucking intense," I said, and Kevin and I both laughed.

"He is."

"I feel better after talking to him, like we're getting something accomplished."

Kevin nodded but seemed a little doubtful. "I don't think he'd really choose palliative care if it was his kid," he said.

"I do. He knows the path these kids take, the survivors and how they fare in life. He's seen how families are destroyed by the stress of having a child who's always knocking on death's door. I don't doubt him for a minute, but I also have complete faith that he will do whatever he can to try to make Colman better."

Kevin hugged me to him and kissed my cheek. "We're going to get through it. We're assembling Colman's team. I feel pretty good about this."

I smiled what felt like my first real smile in weeks. We'd just met hope. And his name was Jack Callaway.

CHAPTER 7

On the evening of March 29, 2004, Kevin and I decided to take Liam and our dog, Lucy, for a walk. We kept a slow pace since I was feeling heavy, with only seventeen days until my due date. Even at that pace, I felt an incessant but painless tightening of my belly. I called my mom when we returned home to ask her advice.

You'd think I'd know all about labor after having one child. Not the case. With Liam, I got my epidural so fast that I never had a chance to experience real labor. I'm not complaining. The problem is it didn't really prepare me for baby number two.

"Hey, Mom," I said, when she answered the phone.

"Hey, sweetie, what's up?"

"I don't know. We went on a walk tonight, and I'm feeling kind of funny."

"Are you having pains?" she asked, sounding panicky.

I rolled my eyes. The way she said "pains" and the pitch of her voice—God, she could be annoying sometimes. And I hate that word. Pains. It ranks right up there with "budget," "womb," "panties," and "moist." The worst? Moist panties. Ugh.

"No, no pains," I said, internally cringing.

"Well, when you went on your walk, did they go away or become more frequent?"

"They got more frequent."

"Are you or Kevin timing these?"

"Hell, no. Nobody is timing anything."

"I think you should go to the hospital. Your dad and I will be on our way."

"Hold on a second. You really think I should go?"

"Yes. I'm scared you're going to go really fast this time. Just head to the hospital. If they send you home, fine. But I bet they keep you there. Dad and I are coming."

"I'm going to call Esme, and then I'll head to the hospital. But wait until I call to tell you they're keeping me. What if you come all this way and they send me home?"

"We don't mind. We just want to be there for you."

"But you'll wait until I call you?"

I heard her sigh. "We'll wait."

I went into the bedroom in search of Kevin. "Hey, babe, we need to go to the hospital."

"Why?"

"Because I'm having your baby," I said, gesturing at my huge belly.

He scowled at me. "Very funny."

"No, seriously. I feel kind of weird. We need to go."

"Do you think you're in labor?"

I shrugged. "I don't know."

"How can you not know?"

"I just don't, okay? I feel strange, though. Esme's on her way to watch Liam."

Kevin stared at me as if assessing the validity of my claim. We'd had a close call a couple of weeks earlier. My right leg had swelled to double the size of my left. I was positive it was a blood clot. Upon arrival at the hospital the intake nurse took one look at my leg and admitted me. She phoned the doctor on call, who ordered a sonogram of my right leg and hip area. Thankfully, it turned out to be nothing. They released me a few hours later, and the swelling subsided after a few days.

"Okay, but isn't this too soon? We don't even have the baby's nursery completed."

Not this again. Kevin had been nagging me about how I hadn't finished decorating Colman's nursery. We had all the stuff; I just hadn't put it together. Decorating is not my thing, and I didn't have the heart to tell Kevin I wanted to be sure we'd be bringing home a baby to put in it. Anyway, babies don't sleep in their nurseries for the first six months. We'd have plenty of time.

"I need to call my parents," Kevin said.

No big surprise that there was no answer. It'd taken them four days to call Kevin back when we found out about Colman's heart. In the intervening four weeks, I'd had two phone conversations with Kevin's mom that didn't end well. Granted, two calls in four weeks were two more than I would normally have with her, but we were in crisis.

I always thought I'd enjoy a good relationship with my mother-in-law, although we have nothing in common, except maybe our love for Kevin (and I sometimes wonder about that). The first time we met, I overheard her say to him, "She seems nice, but your problem is you always go for pretty girls and they don't make the best wives."

Moving forward, she's made it perfectly clear to me that she doesn't think I'm a good wife by saying things like, "Kevin may be more successful than my other children, but he's just not as happy."

I've tried to give that statement and its many variations the benefit of the doubt. But I don't know how to interpret it other than catty and mean and directed at me. I wanted to say, "You know, it's funny. I've noticed that too, but only when you're around." But it's not worth getting into.

When Kevin told his parents about Colman's heart, he asked his mother about her brother's daughter—the one who died shortly after birth—but his mom wasn't forthcoming with answers. So Kevin handed the phone to me, and I explained that any information she had might provide some insight to the doctors who would be treating Colman.

"That baby didn't have this," she said.

"Okay," I said. "What did she have?"

"I don't know, but it wasn't this."

"It seems to fit the timeline of a congenital heart defect," I continued. "If she had some sort of chromosomal abnormality, sometimes heart defects can be a major underlying problem. It may not be this, but Kevin and I were thinking it might be related. Our doctor said these defects usually run in families."

"This did not come from our side of the family," she said. She may have stomped her foot as well, but I can't be certain.

"Here's Kevin," I said and handed the phone to him. I had nothing left to say to her.

Kevin's mother called to talk with me a few weeks later. "I just wanted to let you know," she said, "that we have the whole church praying for you guys that all this stuff with the baby is not true."

You've got to be fucking kidding me! How pleasant it must be to live in la-la land. I've often joked with Kevin that his mom must have *The Sound of Music* soundtrack on a loop in her mind. You got bad news, you say? Hold on while I turn up "My Favorite Things."

If you haven't already guessed, I'm a grab-the-bull-by-the-horns kind of person, and Kevin's parents are more the stick-your-head-in-the-sand type. One does not mix well with the other. I hate denial and dishonesty, and unfortunately those two things go hand in hand.

"Look," I told her, "I appreciate that you're praying, but don't pray that it's not true. It's true. Pray for something constructive, like that the surgeon doesn't hit his hand with a hammer the night before Colman's surgery and we have to scramble to find somebody else. Or pray for the team who will be taking care of Colman in the hospital. But don't be jamming up the lines to God by praying it's not true. It is."

"Well, doctors aren't always right. They don't know everything. We won't really know anything until he's here."

"Kevin, telephone," I called to him in the next room. As much as I didn't want to sound pissed, I couldn't help it, and I knew Kevin heard the edge in my voice. I rolled my eyes at him and circled my finger in the air beside my head. Kevin had to stifle a laugh as he took the phone.

The irony of the conversation was not lost on me. I was hypocritical in telling Kevin's mom how she should pray when I hadn't been able to utter a single prayer for my own child, but her blatant refusal to help us with our family medical history was irksome. Telling me she was praying the doctors were wrong was a total disregard for our feelings. As much as Kevin and I would have loved to believe this was all a big misunderstanding, it wasn't.

Kevin needed more of a support network, and it wasn't there. He has lots of great friends, but talking about the birth of your child with fatal heart defects is a deeper and more painful conversation than most guys are willing to have with a buddy over a beer.

In contrast, my family had sprung into support mode. I could hash this out with my family and a couple of great girlfriends. Every one of my friends and family said some version of this: "Hey, let's be clear, if I say the wrong thing, please just tell me to fuck off. Okay?" That one statement had the ability to take the pressure off of devastating conversations and make me laugh. It was an awesome way for them to let me know how much they loved me and wanted to be there for me.

I never felt the need to tell them to fuck off. I can't say the same about other people. There have been times I've bitten my tongue until it bled.

Anyway, on the night before Colman's birth, Esme arrived within twenty minutes of my calling her. I drove to the hospital while Kevin tried calling his parents again. Finally I said, "Hey, don't worry about trying to get in touch with them until we're sure the hospital is going to keep me. I'd hate for them to drive all the way from Missouri for a false alarm."

Seriously, if I got sent home from the hospital, the last thing I needed was my in-laws sitting around my house waiting for me to have my baby.

At the hospital they whisked me into a labor and delivery room and hooked me up to monitors to check the baby's heart rate and my contractions. When the nurse checked me, I was already three centimeters dilated. Dr. Voigt called the hospital and told the nurse I could stay the night if I wanted, and she'd induce me in the morning.

I texted my mom with the news. The plan was for them to relieve Esme, stay with Liam overnight and come to the hospital the next morning when Esme arrived.

Kevin and I tried to settle in, but we were both feeling antsy. By choosing to stay in San Antonio, I felt like we had slammed the door on the possibility of a heart transplant. Would Colman even be a candidate for the three surgeries with his tricuspid valve leak? Would we be making arrangements for a funeral or for transfer to South Texas Medical Hospital after he was born?

Kevin and I had read the two books on HLHS that Dr. Callaway's nurse had given us by Anna Jaworski. *Hypoplastic Left Heart Syndrome: A Handbook for Parents* explained HLHS and the staged surgical palliation, and *The Heart of a Mother* was an anthology of essays by mothers of HLHS babies. The books were very informative but also pretty depressing.

As I was drifting off to sleep, Kevin tried to phone his parents one more time. He must have remembered how Alicia, our sister-in-law, got in touch with them the night before Liam was born, because he started calling casinos near their town in Missouri to have them paged. And he found them.

Not even kidding.

I could not get comfortable. I must have dozed off, though, because I awakened to overhear the nurse whispering on the phone to my doctor in the early morning hours. I guess they were getting ready for a shift change.

I met my new nurse soon after, and she was nothing short of fantastic. She was bubbly and funny. When I told her about Colman's in utero diagnosis, she didn't get weird like some of the nurses had. She was attentive and practical about the steps we needed to put in place for the baby's arrival. We clicked right away.

About 7:30 a.m., Kevin announced that he was going home to take a shower and have breakfast with Liam, since it looked like it might be a long day. Thirty minutes later, Dr. Voigt came into the room to check on me. The nurse was giving her a recap of my progression or lack thereof when Dr. Voigt said, "Well, you're already six centimeters dilated."

"Can I have the epidural now?" I asked.

"Oh, my gosh!" the nurse said. "The night nurse said you weren't in labor. Have you been hurting all this time?"

"No. But I don't want to be," I answered.

"I'm going to go ahead and rupture your membranes," Dr. Voigt said. "So any time you want to have the epidural, just let your nurse know. Okay?"

I'm sorry. Wasn't that what I'd just said?

I looked at my nurse and said, "I think I'd like the epidural now," and she giggled like I was the biggest tease on the planet.

Dr. Voigt and the nurse left to make some notes and discuss my case in the hall, and I waited about five minutes. No anesthesiologist. I got up to pee and then got back in bed. Then five seconds later, I felt like I needed to pee again, but then I started to shake. I pushed the call button.

The nurse came right away. "Are you okay?"

"I don't know. I can't stop shaking. Do you think I could get the epidural?"

"Are you hurting now? Just point to one of the faces." She gestured to the pain scale on the wall with six faces in various stages of distress.

I don't know why I didn't just lie. It's not like I was faking, and I was at six centimeters already. I said, "I don't know how to explain what I'm feeling. I'm not hurting, but I just don't feel right."

She took one more look at my face and said, "I'll be right back." Less than thirty seconds later, she came back with the anesthesiologist.

As soon as I finished getting the epidural, I felt really drowsy, but the nurse came in to see if I'd dilated any more. "Oh, my gosh!" she said.

"Am I at ten?" I said.

"You must be because the baby is right there. I knew from the way you looked that something was up. I'm so glad I didn't check you before I got the anesthesiologist. I would've hated to have to lie to him."

"You would have lied to him for me?"

"Of course," she answered, and flashed me a huge smile. She crossed my legs and moved the bottom half of my body to the side so I was twisted at the waist. "Now don't move a muscle. Okay?"

"Got it."

She ran out of the room to grab her cordless phone and then came back in and started making calls. In a matter of minutes, medical personnel were lined shoulder to shoulder against two walls. I think I counted fourteen people at one point.

Dr. Voigt came in and told me to push. The nurse exclaimed, "Wait! Where's your husband?"

"He went home to take a shower."

"We've got to call him. What's his number?"

I gave it to her, and she dialed frantically.

"You can call him, but I don't think this baby is going to wait. Let's just do this." I was feeling pretty bold with the epidural.

At some point during all the craziness, I heard Kevin say, "What's going on?"

The nurse said, "Oh, thank God! You made it. Where have you been? I've been calling you."

Kevin made it to my side with tears in his eyes just as Colman made a screaming entrance into the world at 8:41 a.m. He was nineteen inches long and six pounds thirteen ounces. He'd barely given his daddy enough time to get a shower.

The neonatal intensive care unit team was quickly assessing Colman and getting him ready for transport to the NICU, and I heard the nurse give Apgar scores of nine and eight. I said, "I'd like to hold him before you take him to the NICU."

"I don't think that's a good idea," the neonatologist said.

"He should be okay for a few minutes," I said.

Dr. Voigt spoke up and redeemed herself a little. "I don't see any harm in her holding him for a bit."

The doctor reluctantly placed Colman in my arms. He ceased crying as I snuggled him to my chest so he could hear my heartbeat. He looked exactly like Liam and had the sweetest features. I counted ten fingers and ten toes. He looked like a perfect baby, which did not correspond with the half a heart I knew was on the inside.

Peace and relief washed over me. I'd been so worried about my ability to bond with Colman, but I loved that little boy instantly as I held him in my arms.

Colman needed me like no one ever had before.

CHAPTER 8

"**A**re you okay?" Kevin asked. The neonatal team was wheeling Colman out of the room in a clear bassinet.

I gestured toward the exiting hoard of medical people. "Just follow that baby."

"Done." Kevin smiled and gave me a quick kiss on the forehead.

I'd held Colman for a total of ten minutes before they whisked him away. Kevin seemed fine with not getting to hold him, but I could tell he was a little disappointed. I really hoped he would hold him before Colman had to undergo surgery.

Dr. Roberts stopped by when I was recuperating in labor and delivery to say he was on his way to the NICU, which was a huge relief. I didn't want to wait any longer than necessary to find out about the tricuspid valve leak, which would determine if we were moving forward with surgery.

My sister and brother had arrived and were keeping me company, along with my parents, while Kevin went back and forth to the NICU to make sure things were going as smoothly as possible. Holly disappeared for a couple of hours. She finally returned looking a little teary-eyed. "What's wrong?" I asked.

"Sweetie, do you need a Xanax?" our mother asked her as she riffled through her bag.

Mom hands out Xanax like breath mints. She can't stand to see anyone hurting emotionally or physically.

"No, not right now." Holly rolled her eyes at me and changed the subject. "Your mother-in-law is such a freaking weirdo."

"Tell me something I don't know," I said with a sigh. "What did she do now?"

"As I was coming out of the chapel I saw your in-laws, and your mother-in-law said, 'Oh, hey, I heard we have a new baby!' and she clapped her hands together. Like there's nothing wrong. Oblivious that he's lying in a NICU surrounded by babies that weigh a pound, crack babies, and God knows what other kind of babies."

"What did you say?"

"Nothing. I didn't know what to say. Her demeanor was so completely inappropriate." She took a deep breath and wiped huge tears from her eyes. "I mean, they saw me come out of the chapel. I'd been in there on my knees making deals with God. I even made a few with the devil, just in case. I'm sorry. I don't mean to bitch to you. I was just startled by the disconnect."

"No. I'm glad you told me. It will prepare me for when I see them. Thank you." I gave her a big hug.

The labor and delivery nurse came by to say that Kevin had inquired about securing one of the fancy rooms like I'd been in with Liam. If that's what I wanted, she would do it, but she'd already put a private room on hold around the corner from the NICU so I would be close to Colman.

I was touched by her thoughtfulness. I definitely wanted the room closest to Colman.

En route to the room we had the good fortune of seeing Dr. Roberts in the hallway. He was in a hurry, but he said, "Echo looks good. The tricuspid valve leak is minimal. We got a line in his umbilicus and started the prostaglandin, the medicine I told you about to keep the ductus in his heart open. He's breathing on his own. I'll come by and see you later today, but so far so good."

I managed a brief "Thanks!" and he was gone. I finally had the information we'd been so desperate for. I felt like a huge weight had been lifted off of my shoulders.

I don't know if it was some kind of high from giving birth or the drugs I'd been given, but I felt strong, like I was taking my life back. I still had a lot to learn about taking care of a baby with complex congenital heart disease, but I was ready to move forward.

I lost something the day Colman was born. You could call it innocence or vulnerability. A strange fierceness was born in its place that I've never been able to shake, nor would I ever want to. I was ready to kick ass. Whose? I had no freaking idea, but I could have slain fire-breathing, man-eating dragons. It's like giving birth to Colman opened up a bottomless well of strength I had no clue existed.

I scarfed down half a turkey sandwich Kevin brought by for me. The combination of the epidural wearing off and the sandwich made me queasy, but I willed myself not to barf and walked to the NICU to check on Colman.

The staff buzzed me in, and I received some quick instructions. Leaning against the deep stainless steel sink for support, I scrubbed my hands and arms up to my elbows with soap and water. After that, I put on one of the pale yellow gowns.

Colman was in the last bay, which required me to walk past an incredible number of shockingly tiny babies. The experience left me feeling completely traumatized.

When I was twenty feet away I spotted Colman, the giant of the NICU at six pounds and thirteen ounces. Then I remembered Jack Callaway saying, "The hardest thing for you to overcome is going to be denial because he's not going to look sick."

I stood at the end of Colman's isolette. Tubes snaked their way in and around him. Up to that point, I must have thought they'd put one intravenous line into his umbilicus to deliver the prostaglandin. Almost every part of Colman's body was covered with tubing or wire, but he still looked fantastic next to the other NICU babies. He sounded awful, though. Every time he breathed in, he shuddered and whimpered the breath out.

"Are you Mom?" asked a woman wearing scrubs. She was probably mid-forties with chin-length blond hair and blue eyes.

"Yes, I'm Heather."

"I'm Rachelle. I'm his nurse today. You can have a seat right there," she said.

I sat down and rolled the chair as close to Colman's bassinet as possible.

"You can touch him, but do not rub or pat him. If you place your hand on him, you can keep it there if you want. Do you understand me?" she said brusquely.

"Got it," I replied.

I reached into Colman's bassinet and placed one hand on his left arm and one hand on his left leg.

"Just like that is fine. No rubbing. No patting," Rachelle repeated as she shifted focus from what I was doing with her patient, my son, and reading the monitors.

Colman's whimpering didn't stop, but it seemed a little better. Rachelle wasn't up for chitchat, but I had questions. "Why is he whimpering like that?" I asked.

Rachelle leveled her gaze. "The medication we use to keep the ductus open makes them feel like they have the flu."

I felt my heart sink. In talking about prostaglandin, nobody mentioned side effects. Of course, I never asked either. In the grand scheme, it's not like we had a choice. Even though we knew he'd have major surgery in a few days, I hadn't counted on the fact that he'd be absolutely miserable until that point. "So he's probably going to whimper like this until he has his surgery?" I asked.

"Probably."

"Is there a smaller dose that would work?"

"We're giving him the dose that Dr. Roberts prescribed."

"As far as how we touch him and interact with him, what's the deal with that?"

"We're trying to keep him stable and quiet. If you touch him too much and in the wrong ways, he can get overly stimulated and his heart rate will rise, and we don't want that."

"Okay."

I sat with Colman—my right hand on his left arm and my left hand on his left leg—and started channeling my newfound strength into him. If I could somehow transfer this feeling, he might have a chance to get through everything he was facing in the next several weeks.

Rachelle interrupted my thoughts, but I didn't hear her.

"We're getting ready for shift change," she said. "You need to leave."

I'd been sitting with Colman for a little over an hour. "When can I come back?"

"We require two hours for shift change and it's six o'clock now, so probably about eight."

I took a long look at Colman and stood to leave.

"His numbers look okay," she offered. "And you mind a lot better than your husband."

What an odd thing to say, I thought. I managed to leave without looking at any preemie babies on my way out, which I counted as a win.

Back in my hospital room, things were settling down. Kevin came by briefly before taking his parents home to see Liam. My mom stayed so I wouldn't be alone.

Dr. Roberts gave me a quick update on Colman. He confirmed that prostaglandin does make people feel like they have the flu. He told me they'd just reduced the dosage to see if that might help Colman feel less miserable. My mom and I checked on him before going to bed that night. He seemed to be doing fine, although he was still making the awful whimpering noises. It was heartbreaking—I couldn't pick him up and soothe him. I couldn't nurse him. I couldn't even comfort him by patting him with my hand.

We made it back from the NICU, and Mom and I both fell into bed. Within minutes Mom was snoring, but I couldn't sleep. The night nurse popped her head in to say hi and and took my vitals. She asked if I needed anything.

"I could use something for pain," I said. My body ached all over.

"What do you want?" she asked.

"I don't know. I think I took Lortab and Motrin after my last baby, and that seemed to work really well."

"Your doctor says you can't have Lortab because that's a street drug."

But we're not on the street. We're in a hospital, and I just had a baby. Did she think I was going to sell it?

"Well, just give me whatever my doctor said I could have."

"I could give you a couple of Percodan."

Like that's not sold on the street.

"Sure," I said. "Whatever."

I swallowed two giant Percodan and waited to drift off to sleep. But I never did because I was high as a freaking kite all night long with my mother snoring beside me. And, God, was I itchy. It was fun itchy, though. I finally forced myself to stop scratching because I started worrying I wouldn't have any skin left in the morning. Then I worried that they were going to circumcise Colman. Surely they wouldn't without a signed consent.

In Anna Jaworski's book of essays, one particular detail stuck in my mind about the infant boys diagnosed with HLHS after birth. Every single one turned blue during their circumcision procedure, which was one thing that alerted the physicians that the babies might have a heart problem.

I hauled myself out of bed and shook my mother's shoulder. "Mom," I whispered, "do you think they'd circumcise Colman?"

"Not sure," she mumbled, and went back to snoring.

I pulled on a pair of yoga pants and a t-shirt and went down to the NICU. Once they buzzed me in, I repeated the process of washing my hands and arms, donned another yellow gown, and made my way back to Colman. I sat down beside him and asked the new nurse, "Do you have some paper and a marker?"

"Sure," she said. She handed me a paper about four inches square and a black Sharpie.

I wrote "NO CIRC" in big, bold letters. The nurse gave me some tape, and I attached my note next to Colman's information at the bottom of his bassinet.

"You know," the nurse said, "they wouldn't do that unless they had a signed consent."

"I figured, but it was worrying me."

I couldn't be there with him every second, but at least I'd made my wishes known.

I placed my hands on Colman as I had before, but he seemed even more miserable than he had earlier. I looked him over to see if there was anything that could be hurting him. It didn't take long to find the source of his discomfort.

"He has a dirty diaper," I said to the nurse.

"I don't think so."

"Can we check?"

The nurse looked and, sure enough, Colman definitely had a dirty diaper.

"Huh. I wonder how long he's had that," the nurse muttered, which made me think it was a long time.

"I'll change it," I volunteered.

"I think it would be better if I did it."

"What does it matter as long as it gets done?"

She finally relented.

Colman seemed to feel better immediately. I propped my chin against the edge of his bassinet and put my hands on him again while I watched his heart rate trend down on the monitor. He seemed to finally be relaxing.

I needed to sober up from the Percodan so I could get a few hours of sleep, but that wasn't going to happen any time soon. I started talking to Colman. I explained everything about his heart and HLHS. I told him all our worries. And I apologized for everything he was going through.

"Look, this sucks in a whole multitude of ways," I said. "I get it. But if somebody told me I needed three heart surgeries in three years to survive, I'd do it. So I feel I should hold you to the same standard, whether you want this or not."

I must have talked to him a long time, my hands never moving from where I'd placed them on his body. When I looked at the clock, it was six in the morning—time for another shift change. I stood and stretched and went back to my room to find my mother still snoring, her mouth slightly agape.

I crawled into the other bed and fell asleep immediately. I'd never felt so achy and exhausted in my life.

CHAPTER 9

I heard a distant ringing and realized it was my cell phone.

"Hello," I answered, my voice husky with sleep—or no sleep, depending on how you look at it.

"Hey, babe, did I wake you up?" Kevin asked.

"Yeah. What time is it?"

"It's seven. We're having breakfast with Liam. As soon as Esme gets here, we'll head over."

"How's sweet Liam?"

"He's fine. Missing Mommy, I think."

"I miss him, too. Give him a kiss from me. Take your time, though. I really need to take a shower. I didn't have such a good night."

"Is Colman okay?" Kevin said anxiously.

"I was just with him an hour ago, and he was fine. It's still shift change, so I'll call and check in a minute."

"Well, get your shower because we're heading that way in about forty-five minutes."

I slowly rolled out of bed and grabbed my bag of toiletries.

"Was that Kevin?" my mom asked.

"Yeah. They're on their way. I'm going to get a shower."

My mom yawned. "I had a shower last night, so I might just fix my hair and put on some makeup while you're in there. Is that okay?"

"Yeah, that's fine."

"Do you have some deodorant I could use? I forgot to pack mine," Mom said.

My mom always forgets something. Always.

I held up my bag and laughed. "Help yourself."

We heard a knock at the door. It was Dr. Voigt. After she finished her examination, I asked why she would tell the nurse I couldn't have Lortab.

Dr. Voigt gave me a puzzled look. "I never said any such thing," she answered.

"The nurse told me she couldn't give it because it was a street drug."

"That's ridiculous. We're in a hospital."

"That's what I thought. However, she did give me two Percodan and I went on what I can only describe as a major drug trip. I was itchy and wound up. I sat in the NICU all night, hoping no one else would realize I was high. I only ended up getting about an hour's sleep."

"Here's the order," she said, and handed me the chart. "As you can see, I checked the box for no restrictions. You can have whatever you want. I'll write orders specifically for Lortab, though, so there's no confusion. I'm really sorry. What an idiot."

"It's okay. I just wanted to get it straightened out."

After Dr. Voigt left, I went into the bathroom and turned on the shower. I'd just pulled my shirt off when my mom cracked the door and said, "Hey, there's a doctor here to see you."

I slipped on my shirt and exited the bathroom to find a huge man in green scrubs.

"Are you Colman's mom?" he asked.

"Yes," I said. "You can call me Heather."

"I'm the neonatologist who will be taking care of Colman today. It looks like he was stable throughout the night. All of his vital signs look good. Dr. Roberts is with Colman right now, and he should be by in a bit to give you a more detailed update."

After the neonatologist left, I went into the bathroom and turned off the shower, which was the right decision because Dr. Roberts arrived seconds later.

"Hi, Mrs. Connelly."

I had to fight the urge to see if my mother-in-law was standing behind me. It happens every time someone calls me that.

"Everything seems to be progressing fine. Colman's oxygen saturations were a little higher than what we like to see, so we've put him under a nitrogen tent to try to lower those a bit."

"I notice he hasn't had anything to eat," I said. "Can I nurse him today?"

"Why don't we wait on that? I'm not sure that's such a good idea. You're being released tomorrow?"

"Yes."

"Good. We have everything set up for Colman to be transported to South Texas Medical Hospital tomorrow morning. I've been talking to

Dr. Callaway, so he's aware of everything."

A quick glance at the clock, which now showed 8 a.m., and yet another knock on the door. This time it was a lactation consultant with a hospital-grade breast pump and information on milk storage for a baby in the NICU.

I felt lousy about it, but I had to cut this visit short if I had any hope of getting a shower. "I really appreciate this. I brought my own breast pump," I explained, pointing to my black Medela backpack. "But you're welcome to leave this one here since it's ready to go."

"Well, I'd really like to go over some of this information."

"Great! Why don't you leave it with me? I can read through it, and if I have any questions I'll give you a call."

"Maybe we could try a quick pumping session."

I took a deep breath and tried to stay calm. "I'm sure I can figure it out," I said. "If not, I'll use my pump. I nursed my older son for a year and pumped every day for ten months."

Although the consultant didn't look convinced, I could tell she was backing down. "You need to remember to pump every two hours, though," she said, "just like you would nurse your baby. If you don't, you risk your milk not coming in."

"I'll get right on that after I shower." I smiled brightly and started walking her toward the door.

"If you have any questions, don't hesitate to call. We're here to help."

"Okay, thanks. I'll let you know."

I shut the door and turned to my mom. "Is that true that your milk won't come in if you don't feed your baby or pump every two hours?" I asked. "Seems a little extreme."

"I don't know. It wasn't true for me after I had any of you. I didn't do anything except wrap myself tightly with sheets, and my milk still came in. I always thought it was pretty unavoidable."

"I'm not going to stress about that right now. Sounds like some crazy La Leche League bullshit to me, but remind me later, okay?"

"Sure. Gosh, it's been a busy morning."

"No kidding. They should put in a revolving door. I have got to get a shower because I feel disgusting. Kevin will be here any minute."

As if on cue, Kevin opened the door, all smiles. "Hi. Can we come in?" he asked.

I was standing next to my bed, and my mother was still lying in hers. She had stayed there since she was still in her pajamas.

"Babe, I still need to get a shower," I said.

"I called you over an hour ago, and you told me you were getting in the shower then. What have you been doing?" he said.

As if all I'd done was lounge around, visit with my mom and rest. If only. "I've been talking to doctors and nurses nonstop."

Kevin rolled his eyes. "You're telling me you haven't had a chance during all that time to get a shower?"

"That's exactly what I'm telling you," I said, managing to keep my voice even.

"So we can't come in?"

"Not until I get a shower. I mean, *you* can come in, but I need a good thirty minutes to get ready."

Kevin came into the room and pulled the door around, I guess to shield his parents from our conversation. "What am I supposed to do with my parents?" he hissed.

Looking back, it's funny that he thought I gave a fuck what he did with his parents.

I shrugged my shoulders. "I have no idea," I said, my eyes wide like I'd run out of brains. He hadn't even bothered to ask how I was feeling or why I'd had such an awful night.

"Heather, they're old. They need a place to sit down."

"That's not my problem," I said. "But you're in luck, because this hospital is complete with these things called waiting rooms chock-full of chairs."

If looks could kill, we would have spontaneously combusted right then. Kevin narrowed his eyes and gave me one last dirty look. "I can't believe this," he muttered.

"Believe it," I said. Then I shot him the bird.

Not one of my finer moments, I'll admit.

After he closed the door, my mom said, "That wasn't very nice. You had a baby not even twenty-four hours ago. If you wanted to sleep all day and not have anybody disturb you, that would be fine. I can't believe he treated you like that."

"Me either. I'm sure his parents are stressing him out," I offered, in an attempt to explain my husband's behavior. "I am getting in the shower now. I cannot imagine who else might show up. I think I've talked to all the important people regarding Colman, but if somebody does stop by, tell them to go away."

"Okay, babe. I'm sorry. I love you."

"I love you, too."

I stepped into the shower, still reeling from my altercation with Kevin. Halfway through hastily scrubbing my scalp with shampoo, I wondered, what's the big hurry? If I shaved five minutes off my shower time, it wasn't going to earn extra points. Kevin was already irritated. My sarcasm didn't exactly make things better.

Don't get me wrong. Kevin had acted like a complete ass, and in front of my mother no less, but we had a lot on our plate. We didn't need to add a fight into the mix.

I wanted to cry.

I let the spray of hot water wash away the few tears that had escaped my eyes and finished rinsing out my hair.

Fuck him. And fuck them. Kevin's parents were supposed to be here to help, but they were already driving Kevin crazy.

After I finished mentally burning bridges, I thought of Colman—with his half a heart—lying among those impossibly tiny babies. My heart squeezed so tight, I felt like I couldn't breathe.

If the fight that morning was any indication of things to come, maybe our marriage wouldn't survive having a child as sick as Colman. With over 70 percent of marriages ending in divorce where a critically ill child was involved, our odds weren't great to begin with.

As much as I wanted to hurry so I could check on Colman, I took my time. I even shaved my legs, something I hadn't really been able to do when I was pregnant. I got out, slathered on lotion, dried my hair and put on some makeup.

It didn't take much to make thirty minutes stretch into an hour, but at least I looked somewhat presentable, even though I was exhausted.

One thing was for sure. I'd never allow myself to be blindsided by my husband again. I'd never again make the mistake of assuming Kevin had my back. My first priorities were my newborn baby and healing my own body.

I'd have to worry about my marriage later.

CHAPTER 10

I'd finished getting ready when Kevin came back to my room. I braced myself, expecting him to still be angry with me, but he acted like nothing had happened and didn't mention our disagreement ever again.

Although my feelings were hurt, I just went with it and chalked it up to him being worried about Colman. It wasn't going to be the last time one of us went schizoid over something stupid.

"I talked to the NICU doctor this morning, and he said Colman's doing well. I guess he's already talked to you though," he said, with a puzzled expression.

"Yes," I answered carefully, still unsure of his mood.

Kevin rubbed his eyes and started pacing back and forth in the entrance to the room. "Colman has that same damn nurse he had yesterday. I was hoping there'd be a different one today."

"Rachelle?"

Kevin shrugged his shoulders. "I don't know her name."

"Blond hair that's cut into a little bob and blue eyes, mid-forties?" I said.

"Yeah, that's her."

"Yeah," I said. "She's not exactly the friendliest."

"She's a freaking Nazi! Telling me how to touch Colman and where. She's driving me crazy. I finally had to tell her to back off. Colman is my son, and I'll spend time with him how I want."

I know this is terrible, but I was relieved that Kevin had refocused his wrath on the nurse.

"I wondered what happened yesterday," I mumbled, thinking back to Rachelle's comment about how I minded better than my husband.

"Well, he's being transferred at ten tomorrow morning. Colman won't have her much longer."

"How do you know what time they're transferring him?"

"Dr. Roberts came by on rounds and told me."

"Just now? Did I miss him?" Kevin scratched his head and looked around.

"No, earlier, before you arrived. He came to the hospital to check on Colman. He said he's been talking to Dr. Callaway regularly, so he's being kept up to date."

"That's a relief!" Kevin exclaimed. "I'll feel better when we get him over to South Texas Medical Hospital with Dr. Callaway and his team."

"Me, too."

After looking at me for a second, like he was seeing me for the first time, Kevin said, "Are you feeling okay?"

"No," I said. "I feel awful."

"Why don't you rest, babe? I need to find my parents. If I don't see you before, meet me at the NICU at eleven. That's when the pastor is baptizing Colman."

"Okay. See you in a little bit."

Mom and I headed to the NICU after Kevin left. The nitrogen tent seemed to be doing its job because Colman's oxygen saturations were in the mid-eighties, down from the low nineties of the previous day and night. I'd been pleased that they were in the nineties, but Dr. Roberts said that because of Colman's unique anatomy, they should be in the mid-eighties.

Normal oxygen saturations are between 98 and 100 percent. In most states, including Texas, there is a mandatory pulse oximetry test for newborns. Anything below 95 percent is a fail and requires further testing to make certain an infant doesn't have a congenital heart defect.

Colman was awake in his isolette, furiously sucking a pacifier Rachelle had given him, and she commented on his fantastic suck reflex. It sounds stupid, but that one compliment made me incredibly proud. It was comforting to see him going to town on the pacifier instead of whimpering with every exhalation. With the pacifier, he sucked ten or fifteen times in a row and whimpered once. I could see he still felt lousy, but the pacifier was definitely soothing him.

After going back to my room briefly to get some rest, my parents and I met Kevin and his parents in the NICU for the baptism. The pastor was already speaking with Kevin when we arrived. Once we gathered around Colman's isolette, the service didn't take long at all.

A young mother sat in a rocking chair in the next bay and held her tiny infant, who had been born six weeks premature. She gestured toward Colman with her head and asked the nurse, "What's wrong with their baby?" She rolled her eyes and added, "He looks fine."

The nurse put her hands on her hips. "That baby?" she said, pointing to Colman. "That baby's the sickest we've got. He's being transferred out tomorrow. Count your lucky stars that all your baby needs is to grow."

I tried to act like I hadn't heard, but I felt like I'd been punched in the gut. I'd only allowed myself to look at the floor when traversing the long path through the NICU to Colman. For the first time, I made myself really pay attention to the other babies. Most were alarmingly tiny, with tubes and wires everywhere. Some had blue lights in their incubators and wore funny goggles. Almost all required some kind of oxygen support, and the very sickest were on ventilators to help them breathe.

That baby's the sickest we've got. The nurse's words echoed in my head. I turned my attention back to Colman, the six-pound, thirteen-ounce monster of the NICU. I studied him from the top of his head to the bottom of his little feet. I counted ten fingers and ten toes. His body was perfectly formed in every way. No apparent signs would alert someone to the disaster of a heart he'd been born with.

I wished then that he had some sort of outward sign, some mark I could see as a reminder, to help keep the denial at bay—the denial that kept creeping in as I looked upon my baby, who seemed so perfect. I knew Colman's heart was full of defects, but it was impossible to reconcile the HLHS diagnosis with the baby in front of me. Maybe if his fingers or toes were webbed, I'd have an easier time believing it.

With a start, I realized I'd soon have my wish. Colman would have a scar. No, in all probability, he would have many scars.

I found Kevin outside the NICU later that afternoon and asked if he'd take a few more pictures of Colman. He'd taken several already, mostly of Colman's face. I wanted photographs of his entire body, including his bare chest. They'd be the only ones we'd ever have of him without his scars.

As Kevin finished taking pictures, he hugged me to him. "He looks so perfect," he said quietly. "Do you ever think to yourself that maybe they made a mistake? Or worse, that this is some sort of crazy conspiracy?"

"Every time I look at him. I have this almost irresistible urge to yank his lines out and run with him out of the hospital doors." I laughed. "That's crazy, huh?"

"It may be, but that's exactly how I feel. This is unbelievable."

Esme brought Liam to the hospital around five that afternoon. I was really happy to see the two of them. Liam had a stuffed animal for his new baby brother, although I was fairly certain he had no idea what a baby brother was. He climbed onto my bed and let me snuggle him for a few minutes. He smelled like outside—part sunshine, part little wet wolf—and I drank him in. It was such a relief to be able to hold and love on him for a little while. I contemplated again the strange contrast of having one child who was deliciously healthy and another who was incredibly sick. Would I be able to parent them both fairly and equally?

Kevin went home with his parents and Liam that night, and I returned to a party in full swing. My Uncle Buddy, who's actually my great uncle on my father's side, was there. Then there was my mom, dad, sister, and my best friend from high school, Theresa. Buddy's visit surprised me, but I was grateful for his presence, which provided a much-needed diversion for my father.

Dad was walking a fine emotional line. He'd broken down on the phone with me the night before, and I didn't want that happening again. Between Mom's seemingly endless supply of Xanax and Buddy, we'd be able to accomplish that.

The atmosphere was loud and raucous. I had a different night nurse, and she kept checking in to see if we needed anything. I expected her to kick everybody out, but then I realized she had the hots for Uncle Buddy. Despite the underlying sadness of the situation, we laughed and talked way past visiting hours.

Holly decided to stay with Mom and me that night. Although I was only supposed to have one overnight guest, the nurse made an exception and dragged a large sleeper chair into the room, along with extra blankets for Holly.

While Holly got her stuff from the hotel, Mom and I went to check on Colman. A different nurse was on duty, so I introduced myself and sat down beside Colman. He was clearly upset. After a little investigation, Mom and I discovered that he had a dirty diaper. I changed him. Then we watched his heart rate trend down as he got over the drama of having dirty pants.

"Have you held him yet?" the nurse asked me.

"Yeah," I answered. "I held him for a few minutes after he was born."

"Would you like to hold him again?"

"Sure. Can I?"

"Yeah. Try not to jostle him too much once I get him in your arms. We don't want him to become overstimulated."

"Okay." I sat in the rocking chair while the nurse gathered Colman's wires and tubes, making sure nothing was tangled. Moving him from one place to another, even three feet away, was no small feat.

The nurse placed Colman in my arms, and I held my baby boy for the second time in thirty-six hours.

"I wish Kevin were here," I said to Mom, my voice low.

"I know, sweetie."

I felt tears prick my eyes at the thought of Kevin never having the chance to hold Colman. I quickly pushed the thought to the back of my mind. Focusing on Colman, I tried to love him as best I could while holding him perfectly still. My inclination was to rock him, kiss him and talk to him, but I could do none of those things. So I sat like a statue and concentrated on transferring all of my strength to him.

Colman's heart rate stayed steady, and he seemed to relax. I held him for close to two hours. Then my arm fell asleep, past the point of pins and needles. The wooden rocking chair was uncomfortable and big, and there was no place to rest my arms. I told the nurse that we better put him back because I thought my arm might give out from the weight.

Back in my room, I slept like the dead. I woke at six the next morning to use the breast pump, which I'd only used twice the day before— much to the chagrin of my lactation consultant, who seemed to relish warning me of the dire consequences of not pumping every two hours. I wasn't trying to be difficult, but I felt like I had bigger fish to fry. There was always someone needing to talk about Colman, consents to sign or something that needed my attention.

I went to find my nurse so I could hand off the miniscule amount of colostrum I'd eked out and remind the nursing staff that I needed my discharge paperwork so I could leave by ten o'clock, the scheduled time of Colman's transfer to South Texas Medical Hospital. We had a huge day ahead of us, so I jumped in the shower, got dressed and packed my things. Then I sat around and twiddled my thumbs; the NICU was closed for shift change until eight o'clock. Shift changes were the one thing that annoyed me to no end. I hated not being able to check on Colman.

Mom and Holly left a little after seven to grab some breakfast. I stayed behind to speak with the doctors when they came by on rounds. As it got closer to eight I started pacing, trying to get rid of some of my nervous energy.

There was a soft knock at the door.

"Come in," I called.

"Hi, Heather." It was Rachelle, the Nazi nurse, holding several binders.

"Is Colman okay?"

"Yeah," she said. "He's fine. The transport team is preparing him for his trip to South Texas Medical Hospital."

"Wow! I didn't realize they'd get here so early."

"These are some binders on hypoplastic left heart syndrome," she said warily.

"Thank you," I said, taking them from her.

"Has anybody talked to you about your son's diagnosis?"

"Yes. We've talked to Dr. Roberts and Dr. Callaway about our options and what to expect."

"So you knew before he was born?" Rachelle asked, surprised.

"Yeah," I answered. "The radiologist noticed an asymmetry in his heart at nineteen weeks and again and at twenty-three. Dr. Roberts made the diagnosis at thirty-two weeks."

"I wondered how you could be so calm. I figured you must be in shock, but I guess you've had a while to process this, huh?"

"I guess. I don't feel calm." I laughed self-consciously. "Thank you for the information. Do I need to get these back to you before I'm discharged?"

"No. I made those especially for you," she said, her eyes getting a little watery.

"I appreciate that," I said.

Rachelle turned like she was going to leave and then stopped and faced me. "You know, you're doing the right thing taking him over to South Texas Medical Hospital. Dr. Callaway is an amazing surgeon," she said, her voice cracking.

"I feel like Colman will be in good hands there," I said.

Rachelle burst into tears.

"Please, don't cry," I said, stunned that the woman we'd been calling "the Nazi nurse" was bawling in my room.

"I'm sorry. I don't mean to." She wiped the tears from her face with the back of her hand. "It's just, I've taken care of these babies for twenty-five years now. For so long there wasn't anything we could do. HLHS was a death sentence. I'd take care of the babies, then swaddle them up and send them home in their mothers' arms to die. I'm so happy your baby is getting this chance. He's a beautiful little boy."

"Thank you, Rachelle," I said, with tears in my eyes. "Thank you for taking such good care of Colman."

She nodded and gave me a brief smile that lit up her tear-stained face. Then she left the room.

I felt a little bewildered. I'm usually a pretty good judge of character, and I wondered how I could be so wrong about somebody. Kevin and I thought she was being mean because she was burned out and unhappy with her job, life or whatever.

I'll always think of Rachelle as the Nazi nurse, but also as Colman's vigilant protector and first true advocate. In visiting me the morning of Colman's transfer, she handed off that baton to me.

CHAPTER 11

The transfer to South Texas Medical Hospital took only about two minutes once they loaded Colman into the ambulance. The hospital, in San Antonio's Medical Center, is only a block from Mercy Hospital, where I gave birth to Colman. The transport team rode in the ambulance with Colman, and Kevin and I followed in our SUV.

Once I knew Colman was safely inside South Texas Medical Hospital's NICU, I called my parents to come get me. Kevin stayed at the hospital to sign paperwork and make sure Colman got settled.

When my parents arrived, I told them I needed to go downtown.

"Right now?" Dad said. "I thought you'd want to go home."

"I need to add Colman to my health insurance policy. I have thirty days, but I don't want to forget."

Dad drove me to Bexar County Human Resources, which was just about the last errand I wanted to undertake, but I figured I might as well get it out of the way.

We arrived home to a house full of people—hungry people. It was already way past lunch, and nobody had made any sort of plan. Kevin's two siblings were there from out of state as well as his parents, and my parents and siblings.

Before Colman's birth, when I imagined our families coming together for his surgery, I would have characterized that as support. But this felt like a monumental cluster fuck.

Somebody—I can't remember who—asked me, "So what are we supposed to do about lunch?" Gah! Fend for yourself? Go hungry?

Afraid of what might come out of my mouth, I didn't answer. I went into the kitchen in search of something to feed the hungry horde. Since I do most of the grocery shopping, I was certain this was a big waste of time, though I felt pretty confident I could find some stale crackers and a moldy wedge of Gruyère. I may or may not have been thinking about cutting the mold off the cheese before serving it.

All I wanted was to drink a glass of chocolate milk and take a nap, and then go to the hospital to see what the plan was for Colman.

Screw the glass. I grabbed the half-gallon from the fridge and guzzled out of the carton. My eyes met Mom's. I hadn't seen her follow me into the kitchen. She was leaning against the counter with her arms crossed, looking slightly amused.

"What?" I said, letting out a little laugh.

"We could put out some sandwiches," she said softly.

"Yeah. That would be great. And where are we going to get sandwiches?" I whispered. It would be close to two o'clock by the time we sent somebody to pick them up.

"I thought we could just put these out," she said, gesturing to two large trays on the counter.

"Where did those come from?" I asked, puzzled.

"Your neighbors brought them over this morning. The lady that lives across the street—what's her name?"

"Anna."

"And the one next door in the white brick house."

"That's Hazel. Wow!" Relief swept over me. "That was so nice of them." I was genuinely touched by their kindness.

"Yeah," Mom said. "They were upset to hear about Colman's heart. But Anna was telling us that her husband plays golf with Dr. Callaway. She assured us that Colman is in good hands."

"Really? Small world, huh?"

About that time Sarah, my judge, dropped off two huge grocery bags filled with salad, fresh fruit, mold-free cheese, crackers and all manner of yummy snacks for hungry people to munch on.

I was near tears at the thoughtfulness of my friends.

As everybody was finishing up with lunch, Kevin asked me, "What do you think?"

"About what?"

"You haven't even seen it, have you?"

"I have no idea what you're talking about, babe."

"This," he said, pointing to an acoustic Takamine guitar.

I'd been toying with the idea of buying a guitar. I started playing when I was eight, but I told my dad to get rid of my guitars in high school after we had a fight about practicing. Now Uncle Buddy's visit made more sense.

"Did Buddy help you pick this out?" I said.

"Yeah. I told him what I wanted, and he went to the music store. He thought this guitar would be perfect for you."

Uncle Buddy only knew three guitar chords and could play probably a thousand songs, which always prompted Dad to ask me, "Can't you just strum a song?"

Sure. I can strum, but it bores me. I had gravitated to complicated lead, fingerpicking and classical pieces, which is probably the reason I completed court-reporting school in sixteen months instead of the usual three years. It was really sweet of Kevin to give me this guitar as a gift, though I think he, too, was eventually disappointed that I don't play sing-along songs.

Kevin went to the hospital while I unpacked and spent some much-needed time with Liam. When Esme put Liam down for his nap, Mom and I headed for the hospital too.

We were walking through the visitor parking lot when we ran into Kevin and his parents.

"Hi," I said. "How's Colman doing?"

Kevin broke into a huge grin that showed off the character lines in his face that I love so much. I realized how much I'd missed his smile over the last several weeks. "He's really great," he said. "I got to hold him!"

"I'm so glad," I said, giving him a hug. "I've been so worried that you couldn't."

"I know," Kevin said. "He's really a pretty cool little guy." So many different emotions passed over his face—love, fear, happiness, grief, anger and worry.

Kevin's mom placed her hands on her hips and exclaimed, "You know, that nurse wouldn't let me hold him!"

I couldn't form an appropriate response, so I ignored her. If only the asphalt would open up and swallow her whole.

"Did you see Dr. Callaway yet?" I said to Kevin.

"He's been in and out of the NICU checking on Colman. I think he's planning on surgery tomorrow morning."

"Tomorrow? That's so fast," I said, feeling my heart speed up.

Waving her arms in frustration, Kevin's mom interjected, "She only let Kevin hold him. Can you believe that?"

I felt my mom stiffen beside me. I gave Kevin a searching look. She wasn't for real, right?

Kevin shook his head and shrugged. Big tears flooded his eyes, but his mother continued on, oblivious to the emotional distress her son was exhibiting. Kevin's dad at least had the good sense to look abashed, but he did nothing to stop his wife's tirade.

"I asked the nurse again and again," she said, "but she just kept saying no. Can you believe that? And Kevin wouldn't hand him over!"

"She didn't," I said under my breath to Kevin. I could barely control my disbelief and anger.

"She did," he answered, shaking his head again.

After the turmoil of the last few weeks, I couldn't believe his mother would badger the nurse or Kevin when he was able to hold Colman for the first time, which very well could be the last time.

I felt my neck and cheeks flush hot. I knew if I looked in a mirror I'd see splotchy red marks all over my face, neck and chest. Some women look beautiful when they're angry. Not me. I look like I'm having some sort of allergic reaction. I felt my eyes fill with tears. I held Kevin's gaze for a few more seconds before I leaned in to kiss his cheek.

"I'm so happy you got to hold him," I said. "I wish I could've been there to see the two of you together. I love you."

"Love you, too." Kevin squeezed my hand.

His mother was like a dog with a bone. "All I wanted to do was hold him for a little bit," she said. "That's all I wanted. I don't know why they wouldn't let me. Heather, did you hear me?"

I composed my features into what I hoped was a mask of impassivity and finally looked at her. "Yes," I said firmly, not wanting to give her the satisfaction of seeing she'd upset me.

"They wouldn't let me hold him. Only Kevin."

"Good," I stated in my best matter-of-fact manner. To Kevin, I said, "I'll see you at the house later." Mom and I started walking toward the hospital entrance.

Once we were out of earshot, my mom said, "Well, I never!" I knew she was searching for something to say, something to make it better.

I was trying to get a handle on my emotions. I wanted to run back and shake Kevin's mom until her teeth rattled clean out of her skull.

"Why on earth would she think they'd let anybody but the mommy and daddy hold that baby?" Mom said.

"I have no idea," I said, feeling drained and a little defeated. I pushed the button for the elevator.

"Maybe she just doesn't understand how serious this is, Heather."

My mom is the ultimate enabler.

I rolled my eyes. "Maybe," I said noncommittally.

"If you gave her the heart books and she read those, she might have a better understanding of what you guys are up against."

I turned to face Mom as we waited for the elevator. "I gave her the books yesterday."

"That's good." She nodded like we finally might be on to something.

"She gave them back to me this afternoon."

"That was fast."

"Yeah, that's what I thought. She said, 'Oh, no, I didn't read them. They're just too sad.'" I gave an uneasy laugh of disbelief.

Mom's face fell. "Oh, honey, I'm so sorry." She put her arm around me and hugged me to her. "Those books are pretty sad."

"They're slit-your-wrists sad. But that's our life now. That's Colman's life," I said. I wasn't being morose; I was being practical.

"I just don't understand how she could say that to the two of you. I'd like to hold Colman too, but I wouldn't dream of taking that time away from you. Colman needs his mommy and daddy right now. If he makes it through this first surgery, we can all hold him. Can't she see how much pain y'all are in? Doesn't she want to understand what y'all are up against, what her grandson is up against?"

"I don't get it either."

The elevator finally pinged its arrival. When the doors opened, there was only one man standing in the back corner. He was some sort of doctor—wearing a white coat thrown over scrubs and drinking a cup of Starbucks coffee.

We got on and stood near the front. "Well, I'm sorry she acted that way," Mom said. "That wasn't right."

"It's not your fault. She's just . . ." I trailed off, examining my palms where my fingernails had made half-moon marks. I must have been clenching my fists.

"Well, I'm proud of how you handled her. I just can't believe you didn't—"

"Can't believe I didn't what?" I interrupted, forgetting we weren't alone. "Tell her to go eat a giant bag of dicks?"

"Heather!" Mom said, and lightly smacked my arm. I heard the doctor behind us choke on his coffee.

I gave him a shrug and an apologetic smile, which made him laugh even harder. He raised his coffee cup to me.

Mom and I got off the elevator on the floor where the NICU was located. "That was embarrassing," I said, feeling my cheeks burn.

As much as I hated Mercy's NICU policies, South Texas Medical Hospital's were worse. You had to check in at a huge reception desk in the center of the waiting room and wait for approval to see your child.

After almost an hour we still hadn't seen Colman. Dad finally showed up and we sat visiting while Mom went in search of snacks and sodas.

Finally I heard my name called. Mom wasn't back yet, so Dad said he'd go in with me. We scrubbed up, donned our yellow gowns and headed to Colman's bay, which was thankfully straight back at the end of a long hallway. I introduced myself to Colman's nurse and got an update on how things had been going. Colman was back to whimpering with every breath, so I gave him his pacifier, hoping to soothe him. He spit it out and glared at me.

"Yeah, he's over the pacifier," the nurse said.

"I'd say so." I was shocked that a two-day-old infant could conjure such a withering stare.

"Has anybody talked to you about his labs?"

"No."

"Well, we just got them in, and it looks like his vitamin K is pretty low."

"What does that mean?" I said.

"It means if they decide to go forward with surgery, he could bleed out tomorrow. Surgery will probably be postponed."

It's difficult to explain what it's like to receive bad news over and over, to realize death is stalking your son at every turn. At some point you become numb from the constant pummeling. At least, that's what happened to me. I didn't feel sad, weak or helpless when the nurse told me this. On the contrary, I felt like I was doing everything in my power to give Colman the best shot at pulling through surgery. I still had what felt like superhuman strength coursing through my veins, and I wished again for some way to transfer it to Colman.

I turned to say something to my dad, who'd been standing right next to me, but he was gone. I caught a glimpse of him throwing his yellow gown in the receptacle and exiting through the double doors.

He wasn't numb yet.

Mom arrived not long after that, and we hung out at Colman's bassinet for a while. Dr. Callaway came by to see how Colman was doing. We spoke with him briefly and learned that Colman's Norwood was scheduled for the following day, first case. When I asked about his low vitamin K levels, Dr. Callaway acknowledged that blood loss was a definite risk, but he felt that Colman needed the surgery sooner rather than later. They would be prepared with extra blood products.

A steady stream of doctors and nurses checked on Colman throughout the evening. I'd wanted to hold him again, but the nurse didn't think it was a good idea since Kevin had held him earlier, so I sat by his side through the shift change and into the early evening.

I left the hospital late that night with a promise to Colman that I'd see him first thing in the morning.

CHAPTER 12

O n April 2, 2004, I woke up at 5 a.m. and was ready to leave for the hospital fifteen minutes later. I'd washed my hair the night before, so I quickly rinsed off in a hot shower and brushed my teeth. I thought I would come out of my skin while I waited for Kevin to finish getting ready.

Kevin insisted on driving, which was probably for the best if the goal was to get us to the hospital in one piece. I would've run every red light on the way.

As we drove down Medical Drive, I felt my heart constrict as I caught sight of the hospital looming on the hill. It seemed so large in comparison to my tiny baby all alone inside. I willed Kevin to hurry. Colman needed me.

We parked the car, and I half-ran to the hospital and on to the elevator.

"Are you going to wait for me?" Kevin called, sounding irritated.

"Hurry up!" I gestured for him to get a move on while I held the elevator door open.

I wanted to scream as I took in the large, mostly empty waiting area and reception desk in the NICU. We were going to have to wait for those clowns to buzz us in.

Please don't let it take an hour like yesterday, I thought to myself. I checked in with the clerk and sat down beside Kevin.

"Hurry up and wait," Kevin said, running his hands through his hair.

Moments later they called our name. Kevin and I jumped to our feet. We scrubbed in and dragged yellow gowns over our heads. We could see down the hallway; there was a lot of activity going on near Colman's bay.

When we finally made it to Colman, the clock above his bassinet read 5:40. Not too shabby, I thought, but that forty minutes felt like four hours. People were rushing back and forth making sure everything was in order for surgery. They were planning on taking Colman into the operating room at seven.

Kevin and I both wanted to hold Colman before surgery, but the night nurse had already bathed him with a medicated soap to guard against infection. We knew holding him was a long shot, but it was difficult to hide our disappointment. We stood in front of Colman's bassinet, trying to stay out of the way of the doctors and nurses.

Dr. Callaway came by to find out if anybody had seen the anesthesiologist. It felt like we'd just arrived at the hospital, but it was already 6:30. Everybody kind of shrugged when he asked about the anesthesiologist, and that worried me.

I asked Dr. Callaway when the surgery would start.

"That's going to depend on when Dr. Stark gets here," he answered vaguely. I must have looked puzzled. At that point in time, I wasn't completely versed in hospital hierarchy, and it seemed odd that an anesthesiologist would keep a cardiothoracic surgeon waiting.

"Don't worry. She'll get here when she gets here. Denise Stark is definitely worth the wait." Dr. Callaway smiled as he left the NICU.

I looked down at Colman and then at Kevin.

"What are you thinking?" he said.

"I'm thinking that we should have checked out the anesthesiologist as carefully as we checked out Callaway."

"Really?"

"Yeah, really." My hand automatically went up to my mouth. I felt the need to chew my fingernails, but I stopped myself because we were in a hospital. Gross.

"You're freaking me out," Kevin said in a low voice. And it was true—I could feel his anxiety climbing.

"I'm freaking out," I said. "The anesthesiologist is a huge part of this whole deal. Do you know how many medical malpractice depositions I've taken of anesthesiologists?"

"No. I don't want to talk about that right now. Here's the deal. She's got to be good if Callaway uses her. Right?"

"Right."

"We trust him. We need to trust that he's assembled the best team of doctors and nurses to work with him on these difficult cases."

I don't think he overheard our conversation, but one of the male nurses who was working with Colman interjected, "Don't worry. Denise Stark is awesome. Dr. Callaway's not lying about her being worth the wait. He'd wait all day for her."

I felt a giggle bubble to the surface; I could tell the nurse relished the thought that somebody could keep Dr. Callaway waiting.

"Dr. Stark lives way out in the Hill Country," he continued, "so she has quite a drive in. Sometimes she gets behind feeding her cows and whatnot. Sometimes her power goes out, but she'll be here."

"Okay," I said, but I knew I didn't sound convinced.

"Hi, there. Y'all haven't been looking for me, have you?" a voice behind me said.

"There she is," the nurse said loudly, letting Dr. Stark know that's exactly what we'd been doing.

Kevin and I turned and came face-to-face with the anesthesiologist. She was probably in her mid-fifties, small and lean. Maybe it was her twenty-plus years of experience taking children away from worried parents and in to surgery, but she had the most calming effect of just about anybody I've ever met. I knew within seconds exactly why Dr. Callaway would wait all day for her. We were placing Colman in capable hands.

We answered Dr. Stark's questions about family history. Then Kevin finished signing the rest of the surgery consent forms.

"It's time to take him down," Dr. Stark said. "We better get going."

"Do you want to say goodbye?" one of the nurses said to Kevin and me.

How do you even do something like that? How do you say goodbye to your baby you barely met two days ago?

I leaned over Colman, kissed him on his forehead and said, "I love you." It struck me that I'd never kissed him before. How many times had I kissed Liam by the time he was three days old? Probably thousands. Tears poured down my face. The nurse we'd been talking to handed me a box of Kleenex.

"Really, I only need one tissue," I protested.

"It's going to be a long morning," he said, his face pinched with concern. "Just take it."

"Thanks," I said.

Kevin and I watched Dr. Stark carefully wheel Colman onto the elevator, followed by the entourage of nameless people in scrubs who seemed to follow him everywhere.

After the elevator doors closed, I looked at Kevin. "That was awful," I said.

Kevin hugged me for a long time in the empty bay of the NICU. I pulled away from him and looked at his tear-stained face. "You didn't read any of those papers you signed last night or this morning."

"What's the point? It's not like we have any choice in the matter."

"True. It's just I've never seen you sign anything without reading it."

One of the NICU nurses gave us directions to the surgical waiting area. Kevin and I stopped by the cafeteria for some breakfast sandwiches on the way. I didn't think I'd be able to eat anything, but it was something to do; we would be at loose ends for the next four to six hours. When Kevin and I turned the corner, we saw Dr. Callaway talking to my parents in the hallway. I think we both panicked a bit, as we didn't expect to see him at this juncture. He turned to us and asked, "Where's Colman?"

"Dr. Stark took him in to surgery a while ago," I said.

As it turned out, everybody was in the surgical suite ready to go. They were just waiting on Dr. Callaway.

Kevin and I settled in with our families. One of the surgical nurses called the main phone in the waiting room to give us hourly updates. The first two times they called, Kevin talked to the nurse for several minutes. When he hung up, he said, "Colman's doing great."

"That's it? What else did she say?"

"That's pretty much it."

"There had to be more than that. You were on the phone for several minutes. What are they doing? Have they opened his chest yet? Do they have him on bypass?"

Kevin gave me a blank stare. "I think they said something about that stuff," he offered sheepishly.

"Seriously, you cannot answer the phone any more," I snapped. "I need to know what's happening."

Kevin's a big-picture kind of guy, which usually works out fine. Just not in this particular case. If he answered the phone again and didn't regurgitate some major details, I was going to strangle him.

I had to race Kevin to grab the phone on the next call. It was for another family. The second call I answered was for us, but there was static on the line, and it went dead shortly thereafter. They tried calling several more times and finally sent someone from the operating room to give us an update and get our cell number.

The next update we received was that the Norwood was complete. Colman was doing well. They were able to bring him off bypass without any problems, but they were keeping him in the O.R. because he was oozing—whatever that meant. We received two more calls after that, letting us know that Colman was stable but still oozing.

Soon after that someone called from the doorway, "Is Colman's mom here?"

"That would be me," I said, going to meet the woman at the door.

"Hi. I'm Loretta. I'm one of the nurses in the PICU. I think they're going to bring your baby up shortly. Can you come with me?"

"Sure. Do I need to get my husband? He went to the restroom."

"No, that's okay," she said. I followed her to the elevator. "We're getting Colman's room ready. I think they're close to finishing with him in surgery. I wanted to show you around the PICU and let you see what a baby looks like intubated and on a ventilator so it's not such a shock. When you see somebody else's baby intubated, then it doesn't seem so bad when you see your own baby."

Loretta and I rode the elevator up to the PICU, and she led me into one of the rooms. Inside was a two-month-old. She had caramel-colored skin, and her hair had the beginnings of loose, black curls. She was sleeping—her long dark eyelashes fanned out against her chubby pink cheeks—and seemed to be resting comfortably.

"She's beautiful," I said.

"Yeah, she is," Loretta said. "She had surgery two days ago. You see the breathing tube?"

"Yeah."

"That's exactly the same kind your son will have. He'll probably have a few more lines since he's just coming out of surgery. And, of course, his chest will be open."

"Yeah." I looked at the baby girl's chest, which had a perfect incision down the middle that looked to be closed with Steri-Strips. "Dr. Callaway told me he'd probably leave Colman's chest open."

"You okay?"

"Yes. Thanks for coming to get me. I appreciate it. I wasn't sure what to expect."

"I know. It seems like everything's not quite so traumatic if it's explained on someone else's baby first. Let me show you Colman's room."

I followed Loretta to Colman's room, which was in the center of the Pediatric Intensive Care Unit in front of the nurses' station. I met Lexi, the nurse who would be taking care of Colman when they brought him out of the operating room. There were also three other people helping to get the room ready.

The phone rang, and Lexi answered it. When she hung up, she said, "That was the O.R. They'll bring Colman up in the next half hour."

Loretta turned to me and said, "I'm going to finish helping them up here. Can you find your way back to the waiting room?"

"Yeah. I got it. See you in a bit," I said.

When I was just steps from the waiting room, the double doors that led into surgery flew open. An array of medical personnel poured out, and I flattened myself against the wall so they could pass. I recognized Dr. Callaway. I stood on my tiptoes for a glimpse of Colman.

I freaked out momentarily. Not because of how Colman looked— he actually looked great, all things considered—but because of the person tending to him. I'm not sure if he was a nurse, surgical tech or respiratory therapist, but he looked like he belonged in a biker bar. His muscled arms were covered in tattoos that disappeared into the short sleeves of his scrubs, and his hair was pulled into a low ponytail tucked beneath his surgical cap, which showed off more tattoos on his neck. One of his large hands worked to constantly squeeze the bag artificially ventilating Colman, while the other rearranged some of Colman's tubing so it wouldn't get caught on anything.

I took a deep breath. Tough Guy's blue eyes locked on mine. "You must be his mama," he said.

I nodded, but I was at a loss for words. All I could think was, The guy in charge of making sure my baby is breathing has neck ink!

A couple of months before I had realized I was somewhat biased against people with tattoos. I'd never given it much thought, and the realization hit me like a ton of bricks. One day when I came home to check on Liam during lunch, I noticed that Esme had a tattoo. I called my sister, Holly, on my way back to work. I blurted out, "Esme has a tattoo."

"Okay."

"I'm totally freaked."

"Why?"

"I don't know. I didn't know she had one."

"What's the big deal?"

"If I'd known she had a tattoo, I wouldn't have hired her."

"Are you going to fire her?"

"No way."

"Well, what is it?"

"I'm such a bitch."

"No, stupid. What's the tattoo?"

"Oh, it's a tiny butterfly in the center of her back, between her shoulder blades."

"That sounds okay. I'd be worried if it was a rose with a snake around it. But a butterfly sounds nice."

"It's a pretty little tattoo. God, I feel like such an ass. She's so awesome. And to think I would have missed out on knowing this amazing person because I have a hang-up about tattoos," I said.

"Yeah, that would suck."

"I'm a tattoo racist," I said, horrified.

Holly laughed. "You're not a tattoo racist."

"Yes, I am. It's awful. I'm a tattoo racist."

"Whatever, Heather. At least you're being honest with yourself. Maybe you can work on that."

"True," I said.

Obviously I still had some work to do, but those weren't butterflies on Tough Guy's neck.

I took another deep breath and focused my attention on his eyes.

"He did great in surgery, Mama. You should be really proud of him," he said, smiling.

Dr. Callaway said, "We're taking him up to the PICU. Give us about thirty minutes to an hour to get him settled, and you can come up and see him."

"Circulatory arrest?" I questioned, hoping they hadn't needed to stop Colman's heart.

"Eleven minutes."

"Okay."

As I looked Colman over, I noticed a square piece of gauze covering the opening in his chest. There was a giant tube sewn into the left side of his chest down by his bottom ribs. The tube was attached to a large bag full of blood hanging from the stretcher.

"Is that why you said he was oozing?" I said, gesturing to the bag of blood. "That looks like he's hemorrhaging."

"We've had to give him quite a lot of blood. We just started his fifth pint."

Four pints didn't sound too bad. "How much blood did he have in his body to begin with?"

"Probably about half a pint."

It didn't take long for me to do the math. They'd given Colman at least eight times his body's blood volume. I felt a little queasy. "Is he still mine?" I joked.

Dr. Callaway chuckled. "Yeah. He's yours."

I watched them wheel Colman away and felt relief wash over me. He'd made it through surgery. Now I could focus on the critical next twenty-four hours. My mind began racing. When would they be able to close his chest? What if he got an infection? How long would he have to be on the ventilator? What if he lost his suck reflex because he'd been intubated too long? What if he couldn't eat?

I had to remind myself to focus on one thing at a time. Because if we managed to make it out of the hospital after this heart surgery, we could look forward to repeating this whole process in six to nine months. My eyes welled up with tears again.

Maybe I would need that whole box of Kleenex after all.

CHAPTER 13

After visiting briefly with a few friends who had shown up at the hospital, I decided to find out how Colman was doing. I walked into the PICU and stood outside his room. The sliding glass door was cracked and the curtain was drawn, so I could catch only small glimpses of what was going on. Things seemed to be calming down. Just a few doctors and nurses were going in and out. I knew Lexi and Dr. Callaway were there because I could hear their muffled voices.

Linda, Dr. Callaway's nurse, found me outside the door. "There you are. Dr. Callaway sent me to find you guys."

"I don't know where Kevin is right now, but I'm sure he'll be up in a minute."

"Let's go in."

Linda pushed open the sliding glass door and pulled back the curtain. I wanted to take a step inside, but my feet felt like they were glued to the floor. I was glad Loretta had taken the time to show me somebody else's baby. Colman had so many tubes, lines and wires I couldn't even count them. There were at least a dozen medication pumps hanging behind the head of his crib. The medical paraphernalia needed to keep him alive took my breath away.

Dr. Callaway was sitting in a chair at the foot of Colman's bed. "Come on in," he said, gesturing for me to come inside the room.

Somehow my feet managed to obey him. I found myself at Colman's side as Lexi quietly began explaining the different medications and monitors. Then Kevin showed up and Lexi went over everything again, which I was grateful for. It started to make a little more sense.

"Now that you know what all that stuff means," Dr. Callaway said, waving a hand at the equipment, "would you do me a favor?"

Kevin and I nodded.

"Watch the patient," he said. "We need to pay attention to Colman and what he's doing, not rely on some monitor to tell us. You're not going to have these monitors when you take him home. It's the same for me. I watch him. I don't watch the monitors."

"Okay," I said.

I'm not sure why I agreed not to look, because it was impossible. The monitors convey all sorts of interesting information, such as heart rate, oxygen saturations, breaths per minute, blood pressure and body temperature. They're there for a reason. Dr. Callaway busted Kevin and me staring at them more than once that day.

"Watch the patient, not the monitor," he said again and again, his voice stern but gentle.

He had, in essence, given us permission to spend time with Colman, and I was able to study my baby in a way I probably wouldn't have otherwise. It didn't take long for me to start detecting subtle changes in Colman's color, even before the monitor alarms sounded.

Dr. Callaway came around to the bedside. He adjusted some of Colman's tubing, checked chest drain output, listened to Colman's heart with a stethoscope he'd swabbed with alcohol and checked Colman's pulses in his hands, feet and groin. He said the surgery had gone perfectly. It was a textbook Norwood with a Sano modification, and he found nothing unexpected or out of the ordinary, which was good news.

"Would you like to see his heart?" he said.

"Sure," I said, at the same time Kevin said no.

Dr. Callaway snatched off the gauze covering Colman's open chest, which was sealed with some sort of clear plastic membrane—it reminded me of cellophane—and we saw our son's tiny heart beating inside his chest.

"Pretty cool, huh?" Dr. Callaway said.

"Wow," I said. Holding my breath so I wouldn't exhale dirty germs into my child's open chest, I leaned over to get a better look. I heard Kevin make a noncommittal grunt. Out of the corner of my eye, I saw his hands gripping the side of the bed, his knuckles white. I hoped he wouldn't faint, but when I looked up he seemed to have recovered from the initial shock.

Dr. Callaway replaced the gauze covering and sat back down. Kevin left to return some phone calls—cell phone usage was strictly prohibited in the PICU, something about the phones interfering with the delicate monitoring equipment—while Dr. Callaway sat and returned phone calls . . . on his cell phone.

In between calls, I asked, "You don't have any other surgeries scheduled?"

"Nope. Colman was my only surgery today. I wanted to make sure this little guy got off to a good start."

And that's exactly what Dr. Callaway did. He stayed through the 7 p.m. shift change and into the early evening, making minor medication adjustments, checking Colman's pulses and heart rate and probably a million other things I didn't realize he was doing.

Kevin came by to see what I'd decided. I wanted to go home with him, check on Liam, take a shower and then come back to the hospital for the night. Dr. Callaway overheard our conversation and said, "Go home and get some rest. You'll be of no use to Colman if you're tired. If things take a turn for the worse tonight, we're going to kick you out anyway. Tim will call you immediately if anything goes wrong. Right?"

Colman's night nurse, Tim, nodded. "I'll call you first thing. Well, actually, I'm calling him first," he said with a chuckle, pointing to Dr. Callaway. "But I promise I'll call you second."

I laughed. "Yes, please call him first."

Dr. Callaway was right. I hated the thought of leaving Colman, but he was completely paralyzed and heavily sedated. In addition, the past three days had taken their toll on me, and I was drained.

Then there was the matter of my boobs to contend with. Despite the dire warnings from the breastfeeding consultant at Mercy Hospital, I was pretty sure my milk had come in. Either that, or my breasts had turned into concrete that could expand exponentially with every passing minute.

We made it home a little after nine that evening, and Liam was still up. It felt surreal to indulge in a little bit of normal after the day we'd had. I read him a story and tucked him into bed with a regular kiss, an Eskimo kiss and a butterfly kiss, in that order. Then Kevin and I ate the dinner Mom had prepared. It was some kind of King Ranch casserole one of our many friends had dropped off, and it was delicious.

After expressing a whopping ten ounces of breast milk in less than ten minutes, I called Tim. Everything was pretty much the same. Colman was still critical but stable. I fell into bed and slept soundly until two, when I used the breast pump and called the hospital to check on Colman again.

Over the next couple of days, I fell into a routine. I made sure I was home with Liam in the mornings for breakfast and at night to tuck him into bed, but I spent all day by Colman's side. Liam has always been an early riser, which was fortunate because it enabled me to get to the hospital in time for seven o'clock rounds. After Esme arrived to take care of Liam, my mom would usually meet me at the hospital. Kevin had court settings and work appointments, and his parents were still in town, so he was in and out several times a day.

The black Medela backpack breast pump was my new best friend. It went everywhere with me. I pumped for ten minutes and expressed ten ounces every four hours like clockwork. I was a milk machine. After a couple of days, the section of the PICU refrigerator assigned to Colman was full, so I started tossing packets of milk into our deep freeze at home.

A few days after Colman's surgery, I walked into his room. "How's my sweet boy doing today?" I said to the nurse.

She looked at me, placed her hands on her hips and said, "I don't want you to take this the wrong way, but I don't think there's anything sweet about this kid. He's totally pissed."

I laughed, kind of stunned. "How can you know that? He's six days old, on a ventilator, paralyzed and sedated."

"My point exactly," she said. "Watch this." She walked over to Colman's bedside and leaned in close, never actually touching him, and motioned for me to look at the monitor. Colman's heart rate and blood pressure climbed while his oxygen saturations trended down into the low seventies. When she moved away from his bedside, his numbers settled back into a normal range. "See? He shouldn't be able to do that. He's on high-powered paralytic and sedation medications."

"I'm sure he's sick and tired of everybody messing with him," I said.

"Maybe. But mark my words, you're going to have your hands full with that one."

I'd missed rounds that morning. Usually I was there when the cardiac team rounded, and Dr. Callaway made sure I was included in the conversation. Since we were at a teaching hospital, it went something like this: Some resident would recite Colman's medical history and what had happened the previous day and night, and the team would discuss the best course of action for the day ahead.

Colman wasn't peeing, so the plan centered on increasing his nonexistent urine output. His doses of Lasix would be increased to try and pull some fluid off of him.

It didn't work. We went all morning with little urine output while I watched my baby boy become more swollen. Colman's skin was becoming stretched and shiny. Even his eyelids were puffy.

Kevin came by the PICU around noon. "Hey," he said to my mom and me, "why don't you guys come to lunch with us? My parents are leaving to go home today."

I looked at my mom, who didn't exactly seem thrilled, and back at

Kevin. "I don't think so," I said. "I don't want to leave Colman."

"Why not?"

"He doesn't seem to be doing so great today."

"He looks fine," Kevin said.

I wondered if we were looking at the same baby.

"You need to eat something," he reasoned. "You've barely spent any time with Mom and Dad, and they're leaving today. Don't be rude."

God forbid anybody think I'm rude with my baby lying in PICU, swelling up like a water balloon. I agreed to go, thinking we were eating someplace close and fast, like the hospital cafeteria.

Wrong.

We ended up at Aldo's for a huge Italian meal. Aldo's is in the medical center, but it's several blocks from South Texas Medical Hospital. When Kevin ordered a bottle of red wine, I thought I might scream.

Two hours later I'd barely touched my meal or the wine. My mom knew I was upset because I couldn't quit fidgeting. Talk about ants in the pants; I wanted to get the hell out of there. The bill finally came, and Kevin offered to finish my wine so as not to waste it, which would've taken another twenty minutes.

"Oh, no, I'll get it," I said, and emptied the wine into the potted plant to my right.

"What is your problem?" Kevin asked in a quiet voice. "You've had a bad attitude this entire lunch."

"Pee." I said, my voice low. "I can't stop thinking about pee and why our kid isn't doing it. And it's now past two o'clock, which is when I pump. I'm miserable. I want to leave."

"That's fine, sweetie. Why didn't you just say so?"

Oh, for the love of God!

Kevin dropped Mom and me back at the hospital. When I made it up to the PICU, Colman looked worse. The intensivists were discussing options. Dialysis was discussed as they ran labs, trying to get a handle on the problem. One doctor said that maybe Colman's kidneys had "taken a hit" during surgery, which can happen when a person is placed on bypass or undergoes circulatory arrest.

After spending the afternoon with Colman, I still had more questions than answers. I needed a break. I went home and had dinner with Liam, Kevin and my mom. Then I tucked Liam into bed. The change of scenery did nothing to help my anxiety. I felt worse. I needed to get back to Colman.

"I'm going to the hospital," I said to Kevin and my mom.

"Honey, I wish you wouldn't go at night," Kevin said. "That parking lot is full of lowlifes. It's dangerous."

"I'll be fine."

"Do you want me to go with you?" Mom asked.

"If you want."

Kevin said, "Who's on shift tonight? Is it someone we know?"

"Yeah. It's Tim."

"Why don't you just call him? I hate to see you run down there in the dark."

That made perfect sense.

I called the PICU and asked to be transferred to Colman's room. Tim picked up the phone and said, "Hey, I was getting ready to call you. Colman's not doing so hot."

"He wasn't peeing earlier today."

"He's not peeing now either. His output has dropped to nothing. I've paged the surgeons, and I'm waiting to hear back from them."

"Okay," I said, trying to process what he was saying.

"Look, he's really sick. I'm not sure he's going to make it through the night. You need to get down here."

"I'm on my way."

I flew out of the kitchen, shoved my feet into my shoes and grabbed my purse. "I've got to go," I said to Kevin. "Tim says Colman's really sick."

"Can't you go in the morning?" Kevin asked.

"No. Tim said Colman may not make it through the night."

"I'm coming with you," Kevin said, grabbing his wallet.

I can't remember anything about getting to the hospital that night, except that I know I drove. It was almost nine when we arrived, and Tim still hadn't heard from the surgeon on call, which was Dr. Callaway.

I didn't think Colman could get much puffier, but I'd been wrong. His body had swollen to grotesque proportions. Even his head looked like it had edema.

I pulled up a chair and laid my head down beside his. My tears started to fall. I wanted to tell him that everything was going to be okay, but I couldn't. I didn't want to lie to him. Watching his chest rise and fall and his heart beating under the gauze, I wasn't sure they'd be able to put him back together.

Kevin paced around the room while Tim hovered over Colman, arranging and rearranging the lines and tubing and checking Colman's medication pumps. Tim was a huge man, well over six feet tall. I wondered, not for the first time, why the medical field hadn't come up with a more manly title than nurse for men who choose that profession.

The hospitalists and residents were in and out of Colman's room, consulting with Tim. Everybody in the PICU was on edge. I was beginning to wonder what the holdup was with Dr. Callaway when he walked through the door.

"I heard Colman's been misbehaving," he said, his voice serious.

"Something like that." I tried to smile through my tears.

Dr. Callaway wanted to place a couple of drain tubes in Colman to try to pull off some of the extra fluid. He hoped that once the pressure on Colman's kidneys was alleviated, they would start working.

"Just do what you've got to do," Kevin said.

"Are y'all going to take him to the operating room tonight?" I asked.

"No. We'll do this bedside. You guys go down to the cafeteria and get a Coke or something. Give me about thirty minutes."

As we turned to leave, one of the residents said, "Wait. I need you guys to sign the informed consents."

Kevin took a step toward her to sign the paperwork.

"No, they don't," Dr. Callaway said. He grabbed the clipboard from her hand and launched it across the room and onto Tim's desk with a loud clatter. Papers flew everywhere.

"They have to sign the consents," she said, obviously flabbergasted.

"They gave me consent," Dr. Callaway said, his voice stern. "Didn't you hear them? You were standing right there. Dad told me, 'Do what you gotta do to make the boy well,' and that's exactly what I'm going to do."

"We'll be happy to sign the papers," Kevin said.

"Don't worry about them," Dr. Callaway said, irritated. "I've got this. Be back up here in thirty minutes."

Kevin and I walked away slowly, and I overheard Dr. Callaway say to Colman, "Now, son, why do you have to go misbehaving like this? You've got your mama and daddy all upset."

I'd managed to keep my emotions in check during the last couple of weeks, but now I laid my head on the cafeteria table and bawled my eyes out, and I didn't once think how disgusting that was—to lie facedown on a community surface in a hospital.

I heard Kevin say, "Heather, what's wrong? I've never seen you like this."

"I can't stop crying."

"I see that," he said, probably in an attempt to make me laugh. When it didn't work, he grabbed my hand. "Colman's not going to die tonight. He's going to be okay."

"No, Kevin, he's not. He's not okay. Our baby is lying upstairs, and he is sicker than I ever imagined anyone could be and still be alive. He has a tube down his throat that's attached to a machine that is breathing for him, his chest is open and he has a PICC line, arterial line, catheter, pacer wires—he even has a little probe up his ass twenty-four hours a day to check his fever. I realize in the grand scheme of things the fever probe is not a big deal, but it's not okay. And now Dr. Callaway is going to put in more tubes because Colman is swelling up like some sort of Stay Puft Marshmallow man because his fucking kidneys are on the fritz."

"We didn't have a choice."

"We did," I said.

"What—to let him die?"

"It would have been better than this. If he dies tonight, I will never forgive myself."

"But he would have died anyway," said Kevin.

"Right. But I wouldn't have turned him over to be mutilated first," I said. "I'm his mother. I'm supposed to protect him, and all I've done is stand by while he's being tortured in the name of saving him. That's bullshit."

"You're not thinking straight. He's going to be okay. I know it."

"I'm glad you do, because I don't. Right now I feel like we've done the most selfish thing in the world, and I hate it. If he was only going to live a week, it should have been at home with us. He should've been wrapped up in cozy blankets and held by us. It shouldn't have been this way. And if he does live, we'll be back for two more rounds. There is nothing okay about this."

"I know what you're saying, Heather. I do." Kevin stroked the top of my head as I tried to mop the tears and snot off my face with a napkin. "But you and I are a good team. There's nothing we can't handle together, including this."

"I'm not leaving him tonight. You and Dr. Callaway can't make me," I said, wiping the last of my tears away and crossing my arms in front of my chest.

"No, baby, we're staying here tonight. Let's get back up there and see what's going on."

CHAPTER 14

Dr. Callaway placed three drains that night—one on each side of Colman's chest and one in his abdomen. Although Colman looked worse to me with the drains, I could tell he was improving. His numbers were better than they had been less than an hour before, and Tim's hovering had gone from constant to intermittent. I figured these were all good signs. Now the only thing to do was see if Colman's kidneys would kick in once the excess fluid was drained off.

The fluid coming from Colman's chest drains was a clear, light yellow, and the fluid from the drain in his belly was a dark amber that made me think of poison. I felt ill looking at it.

Kevin and I finally left the hospital around four o'clock. After sleeping for a couple of hours, I called the hospital to get an update from Tim. Then I took a hot shower and dressed in what I'd begun to think of as my hospital uniform: a long-sleeved tee, black yoga pants and running shoes.

I stopped at Starbucks on the way to the hospital and ordered the biggest cup of coffee they offered. In my tardiness, I'd missed rounds again, but the plan was the same as the day before, which meant crossing my fingers and hoping for pee.

After hanging out with Colman for a couple of hours—my heart racing from all the caffeine I'd consumed—I needed a break. Maybe the coffee hadn't been the best idea. I was either going to conquer the world or drop dead, nothing in between.

I went on a quick walk around the hospital and grabbed something to eat in the cafeteria before going to the PICU quiet room to use my breast pump. When I returned to Colman's room, his nurse gave me a huge smile. "We've got pee, Mama! Lots and lots of pee."

"Really?" I said. I looked at the rubber tube full of pee snaking its way out of Colman's diaper. "Oh, my gosh! You weren't kidding. That is a lot of pee."

"Yeah, he started right after you left."

"I'm happy I left then," I said. "Who knew I could feel so proud of Colman for something as silly as peeing?"

"I get it. I'm proud of him, too. It's been a scary thirty-six hours."

"Yeah," I said, happy we weren't dealing with some crazy kidney problem on top of everything else.

Colman continued to pee like a champ over the next few days. As the swelling subsided, he began to look more like himself, and Dr. Callaway decided it was time to close his chest.

Kevin and I waited in the hall outside the room during the procedure. I'd be glad to have his chest closed, although I felt queasy when I thought about the surgery. The skin around Colman's sternal wound had healed up after a week of his chest being open, and I wondered how well the skin would go back together. Would they have to roughen the edges to get them to stick?

Mom and Dad met up with us outside the PICU. Kevin headed to the cafeteria for drinks since my parents were there. Not long after he left, we were allowed back in his room.

Colman's incision looked pinched and angry. I knew there were dissolvable sutures along the inside that we couldn't see, but there were also big, black catgut stitches along the outside. I tried to imagine what it might look like once it was healed and thought, Oh, shit.

Dad must've seen it at the same time. From the corner of my eye, I saw his head move. I cast him a quizzical look.

"I think his nipples are crooked," Dad said, his features screwed up in a pained expression.

"I see that," I said. "Do you think it may be the way Colman is lying in the bed?"

Dad turned his head to the side. "I don't think so. They look pretty crooked to me."

"You'd think that's something a heart surgeon would check, whether the nipples match up."

"You'd think," Dad said, clearly exasperated. "Are you going to say anything to Dr. Callaway?"

"Hell, no," I said with a laugh. "He's got two more shots to get it right. If Colman comes out of the Glenn with crooked nipples, then I'll say something so he can match them up after the Fontan. It might be the way Colman is lying and the extra fluid."

"They're crooked," Dad said.

"Fine. Whatever. But don't say anything about it in front of Kevin. It will upset him."

"Like he can't see for himself," Dad said. "They're really crooked."

"He won't notice," I said. "Trust me."

We fell silent when Kevin walked in the room with our drinks. I was right. He didn't notice.

Crooked nipples were the least of our problems, but as Colman's swelling subsided over the next couple of days we could see that Dr. Callaway had matched Colman's nipples up perfectly.

The plan was to make sure he got used to life with his chest closed and then start weaning him off some of his heavy sedation and paralytic medications. Hopefully, he would show us some signs that he was ready to come off the ventilator and breathe on his own. To our relief, he did.

One of the signs was overbreathing the vent, which involved Colman taking extra breaths in between the ventilator breaths. Another was a slight whistle in his airway, which was encouraging to the nurses—I could never really hear it—because it meant he had extra room surrounding the tube. That's a great sign for extubation.

It was reassuring to see Colman getting better, though he was still in a fragile state. I couldn't hold him because of the ventilator, but it felt like we were making progress. Almost daily one of the medication pumps was removed or a medication was replaced with a less potent one.

Respiratory therapists began coming in to do percussion therapy, which consisted of cupping their hands and alternately clapping on both sides of Colman's chest, over his lungs, to loosen any secretions. The therapists assured me that it didn't hurt, and that older children said it felt quite nice.

Colman hated it.

During one of these sessions things went awry for him. A respiratory therapist—a woman I'd not met before—came in with two students and began Colman's chest percussions. I sat in the corner and thumbed through a magazine to give them a little space. I hated watching Colman have the chest percussion therapy. He would get so pissed and give a soundless cry because of the tube down his throat. It was awful.

The respiratory therapist instructed her students on percussion techniques and on Colman in particular. We were at a teaching hospital, so I was used to having students, interns and residents ask questions.

I noticed that Colman's color didn't look so great.

"Hey, guys," I said. "What's going on?"

Right then the alarms on his monitoring equipment sounded, and his oxygen saturations went into free fall. Colman's nurse took one look at him and called for backup. A stampede of doctors and nurses swarmed into Colman's room, each person jockeying for a better position.

The respiratory therapist kept repeating, "This baby always does this." She got louder and louder.

"He's never done this," I said.

"Oh, yes, he has. He does this all the time," she yelled.

"When?" I asked.

"He does this every night. All the respiratory therapists are talking about it. We didn't do anything!" She sounded hysterical.

"Every night?" I asked, incredulously.

"You're not here," she spat. "How would you know?"

She had me there. My cheeks flamed with shame and anger. Except for the one night Kevin and I stayed until 4 a.m., I wasn't at the hospital in the middle of the night. I was snuggled in my comfy bed, trying to get a good night's sleep.

I watched the doctors and nurses tend to Colman. I thought they'd kick me out, so I tried to be as invisible as I could. I needn't have worried. All eyes were on Colman.

They'd unhooked his breathing tube from the ventilator and were bagging him while trying to suction his airway, but his oxygen saturations dropped into the fifties, forties, then thirties.

I should be panicking, I thought. But I stood in the corner and tried to project my strength out to Colman. I chanted in my head something like, "I'm here, baby. Get it together!"

I focused on watching Colman and nothing else. His color looked okay. When I did glance at the monitors, his oxygen saturations were back in the fifties and his heart rate and blood pressure were still out of whack, but not as bad as they'd been. After what seemed like hours—probably less than two minutes in reality—Colman's oxygen saturations were back in the high seventies and his heart rate was trending down to where it needed to be.

Everybody stood around for several minutes, not saying a word, to make sure he was going to behave. Then they filed out of the room.

I stopped one of the hospitalists and said, "Has he done this before?"

"Not to my knowledge. I've been here in the PICU since his surgery, and I've never seen him do anything like that."

"What was the therapist talking about?"

He shook his head. "I don't know. Like I said, I've never heard anything about Colman having a problem."

"What was that?"

"I don't know," he repeated, sounding baffled. "He desatted, and his heart rate went crazy. I'm not sure what that was. He worked it out himself with not much help from us."

"I want to see his chart," I said.

"Okay." He studied my face.

"And I don't want that respiratory therapist to step foot in Colman's room again. I realize it may not be anything she did or didn't do, but she was way too defensive. The yelling was very unprofessional."

"I agree," he said.

"Thank you." I glanced at Colman to reassure myself he was okay and stepped into the hallway to take a deep breath. I ran into Loretta, the nurse who had been so kind to me on the day of Colman's Norwood.

"You doing okay?" she asked.

"Yeah. I guess so. I'm trying to process what happened in there."

"I think we all are. That was weird. You sure you're okay?"

"I think so. As okay as I can be."

"You're made of some pretty tough stuff, aren't you?"

"Why do you say that?"

"Everybody thinks so. We were saying the other day that nobody's ever seen you cry," she said.

"You're not asking the right nurses," I said. "Tim's seen me cry."

Any other day this conversation would have made me feel like I was keeping it together, but after the public shaming I'd endured, I felt shitty.

CHAPTER 15

A couple of days after Colman's chest closure the doctors decided to take him off the ventilator. I was looking forward to seeing his face without the tape that kept the breathing tube in place.

I was able to hold Colman afterward, for the first time since he'd been intubated. He still had several lines and IVs, so I couldn't snuggle him without help from one of the nurses, but it was a huge moment for us.

I held Colman for a little over an hour, and the nurse helped me put him in his crib. I happily babbled about Colman for a few minutes, and then I realized she'd grown quiet.

"What's wrong?" I asked.

"Do you see the way he's tugging?"

"Tugging? No. What does that mean?" Every time I thought I'd been thoroughly immersed in medical lingo they threw me a curve ball.

"You see how his stomach is retracting?"

"Yeah. It looks like he's breathing."

"Sort of, but it's different. Look at what happens to me when I breathe," she said, demonstrating.

"Okay."

"Now look at Colman."

"I see that it's different, but what does that mean?"

"We're going to watch it. But I don't want you to be upset if we have to reintubate him."

"Put him back on the ventilator? We just got the tube out."

"I'm just saying sometimes they need a little extra help. Some babies fail extubation several times."

My heart sank. "How long could he be on the ventilator if he has to be reintubated?"

"Hopefully not long, but we have one Norwood who has been intubated for over six weeks. That little guy just hasn't been able to come off the ventilator."

"Six weeks?" That wasn't going to be my baby. I excused myself and took a short walk downstairs to clear my head. Then I called Kevin with the news that Colman was extubated, but the nurse was cautiously optimistic that he'd stay that way.

I just kept thinking, six weeks?

There was still no affirmative decision about the breathing tube, so I waited with Colman until late afternoon. It seemed likely that he would go back on the ventilator. His breathing had become more labored, and he was struggling to maintain his oxygen saturations, even with the help of oxygen.

The decision was made to reintubate him early that evening. Since I was forced to leave during the procedure, I went home to have dinner with Liam, Kevin and my mom. I was happy for the respite; I was tired of hearing the nurses and doctors discussing Colman's "failed extubation" like it was something within his control.

I tucked Liam into bed, and Mom and I returned to the hospital. The breathing tube was back in place.

In twelve short hours I'd gone from feeling like we were making progress to feeling like there was no end in sight.

At least Colman was still here. Earlier that day, our nurse had responded to a code in the next room. When she came back in, I knew from the look on her face that the baby hadn't made it.

"I'm sorry," I said, my heart aching for the family.

The nurse shrugged and blinked back tears. "It's one of those days," she said.

To change the subject, Dad said, "Isn't this the hospital Genene Jones worked in?"

"Yeah, on this floor. In this unit, actually," she answered.

"Genene Jones?" I asked. "You mean that crazy nurse?"

"Yeah," she said. "Genene would inject the babies in her care with digoxin and heparin. Then they'd crash, and she'd try to save them."

"God. That's awful," I said, feeling sick to my stomach.

Seeing the stricken look on my face, she said, "There's no way that could happen nowadays with the way the medications are administered."

"I thought this was the hospital she worked at," Dad said.

"I was a witness for the state at her trial," the nurse said.

"Really?" Dad and I said at the same time.

"Yeah. I'd just started working as a nurse. I was on nights, and she and I shared the same patient, who was really sick. I would come in at night and she'd say, 'Maybe tonight will be the night this little one will fly high with the angels.'"

"That's sick," I said.

"Tell me about it. I'd worry all night that he'd die, but he remained stable. Then the next day I'd hear that he had all sorts of problems during her shift. It didn't make any sense. That's when we started to suspect she was doing something to the babies."

"One of the judges I've worked with had some sort of involvement in that trial," I said. "I don't know if he was part of the prosecution or defense, though."

"I don't remember any of the attorneys. It's been almost thirty years."

"I'll have to ask next time I see him," I said, rubbing my arms in an attempt to warm up. When I'd heard about the case in the past, I'd thought of someone mentally ill, suffering from Munchausen syndrome by proxy. But in the PICU, looking at the helpless babies fighting for their lives, I knew Genene Jones was pure evil. The fact that she'd walked these halls chilled me to the bone.

The next day Mom and I were back at the hospital early for rounds. Colman had improved overnight, so the plan was another extubation attempt. I didn't get my hopes up, but he did much better on the second attempt.

Once he was off the ventilator, he started making progress at a startling rate. They placed an NJ tube—a nasojejunal feeding tube—to see how he tolerated breast milk, and he did great. Much to my chagrin, though, after a couple of good days he was back in NICU to work on bottle-feeding and breastfeeding, which meant I lost the privacy and freedom that came with the PICU. We were one step closer to going home, but it still sucked.

It took a few days for Colman to get the hang of eating from a bottle. The NICU nurses acted like it was not that big a deal because he could always go home with a nasogastric feeding tube. Eating from a bottle and being able to breastfeed were huge deals to me, though. I didn't want to take my baby home on the NG tube. I wanted the tube out of his nose. The damn thing terrified me.

I made sure I was there for all the assigned feeding times, except for two in the middle of the night. I didn't trust the busy nurses to really work with Colman on his feedings.

Colman and I had a lot of long talks. People laugh when I say this, but it's true. I tried bringing some of Liam's favorite books to read out loud, but I couldn't get through *Goodnight Moon* or *The Owl and the Pussycat* without breaking down in tears. Then I tried singing Liam's favorite songs to Colman. "You Are My Sunshine" seemed to go okay until I got to "Please don't take my sunshine away." I blamed the pregnancy hormones for making me feel weepy, though a baby who's undergone major open-heart surgery with at least two more in his future seems as good a reason to cry as any.

Instead of reading or singing, I told Colman how I needed him to do his part and eat and act as much like a normal baby as possible. Fortunately, "hard-ass" wasn't in Colman's vocabulary, but I'm sure he thought I was one. He seemed to understand what I was telling him, even though he had no voice. Poor guy couldn't make a sound when he was crying because of his intubations.

After a few days in the NICU, Colman seemed to have the hang of both bottle and breast. He still looked really skinny, since he'd lost close to a pound since birth. When I changed his diaper, I couldn't help but feel sad as I picked up his spindly legs and looked at his wrinkly little old-man bottom.

Kevin, Esme and I had to take an infant CPR course before he could come home. I absorbed some of what was said during the class, but mostly I remember thinking, Please don't let me have to use any of this on Colman.

You know what would be helpful for hospitals to teach when you're taking your new baby home? A tracheostomy. I can't tell you how many times one of my kids has choked while eating. If pounding on their backs and the Heimlich doesn't work, I'm going to poke a hole in their throat as a last-ditch effort. They might as well show me the correct way to do it.

The day of discharge came, and I saw Dr. Callaway as we were both going into the NICU. "I need to show you something real quick," he said.

"Okay."

We walked over to Colman's NICU incubator, and Dr. Callaway pulled back the bandages where Colman's abdominal drain tube had been. "This is an omental hernia," he said. What can only be described as a pink mushroom of guts spilled out of my son's belly, about the size of the end of my pinky finger. "When I pulled the tube out of his abdomen, a little bit of the stomach lining, the omentum, was stuck to the tubing and came out along with it."

"What am I supposed to do about it?"

"Nothing, really. The omentum is a great sealant, so you don't need to worry about germs getting in there. You just need to change the bandages every couple of days. Give it a week, maybe two. It should shrivel up and fall off."

"Okay," I said, feeling slightly ill. "So I just change the bandages every two days and it's going to fall off?"

"Yeah. I wouldn't worry about it. Okay?"

"Okay," I said, nodding.

Kevin and I waited most of the day for Colman's discharge paperwork and medications. Finally, around six, Kevin went home to Liam. My mom had returned to Victoria a few days earlier, so it was just Colman and me.

I was feeling somewhat frustrated after standing in line for almost four hours at the hospital pharmacy to get Colman's medications filled. When the pharmacist asked for my Medicaid or Medicare card, I handed him my Humana card.

"This is private insurance," he said.

"Yeah. NICU told me to come here so I could get my son's meds for discharge."

"We don't take this. Go to Walgreen's or something."

"Look, I've waited in this line all afternoon. Can I just pay cash for his meds so we can be discharged?"

"I can't help you," he said. "Next!"

When I told the NICU nurse what had happened, she rolled her eyes and wrapped up a day's worth of meds. Then she showed me how to compound Monopril, which was Colman's blood pressure medication. I had to crush and dissolve a 10-milligram, adult-sized pill in 10 milliliters of water, then draw out 0.4 milliliters of the solution to give to Colman. I guess it shouldn't have come as a surprise that drug companies don't make blood pressure medication in infant dosages.

In addition to the Monopril, Colman had to take a quarter of a baby aspirin daily, along with Zantac and Lasix.

After the medication lesson, I went to check on Colman. I was shocked to find him in baby clothes—ugly baby clothes. Up to that point, because of all the tubing and gear, I'd wrapped him in soft baby blankets I brought from home.

"Doesn't he look cute?" a nurse asked, coming up behind me.

"Yeah," I lied. "I have a going-home outfit for him. Where did these clothes come from?"

"Oh, they were just some extras we had around here. I think he looks so handsome."

So much for that. I'd wanted something with snaps in the front because of his chest incision, and I'd found the perfect outfit at Bambino's, a baby boutique in Alamo Heights. I'd fallen in love with the soft white material and hand-stitched boat on the front.

After the nurse moved on, I leaned over Colman and said, "You have some great stuff at home. Mama will get you all fixed up when we get there. Okay?"

Colman stared at me with his big blue eyes.

"Ma'am?" a woman said, startling me.

"Yes?" I turned around to see one of the NICU residents.

"I need to show you something."

"Okay."

She pulled up the bottom of Colman's onesie. Then she carefully loosened the dressing where the abdominal drain had been. "Have you seen this?"

"Yes, I saw it this morning."

"Well, it's very concerning."

"Really?" I said, wondering how her take would differ from Dr. Callaway's.

"Yes, really. These kinds of hernias are extremely dangerous. What are you planning on doing about it?"

"Well, Dr. Callaway said it should shrivel up and fall off in a couple of weeks. He didn't act like it was a big deal."

"He said that?" she asked, her eyes round in disbelief.

"Yes."

"Are you sure?"

"Yes."

"I don't think that's possible. Look at this," she said, poking around the edge of the hernia with her gloved fingertips. "It's fresh and pink and looks like it has pretty good blood flow. This is going to need to be fixed surgically."

"So it's not going to fall off in a couple of weeks?"

"Who told you that again?"

"Dr. Callaway, the cardiothoracic surgeon."

"You're saying Dr. Callaway told you not to worry about it?"

"Pretty much, yeah."

The resident put her fingers to her temples as if fighting off a major headache. I wanted to do the same.

"I will have our pediatrician look at it and make any referrals we might need," I said, hoping to make her feel better.

"Okay. You promise you'll ask about that?"

"Absolutely," I said.

On April 20, 2004, after a crash course in infant CPR and compounding medications, we were on our way home. Colman was twenty-one days old. I carefully loaded him into the backseat and started the car. The stereo blared Sheryl Crow and Kid Rock's duet,

"Picture," which seemed to be on every time I got in the car. The lyrics had taken on a completely different meaning to me. Talk about overplaying a song. I switched it off.

I took a deep breath and checked on Colman one last time. His eyes were wide open until he decided he disliked being in the car. He scrunched up his face and launched into a soundless cry.

In a matter of seconds, his skin turned an awful gray as his oxygen saturations dipped low. "Let's get home," I said. "You'll like it there. It's going to be okay, sweet boy. We're going to be okay."

I'm not sure if I was trying to reassure him or myself. I felt like I'd just been sent on my way with a ticking time bomb.

CHAPTER 16

In my haste to get Colman home, I didn't drive through Walgreens to pick up his prescriptions like I'd originally intended. Once we pulled into the driveway, I unbuckled him from his car seat and held him in my arms. He calmed down quickly, and I thanked my lucky stars as I watched his color turn from a Smurf-like blue to his normal dusky gray.

Kevin met us at the door and retrieved all the bags of random stuff we'd collected during Colman's hospital stay. When he came back in, he gave me a smile that meant "I can't believe we're all home" and a kiss on the cheek. When he went to kiss Colman on the top of his head, he said, "What is he wearing?"

"Random hand-me-down NICU clothes," I said. "Don't ask. It was meant with the best of intentions."

"Liam is playing in his room," Kevin said. "Let's introduce Colman to his big brother."

"Sounds good," I said, following Kevin to Liam's room.

Liam was happy to see me. Even though I'd spent time with him every night, he seemed to know that me being home was a pretty big deal. I knelt down with Colman in my arms and said, "Liam, this is Colman. He's your baby brother."

They stared at each other for a few seconds. Then, very gently, Liam leaned over and kissed the top of Colman's head, and I felt my heart melt.

We sat in Liam's room to watch him play with his train for a bit. I told Kevin about the fiasco with the hospital pharmacy and how I'd planned to get the meds.

"I'll get them," Kevin offered.

"Right now?" I said, as he got up to leave.

"Yeah. I mean, he needs them, right?"

"Yes. I just . . ."

"What's wrong, Heather?"

"It's nothing," I said, trying to swallow the panic I felt at being left completely alone with my two children.

"I'll be right back."

"Okay. The insurance card is in my wallet."

"Got it."

Baptism by fire, I thought. Is there ever any other way? Colman and I sat in the rocking chair and watched Liam. Eventually Liam became hungry and we went downstairs to the kitchen. I managed to put a meal together for him one-handed, since Colman had taken up residence in my left arm.

Kevin's short trip to the H-E-B pharmacy turned into a two-hour ordeal. The pharmacists refused to fill the prescription for the blood pressure medication, even though the instructions on how to give it were written on the prescription. They said they could be held liable for giving adult medication to an infant, and they couldn't be sure we'd administer it properly.

That didn't make sense to me. Isn't it always possible that people will misuse a medication, or abuse it?

Kevin told the pharmacists that they could count on being held liable if they didn't fill the prescription written.

After several rounds of this, I called the NICU and spoke to one of the residents on staff. She was able to put the pharmacists' concerns to rest, and they filled Colman's prescriptions.

Kevin looked like he was on the verge of a heart attack when he got home. We set up the bassinet for Colman on my side of the bed, and Kevin showed me the nursery he'd completed—with no help from me. All of Colman's things had been put together perfectly.

After giving Liam a bath and tucking him into bed, we spent some time with Colman. I wanted to wash off the hospital smell, which was a foul combination of betadine, hand sanitizer and never-been-washed baby. I couldn't submerge him because of his incisions. Kevin helped me hold him so I could wash his hair and give him the best sponge bath possible. I could foresee it taking several weeks, maybe even months, to get the tape residue off his little body.

"You were a dirty, dirty little bird," I said as I wrapped Colman in a hooded towel.

I put a fresh diaper and pajamas on him and then nursed him before going to bed. As I was lying there, drifting off to sleep, I sat up with a start. How would I know if he woke up if I couldn't hear his cries?

I fretted about what to do, then set my alarm for an hour so I could check on him. I fell asleep with my hand resting lightly on his belly, hopeful that I would feel his movements if he woke up before the alarm went off. That worked pretty well in alerting me to his periods of wakefulness. He woke up almost every hour, if not before.

At the 2 a.m. feeding, I propped myself on the pillows to nurse Colman. The house was so quiet I could've heard a pin drop. It took me a few seconds to recognize that the "whoosh" I heard was Colman's heart beating. I'd been told by one of the residents at the hospital that his heart murmur was considered a stage 5 and was accompanied by a palpable thrill, which was a pretty significant murmur. This was due to the blood moving through his shunt. A stage 6 murmur is audible without a stethoscope.

When the resident gave me this information, I asked if I could borrow her stethoscope to listen for myself. Not that it really mattered, but I wanted to know what my baby's heart sounded like.

As I nursed Colman, I began to grow nauseous with the rhythmic whooshing. I took a deep breath. Instead of focusing on how sick Colman was, I tried to remind myself that hearing his heartbeat should be reassuring. I can't say it helped a lot.

We tried to get settled in a routine the next day. I nursed Colman frequently and counted wet and dirty diapers to make certain he was taking in enough milk. His doctors were not exactly exuberant over my idea to breastfeed him exclusively, but I was determined that we could make it work.

That evening Liam woke from his nap crying and making a terrible barking sound I'd never heard before. Kevin went to get him, but he was crying for me. Kevin and I traded babies. Every time Liam tried to inhale he'd start coughing, which would make him cry. I could tell he was starting to panic because he couldn't breathe very well.

"Sounds like croup," Kevin said.

I'd never had croup as a kid, nor had any of my siblings, so I was skeptical of what Kevin said. Besides, croup was his go-to illness whenever he heard a kid cough. I knew steam or night air was supposed to help, and I figured it wouldn't hurt, so I turned the shower on hot and sat with Liam in the steamy bathroom until he started to feel a little better.

When Liam had calmed down, I called Frank. Based on hearing Liam's cough over the phone, he called a prescription for steroids in to the pharmacy. It was definitely croup.

I called my mom in a panic. I couldn't imagine Colman getting a cough like that right after having his chest put back together. As it was, it seemed he would do just about anything to avoid coughing. If he had to, it was usually one big cough that seemed to take him by surprise, followed by a series of little coughs that sounded like small grunts.

Mom wasn't able to come to San Antonio. She'd taken off too much time from work to help out while Colman was in the hospital. Plus, Nana, my maternal grandmother, had been diagnosed with cancer, renal cell carcinoma, about nine months earlier with a prognosis of six months to live. She was definitely on borrowed time, having outlived that estimation by about three months. My mom needed to save some leave to help Nana with trips back and forth to M.D. Anderson.

Kevin and I tried to sort out what to do. I was tempted to check into a hotel with Colman until Liam was better, but I didn't want to leave Liam after we'd just gotten home. Eventually we'd have to figure this kind of thing out anyway. I couldn't just go to a hotel every time Liam came down with something I was worried Colman could catch.

Kevin volunteered to help out with Liam. He was pretty uncomfortable with Colman. When he tried to hold him, Colman would commence his soundless crying and turn blue, and Kevin would say something like, "Here. You take him. I don't think he likes me."

This division of children worked well enough, but Liam would still become panicked when his cough got bad and cry for me, which broke my heart. I spent a lot of time washing my hands *Grey's Anatomy* style and changing my shirt in between babies late into the night. To say I was frazzled the next morning would be the understatement of the year.

It had been two days since Colman's discharge from the hospital, which meant it was time to change the bandage on his hernia. This seemed easy enough to do, until I began changing it. I loosened the tape surrounding the gauze like a pro. Colman didn't even flinch. As I went to lift the gauze from his abdomen, though, the gauze stuck to the hernia and sent him into silent hysterics. I swallowed a wave of panic and called Kevin to come help me. He'd just finished shaving and walked over with only a towel around his waist to where I'd put Colman on the bed.

"What's the big deal? You're just supposed to change the bandage, right?" he asked.

"Yeah," I said, holding my hands together to stop them from shaking. "But it's stuck." I lifted the gauze to show Kevin the exposed omentum.

"Yuck!" Kevin grimaced. "I wasn't expecting that. What is that thing?"

"That's the hernia I was telling you about. It's his stomach lining. Dr. Callaway called it the omentum. It came out when he pulled the abdominal drain."

"Why did that have to happen?" Kevin asked nobody.

"What do I do? I'm supposed to change this today. I don't want to hurt him, and that's going to happen if I pull this off. What if it pulls out more of his stomach lining?" I was completely grossing myself out.

"Call Frank," Kevin said.

"Hey," I said, as he walked into the master bathroom to finish getting ready for court.

"Yeah?"

"You're brilliant. You know that, right?"

Kevin smiled. "Glad I could help."

I took a deep breath and secured the gauze with another piece of tape. I was pretty sure it wasn't going anywhere since it was glued to my son's body, but I didn't want the bandage to catch on his clothes and hurt him. Then I called Frank and briefed him, trying not to hiccup through the conversation. My nerves were shot.

"Come on down to my office. I'll be happy to change the bandages for you," Frank said.

"Thank you so much. I know I should be able to do this, but it's kind of freaking me out."

"No worries. Oh, and make sure you tell the front desk that you're to wait in my office. Colman shouldn't be in a waiting room."

"Okay. See you in twenty," I said.

I dashed into the bathroom, ran a brush through my hair and pulled on some pants and a long-sleeved T-shirt. Then I loaded up Colman and drove over to Frank's office. Colman hated the car just as much as he did the first time he'd ridden in it.

At the pediatrician's we were ushered into Frank's office to wait. Before long Frank poked his head in and said, "Hey, I have a room available. Come on back."

"Great."

In the examining room Frank said, "Now, you said something about a hernia, but I didn't catch everything on the phone."

"Colman has this omentum hernia."

"Did you say omentum?"

"Yes. Is that a thing? Maybe I misunderstood the word. That's totally possible. I understood it to be the stomach lining."

"Yes, omentum is the stomach lining. I was just making sure I understood you correctly."

"Yeah, I could totally have that wrong." I continued talking at about five thousand words a minute. "But whatever this is, it is the stomach lining. Anyway, I'm supposed to change the bandages every two days, but when I got ready to do it this morning, it got stuck. And I freaked. Then Kevin told me to call you. And now I'm here. Help!" I laughed, feeling a tad foolish.

"Okay. Well, let's see what we've got here."

The tape came off easily since I'd already loosened it. After a few minutes Frank managed to get the gauze free of Colman's body. The hernia looked exactly the same as when Dr. Callaway and the resident showed it to me two days before. This was disheartening, since I was under the impression the grisly thing would eventually dry up and fall off. Damn.

Frank peered down at the hernia and said, "Wow. That's impressive."

For the record, when a doctor uses this phrase it's not a good thing. Think of it as medical-speak for "What the fuck?" You can substitute one for the other and it always makes complete and total sense, even though one is a statement and the other is a question.

"Yeah, that's one way to describe it," I said.

"So what are you supposed to do about this besides change the bandages every two days?" Frank asked.

"Well, when Dr. Callaway showed me this, he said they usually shrivel up and fall off in a couple of weeks."

"He said that?" Frank sounded unconvinced.

"Do you think I misunderstood him? Because this other doctor, a resident, said these kinds of hernias are really dangerous and it would have to be fixed surgically. She couldn't believe Dr. Callaway said that either. I assured her I'd check with my pediatrician. And here I am, checking with you."

Frank laughed. "Yeah, I don't know. When do you see Dr. Callaway again?"

"Thursday of next week."

"So less than a week?"

"Yeah."

"I'd just double-check with him about this."

"Okay," I said. It sounded like a solid plan. "I was wondering about giving him a bath, though."

"I don't think you should submerge him. What if he got a germ through there?"

"Good point. So keep sponging him off?"

"That's what I would do. I'm just not sure about that." He gestured to the bandages.

"Can I bring him back in a couple of days for another bandage change?" I asked, hating that I felt so squeamish.

"Sure thing. I'll change it every two days until it's gone or we figure out what to do with it."

"Thank you," I said. "You're the best!"

I exited the office and went by the front desk so I could pay my $20 copay. It was totally worth it. I'd have paid a hundred bucks.

Colman had a follow-up appointment with cardiology a few days later, but Dr. Roberts was out of town. We saw another cardiologist who'd only rounded once in a while and wasn't as familiar with Colman.

They checked height, weight, blood pressure, heart rate and oxygen saturations and did an EKG. Then the cardiologist listened to Colman's heart with his stethoscope.

"Has he been eating well?" he asked.

"Yeah, pretty good."

"Are you bottle-feeding or breastfeeding?"

"Breast," I said, watching as he pursed his lips.

"Are you supplementing?"

"No. I've been nursing him exclusively," I said.

"He seems to have lost a couple of ounces since he was discharged from the hospital. I'd recommend supplementing him with a bottle. Heart babies, especially HLHS babies, have a very hard time nursing. Breastfeeding requires a lot of energy and hard work. They're just not strong enough."

"Okay," I said, not wanting to listen to his opinion on the subject.

I went home and checked the charts I'd been keeping on Colman's input and output. Everything looked okay, but I had the niggling thought that maybe I should be feeding him from a bottle. He didn't seem to have any of the explosive diapers Liam had at that age, and he was fussy and seemed easily frustrated with breastfeeding. I'd been telling myself he just needed to get the hang of it.

A couple of days later Colman and I had our follow-up with Dr. Callaway at South Texas Medical Hospital. Colman was five pounds, nine ounces, down five ounces from hospital discharge, which was worrisome. I wondered about the accuracy of the scales in all the offices we'd frequented in the past week.

Linda, Dr. Callaway's nurse, came by to see how Colman had been doing. A doctor I'd never met entered the room as we were chatting. He brusquely introduced himself as one of the cardiothoracic surgeons working with Dr. Callaway and began asking questions. He was intimidating and rude.

"I have a question about this hernia," I said, pointing to the bandages on Colman's abdomen.

"Okay," he said, tapping a file against his leg. "What do you want to know?" Clearly, I was wasting his time.

"Well," I said, "I'd like you to take a look at it. Dr. Callaway said it was the omentum that came through when he pulled out his abdominal drain. He said it should fall off, but I wanted you to double-check it."

I started to loosen the bandages. The doctor sighed heavily, handed his file to Linda and walked over to the hand sanitizer he hadn't used when he entered the room.

I'd been on handwashing high alert after one of the cardiologists at the PICU washed his hands thoroughly and then touched the trash can lid to throw away the paper towel instead of using the foot pedal. I didn't even notice until my mom kicked my foot and pointed it out.

I should've asked him to wash his hands again, but he was such a nice guy and I didn't want to embarrass him. I told myself that I would have said something had Colman's chest been open, but since his chest was closed his chance of infection was much less and it would probably be all right. And that shouldn't be the test. Ever.

Dr. Asshat finished sanitizing his hands and came over to examine Colman. He was in a hurry, and his movements seemed rough, especially since they were directed at my baby.

"What did you say Dr. Callaway told you this was?"

"An omentum hernia," I said.

"That's not what this is." He took a pair of tweezers from his coat pocket. "This is granulated tissue," he said, using the tweezers to pull at the stomach lining. Colman immediately commenced his soundless screaming.

"Stop. Just stop," I said, feeling panicky about not knowing where those fucking tweezers had been before he touched my baby boy's insides with them. Amazingly, my words came out sounding authoritative even though I didn't feel that way. I'd obviously misunderstood Dr. Callaway.

Dr. Asshat glared at me. I tried to put as much space between him and Colman as I could without pushing him away.

Linda spoke up then. "Maybe we should get Dr. Callaway to take a look, since he was the one you talked to about this."

"I think that's a great idea," I said, never taking my eyes off Dr. Asshat. If he wanted to have a stare fight, fine by me.

"You don't know what you're talking about," Dr. Asshat said.

"You're probably right," I said icily. "I'm a court reporter. Not a doctor."

"That is not an omentum hernia. That's granulated tissue. See?" He tried to take another swipe at Colman's hernia with the tweezers.

I spread my hands in front of Colman, and Dr. Asshat's tweezers made contact with the back of my hand.

"Don't touch him," I said.

He tossed the tweezers on a tray with a sigh and crossed his arms. His face was set in an angry mask.

Dr. Callaway walked in and greeted Colman and me. I've never been so happy to see somebody in my life.

"I wanted you to look at this again. My pediatrician's been helping me change the bandages because it keeps getting stuck, and he asked me to check with you about it."

Dr. Callaway said, "Ah, the omentum hernia, huh?"

I looked past him through the window at Dr. Asshat, who was standing outside the exam room. He rolled his eyes at Dr. Callaway's back, threw his hands in the air and stalked off.

Fucker.

"Okay. But then that guy was saying granulated tissue, and I'm just not sure. One of the NICU doctors said it was dangerous. When I showed the pediatrician, I told him what you said about it falling off and he said, 'He said that?' like I must have misunderstood you." I knew I was talking fast, and I tried to make myself slow down. "This hernia thing is kind of freaking me out."

Dr. Callaway smiled. In his folksy way, he teased, "Look, if I've told you once I've told you a thousand times. That is an omentum hernia. When the stomach lining, or omentum, comes through the skin like that it makes a seal. The blood supply is cut off. Once the blood supply is cut off, it will shrivel up and drop off."

"What if it doesn't?" I asked.

"If it doesn't, I'll fix it for him when he has his Glenn surgery."

"What about bathing him?"

"You can bathe him."

"He won't get a germ through there?"

"No. That's the best sealant in the world. No germ is getting through. I imagine your pediatrician probably doesn't see many of these, but I do, unfortunately. I would do the exact same thing if this happened to one of my boys."

"Okay," I said, feeling a bit better. "What do you think about his weight? He's down five ounces from discharge."

"I don't know. You've done this before. You're not a first-time mama. What do you think about his input and output? I'm not going to tell you not to breastfeed him, but you need to understand that these heart babies have a pretty difficult time with it. Trust your instincts."

"Thanks," I said. "I'll get it figured out."

"I know you will."

Colman and I went home after our appointment. It was time for him to eat, but instead of nursing him I heated some breast milk in a bottle and fed that to him. He sucked down the entire two ounces in less than ten minutes with no fussing.

After I burped Colman, I laid him down in his bassinet and pulled it into the bathroom with me to pump. After ten minutes of pumping, I was shocked when I looked at the bottles. I'd only expressed half an ounce. The doctors had been right about Colman being too weak to nurse properly. He wasn't strong enough to keep my supply at the level he needed. In my stubbornness, I was starving him.

I checked the freezer and deep freeze and counted almost two thousand ounces of breast milk, which I figured would last Colman until he was almost four months old. Then I retired my breast pump. I'd loved nursing Liam. It was convenient. No bottles to warm and wash. But I would be going back to work in a few weeks; I wanted to have plenty of time to take off for Colman's next heart surgery, and pumping and bottle-feeding were too much for an already overwhelmed mama. I was done.

It took about a week to get over feeling like I'd starved Colman. The guilt hit in crippling waves. Eventually I quit beating myself up so badly. After all, we'd caught it before it turned into something really awful. And he'd started eating like a champ.

A couple weeks into being home, the hernia on Colman's stomach looked exactly the same. I'd resigned myself to the fact that Dr. Callaway would have to remove it during the next surgery. Then one evening I was changing Colman's pajamas, and I noticed that his bandages had come loose. When I went to replace them there was no hernia, just perfect skin. The only reminder was a flat, white scar and a small dimple beneath the skin that was visible when Colman cried.

Where did the hernia go? That's a mystery. I'm guessing it fell off, but I never found it.

CHAPTER 17

Colman was the worst baby ever. There's no other way to describe him as an infant. It took a couple of weeks after discharge for his vocal cords to start working again. In the span of about two days, I went from feeling elated that my baby had finally gotten his voice back to being a jangled bundle of nerves.

Colman was in possession of an amazing pair of lungs, and he used them regularly to emit ear-splitting shrieks that could travel straight up your spine and explode inside your brain. Colman's sleep—and, by extension, mine—consisted of a series of short catnaps. He never slept more than an hour at a time, and when he was awake he wanted to be held. When he wasn't sleeping or being held, he was screaming.

I couldn't lounge on the sofa and hold him either. He liked to be walked around. We tried wearing him in a sling or a Baby Bjorn like we had with Liam, but he hated both. I felt like the Baby Bjorn put too much pressure on his sore chest and made him uncomfortable. I'm not sure what his objection to the sling was, except that he'd turn blue. Arms and legs in constant motion, along with lots of bouncing, were the only things that made him happy. And I use the word "happy" loosely.

We managed to keep Colman healthy through Liam's bout of croup, but I came down with a bad cold during that time. Since most cold viruses last ten to fourteen days, I wore a surgical mask for two weeks whenever I was feeding, changing or holding Colman. When we went on walks, my neighbors were probably thinking, There goes that woman with tuberculosis. It was lovely.

One night I woke with a start and realized Colman was gone. We'd done away with the fiction of a bassinet, and I'd been sleeping with him in bed beside me. I followed the soft light coming from the living room and saw that Kevin was feeding Colman a bottle. I stood there for a minute watching the two of them together. Then I crept back to bed.

Since I wasn't breastfeeding, it made perfect sense that Kevin would help out by taking a night here and there. For the first time in months, I fell back to sleep, hopeful I'd be able to get through the crazy newborn nights. I fell in love with Kevin all over again.

I shouldn't have.

That was the first and last time Kevin woke up for a feeding or to comfort a fussy baby. It was a constant source of strain between us. I'd gone back to work when Colman was six weeks old because I knew I'd need to take off again for a second heart surgery within the year. Kevin used his age and work as an excuse for why he couldn't wake up in the middle of the night, but I thought that was ridiculous. I had to go to work every day too, and the age thing really pissed me off. Everybody knows old people need less sleep, and he was the one who thought it was a good idea to marry someone over a decade younger.

To help alleviate some of the pressure, Kevin offered to hire a night nurse a couple of nights a week, but that just made me angrier. I felt we should be able to take care of our baby at night. Esme was already taking care of him weekdays. Looking back, I had way too much pride. I should have taken him up on the offer. Instead I spent the next several months dead on my feet.

The fact that Colman turned the color of a Smurf when he cried was distressing. It's perfectly acceptable to put a healthy baby in the crib for a few minutes and walk outside to take a breather. I never felt I could do that with Colman. His health was too unpredictable, and we'd been warned at the hospital not to let him cry too long.

I should've had them define "too long."

Esme, Kevin and I were all terrified of this tiny baby and of what could happen if he became too upset. As a result, Kevin spent less time with Colman than if he had been born healthy. Kevin was convinced Colman didn't like him at all, and it was a tough point to argue when Colman's reaction to Kevin was to scream bloody murder. The problem, as I saw it, was that they never had a chance to bond properly in the hospital. They just needed to spend some time together.

My only outlet during those months was work. The rest of the time we stayed home in order to keep Colman healthy, and I was locked down in baby jail like I'd never experienced before.

When Colman was about ten weeks old he contracted a stomach virus, and I was worried about him getting dehydrated. Frank was out of town, so I took him to a pediatrician in Frank's group. "You have a really sick little boy on your hands," he said. "Hypoplastic left heart syndrome is very, very serious."

"Yeah, it is," I said, nodding.

I really didn't deserve a lecture from a substitute pediatrician. Did he think the open-heart surgery three days after birth failed to clue me in?

"Do you know what you're doing and how to take care of him?"

"I'm not sure how to answer that. I'm following the instructions they gave me at the hospital on signs and symptoms to look for, and I'm following my instincts. Do you have any other suggestions?"

"Well, okay, if you're sure."

No, I'm not sure, I thought. I'm not sure about any of this.

"So if he starts throwing up feces, take him directly to the hospital."

I didn't reply. I stared at him. I probably should have thanked him, because I hadn't realized throwing up shit was within the realm of possibility. And how would anybody ever think that was not a big deal? Take him to the hospital? Duh. I would've called 911. The doctor must have thought I was an idiot. Colman and I never went back to him.

When Colman was three months old, Dr. Roberts decided it was time for a heart catheterization. Colman's oxygen saturations were trending in the low seventies—a lot lower than was desired—and Dr. Roberts thought Colman's next surgery, the Glenn, would probably need to be performed soon. The heart catheterization would give doctors the numbers they needed to make that decision.

Colman's heart team had completed their move to St. John's Children's Hospital, so that's where we took Colman for his heart catheterization. When I walked through those sliding doors, my first feeling was peace. I felt as if I was coming home.

My cousin Cody had been treated for leukemia at St. John's when he was ten. I was eleven at the time he became ill, and my parents took us from Victoria to San Antonio, a two-hour drive, to visit him in the hospital on the weekends. After fighting cancer for years, Cody eventually went into remission. He's married now, with two beautiful children. Suffice it to say, I had a lot of memories and good associations with the hospital, and I felt Colman was in the best place possible.

I thought the hardest part of the heart catheterization would be turning Colman over to Dr. Stark, the anesthesiologist, but I was grateful when she came to get him. In preparation for the catheterization, we'd been unable to feed him after midnight. I'd walked the floor with him all night. If I could keep him sleepy and distracted, maybe he wouldn't think about missing a warm bottle of milk. The last two hours were especially trying, as he took short turns furiously sucking his pacifier and screaming at the top of his lungs.

After the hand-off to Dr. Stark, Kevin and I grabbed some breakfast and stationed ourselves in the waiting room. An hour and a half into the procedure, we saw Dr. Callaway go into the cath lab. He didn't seem to be moving quickly, and I took that as a good sign.

Dr. Callaway and Dr. Roberts came out of the cath lab about a half hour later to discuss their findings with us. Colman's pulmonary arteries were narrowing where they were connected to his shunt, and they thought that was causing his low oxygen saturations. They didn't think it was a good idea to try to balloon the arteries and wanted to see if we felt comfortable with them sending Colman home on oxygen until he was old enough to undergo his Glenn.

We discussed our options and decided the oxygen was the least invasive. Dr. Roberts and Dr. Callaway were in agreement that Colman needed to have his next surgery, but they wanted to wait until he was four months old. In their experience, babies who underwent the Glenn before the four-month mark didn't fare as well.

Dr. Roberts sent Colman to the PICU. We met back up with him just as he was getting settled. A pressure bandage had been applied to his groin where Dr. Roberts had inserted the catheter through his femoral artery to look at his heart, and Colman's leg was strapped to a board to keep him from moving it. His leg was pretty swollen from the procedure, and our nurse, Shelly, along with the PICU doctors, was keeping a close eye on it. During all this, the nurse-in-training was telling me how the doctors drew a picture of Colman's heart for her and she couldn't believe he was alive it was so screwed up.

I can't even tell you what that conversation did for my anxiety, but I managed to push my fears aside and focus on being there with Colman.

Other than the babbling nitwit, Colman's post-op recovery was smooth. The swelling in his leg that had everybody so worried was subsiding. Colman's PICU room had a bunk to accommodate one parent, so Kevin went home to pack a bag for me so I could stay the night.

Before being discharged the next day, I was given an oxygen tank— along with instructions and a quick run-through on how to use it—and an appointment for home health to set up oxygen for Colman.

The home health agency arrived at our house at the same time Colman and I did. They set up an oxygen concentrator that would run twenty-four hours a day for Colman's "whiff" of oxygen. A whiff of oxygen sounds like no big deal. In reality, it was anything but.

We put the oxygen concentrator in the living room because it was the central place in our house. The oxygen's concentration was diminished if the tubing was longer than twenty feet, which meant Colman couldn't sleep with me anymore. I dragged the bassinet back out and set it up in the living room, which was right next to our bedroom.

We spent the next five weeks with Colman on a twenty-foot tether or lugging the portable oxygen tanks when we had to take him to doctor appointments—not to mention the craziness of putting him in bed with a long length of plastic tubing. I'm pretty sure taping plastic tubing to your baby's face is a big SIDS no-no, but Colman had to have it.

Colman wasn't turning over yet, but he was getting close. I can't count how many times I woke at night to Colman's screams and found the tubing wound tight around his little body. I tried running the tubing along the inside of his footy pajamas with the snaps up the front, but he almost always managed to get it loose. Sometimes he pulled the nasal cannula out of his nose even though I'd secured it with tape, and that part would be wrapped around his neck so tightly it left an indentation.

We made frequent trips to Dr. Roberts's office for checkups. Colman's oxygen saturations were still low, even on the oxygen. Bath time meant I could see his precious face without the tubes. However, the last few weeks leading up to his second surgery, I started spacing his baths out from every other day to every three days. Then I stopped giving him a bath altogether because he turned a horrible dusky gray, without even crying. I knew his oxygen saturations were dropping into the sixties, which was dangerous.

I didn't have the greatest feeling going into our next appointment. When I took Colman in that afternoon, his oxygen was 65 percent.

"I'm going to admit him," Dr. Roberts said. "I don't think we're going to be able to wait for his Glenn. You should probably know, Dr. Callaway is out of town right now."

"Of course he is," I said, feeling my luck turn. "Who would be the surgeon if we have to do this emergently?"

"Probably Dr. Kaufman."

"Dr. Kaufman would be okay, but I don't want Dr. Asshat touching Colman. I don't even want him assisting," I said.

"You don't like him?"

"No, I don't."

Dr. Roberts looked at me thoughtfully and said, "There's another cardiothoracic surgeon who just joined our team from the West Coast, Javier Saldivar. He's very talented and has a good reputation. I think you'd like him."

"Where is Callaway, anyway?"

"Thailand, I think."

I ran my hands through my hair in frustration. Colman's heart surgeon was just about as far from San Antonio as he could be.

"I really want to wait for Callaway," I said.

"I know you do. I do, too. We'll see how it goes tonight. Colman may have to stay in the hospital until Dr. Callaway gets back."

"That's fine. Do I have time to go by my house and pack a bag?"

"I'd rather you go straight downtown so you don't hit rush hour. I'm calling now to let them know you're on your way."

"Tell them I'm running low on oxygen."

"I will. You tell them too, when you guys get there. It will get you admitted and up to the PICU faster. Drive safely, but go as fast as you can. I'm finishing up a few things, and I'll be right behind you."

I snatched Colman's car seat, my giant purse that doubled as our diaper bag and the oxygen tank and raced out of the office. I snapped Colman's car seat into the base, jumped in my car, turned on my hazards and drove Colman to the hospital. When we arrived, his room was ready.

I called Kevin once we had Colman settled to let him know we were admitted. Naturally, he was upset.

"It just seems like it's always something with him," he said. "Do you think we're ever going to get back to normal?"

"No. Honestly, I don't think so. I think hospital stays are going to be our new normal."

"I'm sorry, babe."

"Me, too. Can you pack an overnight bag for me?"

"Sure. We'll be down there in the next hour."

"That would be great. Thanks."

Kevin and Liam brought my overnight bag along with some dinner. Colman's oxygen saturations were low, but they stayed around the 70 percent mark. He was discharged the next morning.

At the follow-up appointment the next week, Dr. Roberts scheduled Colman's surgery for two days later, first case of the day on August 6.

"I'm surprised they had an opening that fast," I said.

"We had to bump somebody."

"That makes me feel bad."

"Well, he needs this," Dr. Roberts said. "He can't wait any longer."

"Dr. Callaway will be back?"

"He should get into town late tonight, so, yeah, he'll be here to do Colman's surgery."

"Thank goodness," I said, feeling like we'd dodged a major bullet.

I knew Colman was in desperate need of this next surgery, and Kevin and I were ready to get it behind us.

CHAPTER 18

We checked into the hospital on the evening of August 5 for Colman's heart surgery. He was the first case the next morning, which meant they'd take him into the operating room around 7 a.m.

The first order of business, once we were on the intermediate care floor, was to get an IV in Colman and draw blood for labs they'd need for surgery. Colman's nurse came into the room to place the IV, and I asked her, "Are you good?"

She laughed. "I'd like to think that I am. Why?"

"Colman's a really hard stick. You've got one try to get an IV in him. If you don't get it, I want you to find the best sticker they've got in the NICU, and we'll go from there."

"Why do you think he's such a hard stick?"

"Past experience. And he has terrible perfusion. Just look at him." I gestured to my adorable but very gray baby.

"Okay. But you know, other than his coloring, I wouldn't think he was a heart baby. Look at those chubby cheeks!"

"He's a great little eater," I said.

"That's surprising," she said. "Heart babies usually don't have that much chub. If you'll hang on a sec, I'll be right back."

About half an hour later Colman's nurse came in followed by two additional nurses.

"I went ahead and called the NICU. She's the best sticker we've got," she said, nodding to a short round black woman. "I thought we'd start with her, if that's okay with you."

I smiled. "Sounds good to me."

It took all four of us working a solid two hours to get an IV in Colman. They checked his hands and feet and tried vein after vein. No success.

After each attempt I picked Colman up and did my best to calm him. They'd search his extremities for another place. I'd lay him down on the bed and hold him tight so they could try again, and Colman would scream at the top of his lungs. He turned bright blue, and a huge vein bulged on top of his head. I wished that throbbing vein were anywhere else so we could stick it.

"Pick him up, Mama," the NICU nurse said. "He's too blue."

I tried my best to soothe him.

"Let's take a little break," the nurse said, and started to move around. We were all sweating from the stress and physical work involved. Then she said, "Oh, look at him watching me. He's not taking his eyes off of me."

In spite of how stressed out I felt, I laughed. She was right. Colman was furious, and he followed her every movement.

"Let's put it in his head," I suggested.

"No, way. Dr. Callaway won't like that."

"He has a great vein there that pops out the second he starts crying."

"I know. I saw it." I could tell she was weighing her options. "Dr. Callaway will have my hide if I put an IV in that baby's head."

"If he says anything about it, blame me. I don't care. Tell him I said 'the head or nowhere.' I'll tell him myself. We can get what we need for now, and they can place the lines after he's under anesthesia tomorrow in the operating room."

She looked at me for a long time. Finally she said, "Okay, but I'm telling you, Dr. Callaway is not going to like it. Not one bit." She shook her head in defeat.

I laid Colman down one more time, and the nurse had the IV in his head in seconds. We were done.

Colman's floor nurse said, "You weren't joking about him being a tough stick."

"I really hoped y'all would prove me wrong. Poor little guy," I said, kissing Colman on the side of his face where his oxygen tubing was taped.

When the nurse left the room, my brother and sister came in.

"Hey, guys!" I said, hugging them. "I'm glad to see y'all."

"What was going on in here?" Hunter said. "Colman sounded pissed."

"They were placing an IV. He's a tough stick," I explained.

"They put it in his head?" Hunter looked aghast.

"They didn't want to. I made them. His hands and feet will be black and blue from all the places they tried."

"We've been standing in the hallway for over an hour. It sounded awful," Hunter said.

Holly's eyes filled with tears.

"No crying," I said, my tone bitchy. I couldn't handle anyone else's waterworks.

"Sorry," Holly said, hastily wiping away her tears with the back of her hand.

I hugged her again and we laughed through her tears at my meanness.

We visited for the next couple of hours, and Holly and Hunter took turns holding Colman. When he fell asleep we took pictures with our cell phone cameras of each other from behind so we'd all know what we looked like.

I was horrified at my ass and vowed to start doing squats every day, although Holly assured me that Gap jeans make everyone's butts look terrible—something about the back pockets being too small combined with bad pocket placement.

How had I not heard this before? Still, I reasoned, the squats couldn't hurt.

This is what happens when grown siblings are bored out of their minds in a hospital room. No telling what would have happened if Kevin hadn't walked in with his parents and mine.

"Hey, look who I found," Kevin said.

"Great," I said, which was the exact opposite of what I was feeling.

"What were you guys doing in here?" Kevin said. "It sounded like a party."

"Taking pictures of each others' asses."

Everyone laughed. Kevin, however, wasn't amused. "Really?" he said.

"Really."

"Why would you do something like that? That's weird."

"How else are you supposed to know what you look like from behind?"

"What did you say?" Kevin's mom said.

"Nothing," Kevin said, waving her off. "Do you want to go to dinner?"

"I'd love to. I'm starved," I said, thinking Kevin was here to relieve me.

"Let's go, then."

"What do you mean?" I said. "One of us has to stay here with Colman."

"The nurse can't watch him?"

"She's not a babysitter."

"I realize that, but we've left him in the PICU before."

"That was the PICU, and this is the floor. They have other patients."

"It's just an hour."

"I know, but we can't leave our baby in a hospital room by himself while we go to dinner. "

"Do you want us to bring you anything back?" Kevin said.

"No, don't bother," I said, feeling pissed.

Kevin walked over to stand beside me. "What's the matter? I'd be happy to bring you something."

"I need a break. This afternoon has been exhausting."

"Tell me about it. I had client meetings, and Mom and Dad just got into town. They need to eat."

"Client meetings or holding your baby down for sanctioned stabbings that went on for two hours?" I said. "Not even the same thing."

"I need to take care of my parents," Kevin said quietly, willing me to understand his predicament.

"You need to take care of me," I said.

"Don't be mad. We'll talk about this tonight when you get home."

I wished I had something hard to hit him in the head with. "I'm not coming home tonight. I can't leave Colman. Unless you want to stay here with him. What are you not understanding about this?"

"I didn't realize you'd have to stay." Kevin looked at me like I was an overprotective maniac. "I'll call you later."

"Yeah, great," I said. It felt like all of the responsibility for Colman rested squarely on my shoulders.

Since Kevin and his parents were going out to dinner, my parents had to take care of Liam so Esme could go home. I didn't want to sit there feeling angry and dejected. It could be worse, I thought. Kevin could have offered to stay, and I could've had dinner with his parents.

Suddenly I felt much better. Maybe one of them would choke, I thought. That cheered me up immensely.

No worries. I wish death on people all the time. Usually the same two or three people, and I've never been successful. They're all very much alive. As much as I believe in positive energy and its effects, let me be clear that negative energy does not produce even close to the same results.

Holly and Hunter went to Mi Tierra, a Tex-Mex restaurant in El Mercado across the street from the hospital, and brought back chicken quesadillas. Soon afterward, they left to go to a hotel.

I washed my face and got Colman ready for bed. Kevin called to tell me good night, which meant everybody survived dinner—I didn't actually ask—and we made a plan for him to meet us early in the morning. Dr. Callaway needed to talk to us before the surgery.

I set an alert on my phone so I could feed Colman one more time before we hit the after-midnight starvation zone. Then I lay down to try to get some rest. The pulse ox monitor that was hooked up to Colman's big toe went off every few minutes, whenever Colman's oxygen saturation levels went below 75 percent. Sleep was impossible. I asked our night nurse to turn off the monitor, but she didn't feel comfortable doing that. I did succeed in getting her to set the alarm to sound only if the levels dipped below 70 percent.

I heated up a bottle of milk at 11:30, but Colman was so sleepy he wasn't interested. I did my best to wake him up, but no luck.

"You're going to be sorry in a couple of hours that you didn't drink this," I said. Colman looked at me from beneath heavy-lidded baby blues.

I sat there, bottle in hand, watching him. I wondered if he might sleep through the night on account of the trauma he'd endured while getting the IV. He had to be exhausted.

I struggled all night to get my heart on track with my brain. My heart was frozen with fear. My brain kept repeating, The Glenn has the highest survival rate of the three surgeries and the easiest recovery. To a certain extent, I knew what to expect this time around as far as the surgery and the recovery. I'd lived through it once; I could live through it again. But would Colman?

I woke to Colman crying at 1:30 a.m. He was hungry. Not surprisingly, he didn't remember our conversation at 11:30, or if he did he didn't seem to care. I finally rocked him back to sleep around 3:30 a.m., at which time the night nurse came into the room, handed me a bar of medicated soap and instructed me to give Colman a bath at 4 a.m.

"He just went to sleep," I whispered. "Does it have to be right at four?"

"Pretty close," she said.

"You want me to wake a sleeping baby?"

"Sorry," she said, as she headed for the door.

Fuck my life. I waited until 4:45, which is how I defined "pretty close"—still within the four o'clock hour. Colman usually enjoyed his bath, but he didn't like being woken up and placed in a tiny plastic tub. The tub was slick, and he was slippery with soap. I should have asked for an extra towel to line the tub bottom. I did the best I could, and by that I mean Colman didn't drown. I wasn't positive I'd covered every nook and cranny, but I made sure to go over all of his scars and both sides of his groin, where he'd had lines placed in the past.

Once bath time was over, I settled in for the long haul. I was thankful for Colman's pacifier and for the feeling of super-human patience that descended over me. Someone from pre-op came for us at 6 a.m. I was worried about Kevin finding us, but they assured me they'd tell him where we were.

We spent a little over an hour in pre-op holding, but the time flew by. Kevin joined us right before Dr. Callaway visited with us.

He took one look at Colman and said, "I don't like that IV in his head. I wonder why they did it like that?"

"That's my fault," I said. "We spent over two hours trying to get an IV in yesterday. I told them they had to put it in his head or leave. They said you wouldn't be happy about it. I take full responsibility."

Dr. Callaway let out an irritated sigh. "I'll place all the lines myself when we get in the O.R."

"Thank you."

Then Dr. Callaway remarked on Colman's chubby cheeks and introduced us to his new partner. "I'd like you guys to meet Javier Saldivar. He'll be assisting today on Colman's case."

Cue the porn music. Dr. Saldivar was genuinely handsome, with big brown eyes and boyish good looks and the whitest, straightest teeth I'd ever seen. The kind of guy where you're out for drinks and dinner with fun friends—who get a little raunchy when they're tipsy—and they say, "Boom-chicka-bow-wow!" when he walks through the door.

Notice I didn't say I was tipsy. Somebody has to be responsible and drive those drunken bitches around.

I imagined he'd be talking to one of my friends and when they asked what he did for a living he'd say something like, "I'm a thoracic surgeon. I operate on tiny babies' hearts and save their lives every day."

I'd see through his bullshit and say, "Shut the front door. You do not," because doctors who look like him are only actors on TV who play doctors.

I once did this very thing with one of the players for the San Antonio Spurs. I was at a charity golf tournament with the court reporting firm I was freelancing for, and one of the golfers said, "You look so familiar," which led to a conversation about where we might have seen each other. I asked him where he worked.

"I work for the Spurs," he said.

"Cool," I said. "What do you do for them?"

My boss, Janis, leaned over and whispered loudly enough for him to hear, "Heather, he's a Spur."

"Get out," I said, laughing. "Really, what do you do?"

"I play basketball."

After he left Janis explained who he was. How should I know? The dude was tall, but he didn't seem basketball tall.

After we finished speaking to Dr. Callaway and Dr. Saldivar, we waited for Dr. Stark. Instead, another anesthesiologist came to get Colman, and I felt a momentary stab of panic.

"Dr. Stark had a family emergency," she explained. "Dr. Callaway called me last night, and I flew in from Dallas this morning."

I was relieved that Dr. Callaway had sent for an adequate replacement, but it made me wonder about the depth of pediatric specialists in San Antonio.

Kevin and I went over the paperwork with the anesthesiologist and signed the consents. Then we each gave Colman a snuggle and a kiss, knowing this might be the last time we'd hold him for days—and handed him over to her.

CHAPTER 19

Kevin and I met up with his parents and my family in the waiting room.

My parents had brought breakfast tacos from Mi Tierra, and we found a table and settled in to wait. I was expecting the first phone call from the operating room around 8:30 a.m., because they'd been a little late taking Colman back. A Code Blue called over the PA system around nine set me on edge, but it wasn't on Colman's floor. Fifteen minutes later Dr. Callaway came into the waiting room. I swear my heart stopped. Kevin and I flew to our feet, and Dr. Callaway waved his arms and yelled across the crowd, "He's fine. Sit down."

What a relief. But why the hell did he have to scare us like that?

Dr. Callaway walked over. "I wanted to let you guys know we're getting a late start," he said. "We're going to be starting in the next few minutes or so. Okay?"

"Okay," Kevin and I said in unison.

After Dr. Callaway left, Kevin said, "I thought they'd already be an hour into it." He heaved a sigh brimming with frustration.

I never thought I'd meet anyone who hated waiting more than I did—until I met Kevin.

"Me, too," I said. "He could've just called with the update. He didn't have to go scaring us like that."

"I know. Seeing him walk through those doors freaked me out."

"Me, too."

Once they got started, the bidirectional Glenn only took around three hours to complete. Colman was back in the PICU by one o'clock that afternoon.

When we were finally able to see him, I was astonished at the difference. Colman was a lovely shade of pink. Dr. Callaway's face broke into a big smile—one of the few I'd seen from him—and, as if he could read my mind, he said, "He's pink!"

The transformation was amazing. Colman looked like a healthy baby—if you ignored the breathing tube, fresh chest incision, central line, arterial line, peripheral IV's and chest tubes. The floppy IV in his head had been removed.

"I placed all his lines myself," Dr. Callaway said. "Word got around that Colman was traumatizing nurses yesterday, and nobody would touch him."

I laughed. From my point of view, the nurses had been traumatizing Colman, but I could see it from their perspective.

Dr. Callaway said that the surgery had gone well and Colman seemed to be tolerating his new circulation. He'd used some sort of glue to close Colman's chest. From looking at the X-rays they'd just taken, I knew there were four sternal wires holding the bone of Colman's sternum together, as well as some stitches underneath the skin. On the outside, however, there was just a neat, half-inch wide line, approximately four inches long, of bloody-looking glue. Dr. Callaway checked a few of Colman's lines, gave the nurse some brief instructions and went into the hallway to make some phone calls, and Kevin left to update our families.

Among the first things I noticed—besides the fact that Colman was pink—were Colman's chest drains, two small tubes on either side of his sternal incision. His drain after the Norwood had been a huge tube coming out of the side of his ribs.

"What are these?" I asked the nurse, Shelly, the same one who had cared for Colman after his cath procedure.

"Ah, the Blake drains," she said. "Those are new. Dr. Callaway started using those last month when Dr. Saldivar got here. That's what Dr. Saldivar likes to use, and they've worked really well so far."

"I like them a lot better," I said. "The drain Colman had after the Norwood was like a garden hose."

The nurse laughed. "Yeah, I don't know why, but Dr. Callaway has always liked big chest tubes. It seemed the smaller the baby, the bigger the tube."

"These don't seem like they'd be as painful," I said. "They look a lot more flexible."

Thankfully, the next eighteen hours were uneventful. I was surprised that on rounds the following morning, the doctors were already talking about removing Colman's breathing tube. Over the next couple of hours they eased off the sedation and pain medications so

Colman could wake up a little more in preparation for extubation.

About an hour before extubation, Colman became agitated. Out of habit, I moved in to swoop him up in my arms. I quickly realized I couldn't because of the breathing tube. I put my hands on either side of his body. Maybe he was just upset with the tube down his throat.

When he opened his eyes, his head started shaking. His eyes were locked on mine, and I felt like he was pleading with me to do something, but I wasn't sure what he needed. He trembled from head to toe. I got an extra blanket and tucked it around him, but it didn't help.

I shot a quizzical look at Colman's nurse, who was watching him as well.

"I don't know," she said. She helped me swaddle him as best as we could while we checked his numbers on the monitors. Everything seemed okay except his heart rate, which was a little high, as was his blood pressure.

As the sedation wore off, Colman became more alert and awake. His trembling worsened.

"Do you think he's had a stroke?" I said.

"I don't know," she said, still watching him in her thoughtful manner.

"We need to call one of his doctors."

The nurse made some phone calls while I willed Colman's shaking to stop. It didn't.

Thirty minutes later, what had started out as a mild case of the tremors looked like full-on Parkinson's, and I was about to lose my shit. There was no sign of a doctor.

My mom entered the room and immediately knew something was wrong. "What's the matter?" she said.

"He's fucked up," I said quietly, running my hands through my hair and pulling it into a ponytail with the hair tie I always kept on my wrist.

"Don't say that."

"Look at him, Mama. He can't stop shaking."

"Have you called for the doctor?"

"Yeah, but Dr. Callaway is in surgery and there was some emergency in the PICU. Everybody seems to be out of pocket."

"What do you think?"

"I don't know. It seems neurological to me. Maybe a stroke?"

I couldn't stand to be in the same room as Colman for one more second. He was too pitiful, and I was at a loss for how to comfort him in such an unnatural environment.

"I'll be right back," I said. I flew out the double doors of the PICU and headed for the restroom. Once I was safely inside, I stood there a minute and gave myself the opportunity to fall apart.

Nothing.

I understood, at that moment, why people cut themselves. I'd have given anything to feel something besides the overwhelming numbness that had descended over me.

Then a million thoughts ran through my mind. Why didn't I prepare myself better for this? I knew, coming out of Colman's first surgery, that he could have a stroke. How could I forget about that? What if he was totally fucked up? What if he couldn't walk? Or talk? What if he was retarded? I hated myself for even thinking the word "retarded." It's hateful and mean and conjures an image of someone who's irreparably damaged. They aren't, of course. Their challenges in life are immediately visible to others—that's all.

I felt somewhat prepared for the physical aspects of HLHS, but what about dealing with a mental deficit? Would a major mental deficit disqualify Colman from being considered a candidate for the next surgery, the Fontan?

I looked at myself in the mirror. "I did not sign up for this shit," I muttered. It occurred to me that it didn't matter; I was in knee-deep, and I needed to sort this out. I needed to find out how to mitigate the situation, and I couldn't do it if I was in a full-blown panic.

I splashed cool water on my face and dried it with one of the funny-smelling brown paper towels that are ubiquitous in hospitals and schools. Then I went back to Colman's room.

"I need to talk to one of the doctors now," I said to the nurse.

"Let me see what I can do," she said, and made another phone call.

Within a few minutes, a doctor I hadn't met before came in and introduced himself. He was one of the residents in the pediatric program. After he examined Colman and read through his chart, he sat down to talk to me. My mom stayed in the room to hear what he had to say.

"Other than the shaking, his exam seems normal," he said.

"But what about the shaking?"

He looked at Colman and said, "I don't know."

I cut to the chase. "Do you think he's had a stroke?"

"I don't know. If he continues to show more symptoms after he's extubated, we can order a CT scan."

"Why not right now?"

"What, a CT scan?"

"Yeah. Why can't we order one now to determine if he's had a stroke?"

"Well, the scan will expose him to a lot of radiation," he said.

"Colman has had an X-ray every single day he's been in the hospital, sometimes two a day. That baby almost glows from the copious amounts of radiation he's been exposed to. If I'm not present when the X-ray gets taken, most of the radiology technicians don't even shield his genitals. Is the radiation from a CT really that much more?"

"Yeah, it's a lot more. We don't want to do a CT unless it's absolutely necessary."

"It's necessary. Look at him," I said, pointing to Colman, whose shaking had only worsened.

Mom let out a sob, and the doctor and I both turned to her.

"You need to leave," I said.

Mom gave me a look that said she couldn't believe I was throwing her out.

"Go," I mouthed, and she stood to gather her things. It might have seemed harsh, but I needed to get to the bottom of what was going on with Colman, and I couldn't do it with her blubbering next to me.

"Here's the thing," the doctor said. "Even if Colman did have a stroke—and I'm not saying that's what happened here—we wouldn't be doing anything differently at this point. We would be doing everything exactly the same. The way I see it, we would be exposing him to a high dose of radiation unnecessarily."

"But we'd know if he had a stroke," I said simply.

"You're absolutely right. We would know one way or the other. But when you think about someone having a stroke, what's the worst thing you think of?"

"Weakness, paralysis maybe, neurological deficits, rehabilitation, having to relearn how to walk, talk, eat—that kind of thing."

"Exactly," he said, seeming relieved. "Colman's a baby. He won't have to relearn anything because he hasn't learned it yet. That's why children, babies especially, are so amazing. They have this incredible ability to compensate. It's one of the reasons I decided to specialize in pediatrics—because kids' resiliency is so fascinating."

I almost smiled at his excitement. I was amazed by how passionate he could be while surrounded by critically ill children day in and day out. Medical school hadn't beaten the shit out of this guy. But my heart ached; I wished that words like "compensate" and "resiliency" didn't have to apply to my child—to any child.

"I tell you what," he said. "Let's watch him after extubation and see if there are any signs of weakness on either side. Give it a couple of days. We can always do the CT later."

"What could it be if it's not a stroke? What else could cause him to shake like this?"

"Withdrawals," he said.

"Withdrawals? Like, from drugs?" I looked at Colman's nurse, and she nodded.

"Yes. Colman's been given both fentanyl and morphine for pain since yesterday. Both are high-powered narcotics. He probably was on those same medications, but for a longer period of time, coming out of his Norwood a few months ago. Am I right?"

"Yes."

"This could definitely be drug withdrawal. Let me discuss it with one of the attending doctors and see if we can do something to manage his symptoms. I think that's the first thing we should try."

"Okay," I said, feeling minimally better.

As the doctor left, a girl who looked to be three years old was brought into the room next to Colman's on a gurney, followed by Dr. Callaway. I watched through our shared window as the medical team got her situated. She'd had heart surgery. I felt a stab of guilt. Had her surgery been bumped to accommodate Colman yesterday?

Breaking my rule about not being nosy about other patients, I said, "Is she a Fontan?"

Colman's nurse looked through the window. "No, she has Tetrology of Fallot."

That didn't seem so bad, I thought. They've been saving kids for half a century with TOF.

"This is her fourth open-heart surgery," she added.

"Four?" I asked. "That's not normal for TOF, is it?"

"No. For whatever reason her pulmonary valve keeps calcifying, and they keep having to replace it."

That's when I realized it didn't matter whether your baby had HLHS or a simple atrial septal defect—a hole in the heart. Congenital heart defects suck. They're all bad. As I looked at that beautiful little girl, intubated, her blond hair spilling across her pillow, I felt I could weep for her in a way that I hadn't been able to for my own child.

I walked the few short steps across Colman's room to the window and closed the blinds. If I looked at her for one more minute I'd break into a thousand pieces.

Two friends showed up, my judge and our administrative lawyer from work—both named Sarah—and we visited for a little while in Colman's room. Then the nurse informed me that the team was planning to extubate Colman in the next few minutes, which would be a great time to take a break and grab some lunch. The team needed thirty minutes to an hour to make sure everything went well.

I walked over to Mi Tierra with the two Sarahs. We ate and visited about lots of things other than Colman. It was a much-needed and welcome distraction. The margarita I drank helped too.

After lunch I walked back to the hospital. Colman was sleeping.

"He did well," his nurse said. "I gave him a dose of the methadone that was ordered in case he's having withdrawals. He's still shaking, but it's not nearly as bad. I just gave him a bottle of formula. He only drank about twenty cc's, but he didn't spill a drop."

She smiled broadly and added, "That's a really good sign we're not dealing with a stroke."

I felt like we weren't out of the woods yet, but it was nice to hear some good news. "Methadone? Like what heroin addicts use?"

"Yeah. It helps with withdrawal symptoms, and it's also good for pain management."

I picked up the bottle of formula. "This is cold," I said.

"Maybe that's why he didn't want to drink more of it. I wondered about that. I said to him, 'I bet your mommy gives you warm bottles of milk.' He just gave me this crazy look before he pushed it out with his tongue."

"Of course I warm up his milk," I said, faking outrage.

She laughed. "I think if we can stay on top of his pain and withdrawal symptoms with the methadone, he'll do pretty well over the next few days."

"I hope so," I said.

She wasn't kidding about Colman getting better fast. Our major problem was weaning him off oxygen. He had trouble keeping his oxygen saturations where they needed to be on room air only. Dr. Callaway mentioned that it wasn't that big of a deal because Colman could always go back home on just a whiff of oxygen.

"I really don't want to go home on oxygen," I said.

"It's not all that bad, is it?" he asked.

"It's pretty bad," I said.

On the fourth day post-op, Dr. Callaway entered Colman's room early in the morning. "I think we can discharge him today. Let's get him ready to go home."

"Okay," I said. "Is he going to need the oxygen?"

"I don't think so." He tossed the nasal cannula to the side. "Let's see how he does this morning."

"Today?" I mouthed to my mom.

Mom shrugged.

It just seemed too soon to be at home without our safety net of doctors and nurses. Too soon to be without monitors.

Dr. Callaway walked to the crib, peered in at Colman, and said to the nurse, "He looks constipated to me." Then he left the room.

My mom and I looked at each other like, What the fuck? Well, I'm positive she didn't think the word "fuck," but I sure did.

"Do I look constipated too?" I said to Dr. Callaway's back when he was out of earshot.

Mom and the nurse giggled.

"Isn't that just like a man to walk in and look at somebody and announce they're constipated?" Mom said.

"What does he mean?" I asked the nurse. "Is he serious? He didn't even touch Colman. Shouldn't he have palpated his abdomen or at least touched him somewhere on his little body? Can you really tell that a baby's constipated with a glance?"

"I don't know," the nurse said, shrugging and laughing. "Dr. Callaway is pretty amazing. He's usually right."

"I know. But he would have to be a freaking magician to be able to do that. Does he look constipated to you?"

"I don't know, maybe. His face is kind of scrunched up."

"When has he not looked like that?"

"True," she said. "He's in a perpetual bad mood, it seems."

"You're right about that," I said. "That is so bizarre. Is it just babies, or can Dr. Callaway tell by looking whether adults are constipated, too? Because that is quite the party trick."

The nurse shook her head and said, "I don't know."

A couple of hours later Kevin and I were waiting on discharge paperwork and for Colman to poop. He'd been given a suppository because he was, indeed, extremely constipated. From that moment on I would feel a tad self-conscious around Dr. Callaway and his apparent X-ray vision.

I listened closely as the nurse briefed us on last-minute instructions.

"Do not pick him up under the arms for at least six weeks," she said. "You're going to want to scoop him because of his chest incision. He's going to be really sore."

"I'm glad you said that," I said. "I had no idea I shouldn't pick him up under the arms."

"Gosh, Heather, that's horrible," Kevin said. "Why would you ever pick up a baby by their arms?"

"We do it all the time," I said, perplexed he would say that.

"I don't," Kevin said, a look of alarm on his face. "I never pick him up like that. I always scoop him."

"That's good," the nurse said, and Kevin nodded his head like he was the perfect student.

I wanted to kick him in the balls and yell, "What are you talking about?"

I tried not to be annoyed with him as he stood there looking handsome in his suit. He'd been busy as hell at his law office while Colman was in the hospital. On the one hand, it was great that he was making money and not annoying me with the endless when-can-we-get-out-of-here question. On the other hand, I missed him terribly and felt pretty lonely in the PICU. If my mom hadn't been there to keep me company and take my abuse, I'd have gone stir-crazy.

The nurse came in with our discharge paperwork, which I signed.

Kevin bent down to pick up Colman.

The nurse placed a hand on Kevin's arm and stopped him. "What are you doing?" she said.

"I'm picking him up," Kevin replied.

"Not like that," she said. "You have to scoop, remember? You can't pick him up under the arms."

"That's what that whole conversation was about ten minutes ago," I told him. To the nurse, I said, "Maybe you should show us how we're supposed to pick him up so everybody is crystal clear."

The nurse physically demonstrated how to scoop Colman into our arms.

Kevin looked sheepish. "I thought you meant by the ends of his arms, like his hands. I didn't realize it was under the arms. I always pick him up like that."

"I know you do," I said, laughing. "I do, too."

We said our good-byes to the PICU staff, and then we were on our way, with a bag of prescription medication that included Zantac, Fosinopril, Lasix and a tiny bottle of methadone, along with strict instructions for weaning Colman off the narcotic over the next couple of weeks in order to avoid more withdrawal symptoms.

Two heart surgeries down. If all went as planned, we'd only have one to go.

Chapter 20

The first couple of weeks at home were rough after Colman's discharge from the hospital. He had Glenn headaches that worsened when he was lying down flat. The methadone definitely helped manage his pain and withdrawal symptoms, but the hospital pharmacy shorted me six milliliters, the amount I needed to taper Colman off for the last three days. It seemed like a ridiculously small amount—three milliliters one day, two milliliters the next and one milliliter the last day. I called Dr. Roberts to see if I needed a refill.

"Cold turkey would not be a good idea," he said.

Dr. Roberts didn't have any triplicate prescription pads on hand, so I called Frank, and he wrote me a prescription.

You wouldn't believe the hassle involved in procuring methadone for a four-month-old baby. It's not a medicine you can pick up at your neighborhood corner drugstore. I had to go to three pharmacies before I found one that could fill the prescription. They had to call Frank to check my story, all the while eyeing me like I was a crazed drug user.

If I were a methadone junky, would six milliliters be enough to get a grown woman high? Wouldn't I have forged a prescription for sixty milliliters?

After a couple of weeks Colman's headaches seemed to lessen and then completely go away. I, on the other hand, was exhausted. His idea of rest was nonexistent. A ten-minute doze seemed to leave him feeling refreshed but did little to alleviate my tiredness.

To compound the situation, I'd gone back to work full-time as soon as Colman appeared to be feeling better. When I tell people I'm a court reporter, they usually say something like, "Oh, you're the one who types on that funny little machine" and make a motion with their hands that,

I'm guessing, is supposed to mimic that. In actuality, it looks nothing like what I do and more like some kind of disturbed masturbating squirrel.

First, we don't type. We *write* on our stenograph machines with a machine shorthand—whichever version of theory we were taught—sometimes more than 300 words a minute. The word "type" doesn't do it justice. Most reasonable humans speak in the 140- to 200-word-a-minute range, but there are the occasional assholes—I mean, self-important expert witnesses—who speak more than 300 words a minute, and it's our job to make a record, whether that means keeping up at that blazing pace or frequently interrupting to ask them to slow down.

Court reporting machines are small computers that cost about $5,000. They have SD cards and flash drives that store our keystrokes, and they're also equipped with Bluetooth. What we write on our machines is instantaneously transmitted to a laptop with software that translates the steno strokes into English. The English version can then be transmitted by Bluetooth to lawyers' and judges' laptops so they have a live feed of everything said in court.

Then there is the time we spend editing, proofreading and preparing the transcripts attorneys have requested and perfecting appeals on trial work. For every hour spent in court, it takes another two to three hours to prepare the transcripts.

What I'm trying to say is this: a career in court reporting is mentally and physically demanding. There's not a lot of time for goofing off or closing the door to my office so I can take a nap on the floor. When I'm in court I'm the guardian of the record, and it's my sole responsibility to get every word uttered.

And what's uttered in court is, more often than not, heartbreaking and stressful. I've had back-to-back aggravated sexual assault trials where children were the victims.

I believe my work is one reason I've developed excellent coping mechanisms. Or maybe my excellent coping mechanisms are what allow me to do this kind of work. Coping mechanisms aside, working a full schedule and having a baby with major heart issues who doesn't believe in sleep are the perfect ingredients for what Holly and I call "the dark and twisties."

By the time Colman was about six months old, I'd pretty much given up on sleep and stayed perpetually pissed off at Kevin for not waking up to take a shift. Around this time I started kicking the shit out of him on a nightly basis.

"Ouch," he'd mumble. "What was that for?"

"Oh, sorry. My foot must have slipped," I'd say in a sugar-sweet voice.

He must have started sleeping with one eye open, because he managed to dodge my foot at the last second. I had the same swell of satisfaction as when I made contact, though, because I'd made him as miserable as I was; he wasn't getting the deep REM sleep he needed either.

Another huge source of contention was Colman's medication. It started out innocently enough. I'd been giving Colman his medicine for several months and didn't mind it. It made perfect sense that one of us—me—should be in charge of this to avoid any confusion and accidentally administering a double dose.

What worried me was that no one but me knew how to prepare and give them. We were still compounding the blood pressure medication, which consisted of dissolving a ten-milligram pill in ten milliliters of water and giving Colman two milliliters. I taught Esme how to mix and give the meds, and then I told Kevin he needed to know too.

"Why?" he asked.

"I can't be the only one who knows this."

"But didn't you teach Esme?"

"Yes."

"So why do I need to learn?

"Because you're his father. You should know the medications Colman's taking."

Kevin rolled his eyes and sighed. "Tomorrow. You can show me tomorrow."

"Great."

Tomorrow turned into days, then weeks. Kevin saw me preparing Colman's meds every morning and night, but he didn't bring it up.

"Hey," I finally said, "when are you going to let me teach you how to do these meds?"

"Tomorrow."

"Why not today?"

"I'm late for court."

"Yeah? I am, too. What if I get hit and killed by a bus today?"

Kevin scoffed. "Like that's going to happen."

"Okay," I said. "What if I throw myself in front of a bus today? Who's going to give Colman his meds?"

He had to think about that one a minute. "Esme?" he asked sheepishly.

"Who's going to take Colman to doctors' visits? Are you going to have the nanny take him?"

"I don't know. Why don't you get off my case? I'll do it tomorrow."

"Promise me," I said, hating that Kevin was forcing me to nag.

Colman's meds were nonnegotiable, as far as I was concerned. I would get up with the baby every hour of every night for the rest of my life. I might kick the shit out of Kevin. I might be a total bitch from lack of sleep, but I'd do it and not nag him. But Kevin had to know how to give Colman's medication in case I wasn't around.

Kevin rolled his eyes and shrugged. "I promise," he said.

The next morning he was in an awful mood, but I wasn't letting him off the hook. As I was explaining how to mix the blood pressure medicine with water, he dumped the crushed pill into the medicine cup.

"You have to put the water in first," I said, pouring the pill powder out of the cup.

"What does it matter?" he huffed.

It's simple chemistry, bonehead, I thought. But I said, "The pill is ten milligrams. The mixture is supposed to be one to one. If you put the water in after the pill and try to eyeball it, you're going to have less volume because of the pill's mass, which would cause the mixture to be more concentrated than it's supposed to. Unless you measure ten milliliters of water with a syringe, in which case it's no big deal to put the pill in first."

Kevin was completely glazed over by the time I'd finished my explanation. "Do you have to be so pedantic when it comes to this stuff?" he said. He waved his arms, knocking Colman's medicine all over the kitchen counter.

"Just forget it," I said. A tingling anger took over my body as I cleaned up the spill.

"I'm not good at this," Kevin said.

"Yeah, me either, but I don't have a choice."

"What do you want?"

"I want your help. I want a partner in managing Colman's medical situation. I want a break once in a while from the daily grind."

"You're ungrateful and spoiled," Kevin said. "You ask way too much of me. I make good money. I work hard to provide a nice life for this family. I don't go out drinking or carousing."

"Congratulations!" I exclaimed, laughing at his ridiculous speech. "You have just described entry-level husband material. News flash: You don't get bonus points for not being a complete piece of shit."

"Get off my ass!" Kevin yelled.

"Happily," I said. I ignored him as I went about the business of drawing up Colman's medications.

"Can't you understand that I'm terrified I'm going to kill him?" Kevin yelled, running his fingers through his hair in a fit of frustration.

Now we were getting somewhere. I pushed on anyway. The dark and twisties had taken over my soul.

"How dare you put that burden on me?" I said. "What? So if Colman dies you can have deniability and blame me? Fuck you. You're not the only one who's terrified."

"I'm sorry," Kevin said. He sounded sincere. "I'm just not ready."

"Well, neither am I. Get out of here. Go make money. Do what you have to do. I'll do what I have to."

"What does that mean?"

"It means that I hate your guts right now."

Kevin left for work, and I went on to court, wishing I'd never asked him to help with the medicine. If I hadn't asked, he couldn't disappoint. I was overwhelmed by the energy required to care for Colman, but I didn't expect fifty-fifty. I would have happily taken a ninety-ten split.

During our all-night sessions, Colman and I started watching reruns of *Sex and the City*. I'd never gotten into the show during the height of its popularity, but they showed two back-to-back episodes from midnight to one, and the story line was so different from my life that it was a welcome distraction. Plus I had a TV crush on the character Big, which forced me to come to the depressing conclusion that I most definitely have a type: handsome, older and successful rolled into a high-maintenance package.

After one particularly long and stressful night, Colman finally fell asleep around 3 a.m. I was drifting off when I heard Kevin say urgently, "Colman, Colman!" I realized seconds too late he was shaking the baby awake. Colman began to scream.

"What are you doing?" I said. "I'd just gotten him to sleep."

"I thought he was dead," Kevin said, still blurry with sleep, his voice thick with panic. "Oh, thank God he's all right. I dreamed he died. I thought he was dead."

"He would have been dead in the morning," I hissed.

"That's crazy. You're losing your fucking mind."

"Well, aren't you Albert Fucking Einstein? What's crazy is shaking him awake when you know how hard it is for him to sleep. Couldn't you place your hand on his chest to feel for a heartbeat or watch the rise and fall of his chest for five seconds?"

"I'm sorry."

"You woke him up," I said. "You put him back to sleep."

"I can't. I've got court tomorrow."

I picked up Colman and began walking the floor yet again to try to get him back to sleep, and I realized I couldn't live like this much longer. The fact that I'd been okay with the horrifying possibility that Colman might be dead—though I knew in my heart he wasn't—in order to get a few hours of sleep showed the depths of my exhaustion.

At work the next day I contemplated taking a sick day and checking into a hotel so I could get a solid eight hours of sleep. I tried to reserve a room, but it turns out that if you want to sleep for eight hours during the day, you have to rent a room for two nights.

"Can't I just pay for one night?" I said to the clerk at the third hotel. "I only need a room for eight hours."

"We're not that kind of hotel, ma'am. We don't rent rooms by the hour."

Fantastic. Now the reservations lady thought I was a cheater. Or a hooker. Whichever.

When Colman was seven or eight months old, I called Frank to see if he had any ideas on getting him to sleep through the night.

"I think the best way is the cry-it-out method. Is there any reason you can't try that?"

"I'm willing to try anything. Can you check with Roberts, though? I know Colman's not supposed to get too upset."

"I'll call and see what he says."

In the meantime, Kevin and I took Liam and Colman to Victoria to see my family. The two-hour trip ended up lasting closer to four because of all the breaks we had to take. Colman hated riding in the car, and I didn't feel comfortable letting him scream longer than fifteen minutes. We'd pull over on Highway 87, and I'd walk him around until he calmed down. Then we'd drive another fifteen minutes while he screamed.

I didn't realize how incredibly loud Colman was until it was bedtime. Staying in my parent's house meant I had to try not to wake the whole house. I stayed up all night with Colman, who wouldn't sleep a wink in a strange place.

Holly must have heard us because she got up around 6 a.m. and came into the living room. I don't remember this, but she said the minute I saw her I deposited Colman into her arms and said, "I know why some women kill their children. I'm not saying I would. I'm just saying I know how that kind of thing happens."

I went and slept a solid four hours, the longest stretch I'd gotten since Colman was in the PICU at South Texas Medical Hospital.

The weekend after our trip to Victoria, while I was making Liam pancakes for breakfast, Kevin came up behind me and gave me a hug. It was one of the first times we'd hugged since our fight over the medication.

"Hey," he said.

"Hey," I answered flatly.

"I love you. I don't want you to be mad at me anymore."

"I don't want to be mad anymore, but I'm angry. I'm angry all the time."

"What can I do?"

"Act right?" I said, laughter invading my attempt at seriousness.

"I had a nightmare last night," Kevin said. "I dreamed you divorced me and I never got to see the kids again."

"Must be nice," I said. "I can't dream. I'm not sure if my subconscious won't allow it or if I can't get enough consecutive hours of sleep to sustain it."

"My nightmare wasn't nice," Kevin said. He looked vulnerable. "You're not going to divorce me and take the kids, are you?"

"Do I look stupid to you? Wait, don't answer that," I said quickly. "I might divorce you, yes, but I'd petition for joint custody. You get a week with the kids, and then I get a week. Nobody pays child support. We'll share them."

"You're kidding, right?" Kevin said, and laughed uneasily. "You seem to have thought this through."

"Fantasized is probably the better word," I said. "You know what that means, don't you?"

Kevin crossed his arms. "What?" He looked like he wished he'd kept his bad dream to himself.

"You're going to have to learn to administer Colman's medicine come hell or high water. And guess what?" I said, kissing him on the cheek. "I'm both, love."

"So will you teach me?"

"What?"

"Colman's medicine."

"Sure. When shall I pencil you in?" I said, thinking he'd say tomorrow or next week.

"Now. I'll learn how to do it now."

Kevin mixed Colman's medicine and gave it to Colman by himself, which was no easy task. You'd think a baby who'd taken medicine since birth would be used to it, but Colman had a whole bag of tricks at the tender age of seven months that included spitting, gagging and sometimes vomiting. I swear that child was born with a puke-on-demand feature.

Kevin and I both ended up getting tickled at what a little stinker Colman could be. Then Liam joined in the laughter. I sat there feeling relieved at Kevin's effort but unsure of what the future held. I watched

Kevin interacting with our boys, and he seemed determined to keep our family together and make things work. Only time would tell whether our fear would bind or repel us. Some people are fright-and-fight, and others are fright-and-flight. The problem is you never know which until the fright happens.

"If you want to lie down for a while, I can watch these guys," Kevin said.

"That'd be great," I said, hurrying to bed before he had time to change his mind.

CHAPTER 21

Over the next several weeks I noticed that Kevin was making more of an effort to help out with Colman, and I was grateful. Dr. Roberts wasn't keen on Colman crying it out at night, so I felt a little stymied on that front. But we had an appointment the following week, and I felt he would have some good ideas.

Doctor appointments were always traumatic for Colman and, by extension, me. When family and friends heard about his heart problems, they said pretty much the same thing: "At least he'll have his surgeries early in life. He won't remember a thing."

If you have to start a sentence with "At least," it's probably better to just skip it, even though I'm guilty of doing it all the time. I hoped they were right, but it didn't take me long to realize they were talking out of their asses. Maybe Colman didn't remember exactly what happened, but he definitely held unpleasant associations with doctors, nurses and hospitals. White coats, scrubs or simply the smell of hand sanitizer and a stethoscope were enough to launch him into full-blown hysterics.

At the appointment, Dr. Roberts was stumped. "I've never had this complaint before."

"You've never had someone tell you that their heart baby doesn't want to sleep through the night?" I asked. He had to be joking.

"No. I'm sure he's going to start sleeping for longer periods pretty soon. He's definitely big enough."

"You don't think the cry-it-out method is a good idea?"

"Not at all," he said. "I don't feel comfortable with Colman crying for more than five minutes at a time."

"Five minutes?" I racked my brain trying to remember conversations about crying. Nobody had ever said anything about five minutes. I would've remembered such a shockingly short period of time.

"Has he cried for longer than that?" Dr. Roberts asked.

"He cries all the time," I said, bouncing Colman on my hip in an effort to keep him calm.

"What's the longest he's cried, do you think?"

"At least fifteen, maybe twenty minutes," I said, feeling like a liar because Colman had cried at least thirty minutes straight the day before.

"That's not good," Dr. Roberts said. "Have you tried Benadryl to get him to go to sleep?"

"The problem is not so much that he won't go to sleep. It's that he won't stay asleep. I don't want to add yet another medicine to the mix."

"I don't know what to tell you. I'm sorry. I know it's got to be hard, but between you and your husband taking turns—"

"The only person taking a turn would be me," I said, wishing I could get rid of the bitterness that I felt oozing out of my pores.

How could I tell Dr. Roberts that if I didn't come up with a solution, I was going to end up in a family violence case against my husband, that if I didn't get this figured out I'd need a one-way ticket to Crazytown?

There was no doubt in my mind that Dr. Roberts would have been shocked by the playlist in my car. "Bitch" by Meredith Brooks, everything by Eminem. I had a particular fondness for "Puke" and kept it on repeat. When I was feeling less angry and more sad, I listened to the Dixie Chicks.

When I'd lie down at night, I could feel my heart skipping beats; I was that tired. What if my heart stopped, I wondered, and I died? When the thought didn't make me panic, I realized my own death was somewhat appealing. I wasn't suicidal in any way, shape or form. I just wasn't scared to die. There was the added bonus—albeit incredibly selfish—that I'd be spared having to survive my child's death. Even more compelling was imagining Kevin taking care of Colman and Liam, who was in the middle of the Terrible Twos, by himself. (Then again who was I kidding? What's the old saying—women grieve and men replace? I'm confident Kevin would have another wife in under a year. He's no dummy!)

What I really wanted to do—as long as we're talking fantasy—was fake my own death. I've always been fascinated by stories about people who have done that. But they always seem to get caught and end up going to jail, which leads me to wonder, is it illegal to fake your own death or are the people who fake their own deaths already facing legal trouble? Hence, the need to fake their deaths.

You know who would probably know the answers? Kevin. But I

couldn't ask him without tipping my hand. Maybe I could just stockpile some cash and disappear for a month and say I bumped my head. Who could argue with a poor mother who'd gotten a horrible case of amnesia, even if she did come back with a great tan?

"So you don't want to try Benadryl?" Dr. Roberts said now.

"I'd rather not drug Colman," I said, teasing Dr. Roberts. He didn't seem to find it funny. "You're really against him crying it out?"

"I am. Colman has done amazingly well. I hate to do anything to jeopardize his health."

Reading between the lines, I felt like Dr. Roberts was saying, "Can't you just be grateful he's here?"

I sighed. I'd dug really deep, and I'd hit the wall. I needed sleep.

"Is it really that bad?"

"Yeah, it is," I said. "I haven't had a solid night's sleep since Colman was in the PICU at South Texas Medical Hospital almost eight months ago. I feel like if I could just string together a few hours of sleep each night, I'd be okay. I'm up all night long. Then I go to work, and I have to get every word people are saying. I can't keep up this pace much longer. Colman sleeps an hour at a time. That can't be good for him either, can it?"

Dr. Roberts didn't say anything.

"You've really never had a mom tell you their heart baby won't sleep?" I said.

"Never." He shook his head.

Great, I thought. I have *that* kid.

"Isn't there anyone who could help you?"

"Do you want to take Colman for a couple of nights?" I said. "Four hours. That's all I'd need."

"I don't think that would work," Dr. Roberts said, laughing nervously. "Let me make some calls to a couple of colleagues and see what they say. I'll let you know what we decide."

"Sounds good," I said.

I thought he meant he'd call in a couple of hours, best-case scenario. Worst-case, in my mind, would be a couple of days.

Nothing.

I did end up getting a solid eight hours of sleep three nights in a row thanks to Kevin. He'd planned a couple of days in New York City for my thirtieth birthday, and he arranged for my parents to watch Liam and Colman with the help of Esme during the day.

My birthday sometimes falls on Election Day, which was what happened in 2004. I felt pretty good about leaving Liam and Colman with Mom and Dad. I gave Mom a crash course on Colman's meds, plus

Esme would be there to answer any questions she might have. Then we were off.

I felt like I was forgetting something (two kids, maybe?) as we made our way through the security line, but I relished being footloose and fancy-free for the next several days. No late nights followed by before-the-ass-crack-of-dawn mornings. No meds. No waking up every hour. I felt my spirits lift for the first time in months.

Kevin and I boarded the plane, stowed our carry-on bags, then sat down and buckled our seatbelts for the three-hour nonstop flight to La Guardia. I stared out the window at the tarmac as people filed past to get to their seats. Kevin recognized a federal judge he practiced in front of. They briefly exchanged pleasantries, and Kevin introduced me as the judge was making his way to the back of the plane.

An unbelievable surge of panic burst forth from the base of my brain, flooding down my back, through my arms and legs and to the tips of my fingers and toes. I'd never felt anything like it before, and I couldn't catch my breath. I unscrewed the air vent above my seat and tried to talk myself down, but the waves of fear were too much. I gasped.

"Are you okay?" Kevin asked.

"I hate to do this to you, honey," I said, "but I've got to get off."

"Why?"

"I don't know."

Kevin loves to travel a little bit more than he hates to fly, which is the only reason he gets on a plane, so I didn't want to say anything that would make him worry any more than he already does.

"Are you worried about the boys? They'll be fine with your parents."

"I don't feel like I can talk about this with you, other than to say I need to get off now."

"Heather, this is ridiculous. They're getting ready to close the door. Tell me what's wrong."

Screw it. Honesty is the best policy. "I have this horrible premonition that we're going to die in a big-ass fiery crash," I said, laughing at how bananas I sounded and hopefully lessening the panic-inducing blow I'd leveled at my hates-to-fly husband. "That can't happen. One of us needs to survive. Who's going to take care of Colman?"

"Listen, I feel that way every time I step foot on a plane."

"But I don't," I said. "I've never felt this way before. I think I'm having a panic attack. I can't breathe." I started to unbuckle my seatbelt.

"Sit down. They're not going to let you off. They just sealed the door."

"You want to make a bet?"

Kevin chuckled. "Sit down. Don't you want to go to New York?"

"Yes," I said. "Yes, I do. I want to get away more than anything. I tell you what—I'll take the next flight out and meet you."

"And leave me to die on this plane?" Kevin laughed. "Thanks for that."

"Okay. I'll volunteer to die, and you can take the next flight. You can meet me out there if I make it."

"Taking two separate flights only increases the chances of something bad happening to one of us."

"I volunteer to be the one. We can't leave our chronically ill baby parentless. That's not okay."

"Liam and Colman are not going to be orphans. Calm down. From experience, I can tell you it's too late to get off once they've sealed the door. We're stuck on this plane." He waggled his eyebrows.

Usually that would make me laugh, but my funny had died in the inferno of what was sure to be our airplane.

"I've never seen you like this before," Kevin said.

"I've never felt like this before."

"You're always the one comforting me when I'm freaking out about planes."

"I know how much you hate to fly. I feel terrible for saying anything about this to you."

"It's okay." Kevin put his arm around me and pulled me close.

I closed my eyes and tried to get to the bottom of it. Maybe it's a control thing, I thought. What if I were flying the plane? Would I be this flipped out? Probably not. I'm a freaking badass driver, and I'd probably be a badass pilot.

After takeoff I counted to thirty. A good friend I used to fly with— who was terrified of flying—said that if something bad were to happen it was usually within the first twenty-four seconds. I'm not sure where she got that information, but when our plane didn't disintegrate into a ball of fire, my anxiety lessened.

New York City was a blast, and it was exactly what Kevin and I needed to reconnect. The kids fared well, even though Liam contracted a stomach virus. My sister, Holly, drove to San Antonio to help my parents and was promptly baptized in Colman's vomit.

"He pukes all the time," Holly said, when I talked to her on the phone.

"I know. I think he has reflux. The doctors prescribed Zantac, but I urged them to let me take him off because it didn't seem to help. He always pukes up some of his bottle."

"Heather," Holly said, "you need to get that baby back on Zantac.

This is craziness."

"But the puke was exactly the same as it is now, except now he doesn't puke up the Zantac and his heart meds. It's one less barf a day."

"This wasn't just some of his bottle. I was carrying him up the stairs and his eyes got really big, then his little mouth formed a perfect 'O' and vomit just shot out of it for, like, a whole minute. I was covered."

"Sounds about right," I said. "Sorry."

"It was awful."

"You're making me miss him."

"You miss vomit?"

"Kind of. Well, no, not really."

"I had to change my clothes from head to toe and wash my hair. And I'm pretty sure I'm going to have to throw my shoes away."

"Sorry."

"No, it's okay," she said. "I'm just glad I'm here. Between Liam's stomach virus and Colman's reflux, I think Mom and Dad are a little in over their heads."

"Where's Esme?"

"Mom keeps sending her home."

"Why?" I asked, flabbergasted.

"Because she doesn't want Liam to feel deserted while he's sick and you're not here."

"That makes no sense whatsoever. Liam loves Esme. She's like a second mom to him. She's taken care of him since he was an infant. If he's going to want anybody as his first choice, it'd probably be Esme, then me a distant second."

"That's what I was thinking. I tried to tell her, but she wouldn't listen."

"Great," I said. "Why does she have to make this more difficult?"

"Liam wants to talk to you."

"Okay, love. Sorry about your shoes."

"It's okay." I could hear Holly say to Liam, "Here's your mama."

"Mama?" Liam said.

"Hi, baby," I said. "How are you?"

"I sick. I frow up."

"I'm sorry. Is Mimi taking good care of you?"

"Uh-huh. Bye."

Mom picked up the phone. "Hi, babe. Are y'all having fun?"

"Yeah, but I hate that we left you guys battling a stomach virus."

"Oh, my God. It's been really bad. Anything Liam drinks, especially milk—which is all he wants—just comes right back up. We're making him some toast now."

"That's good. We'll be back tomorrow. Please don't send Esme away, though. You ought to give yourselves a break. Not to hurt your feelings, but Liam would probably rather have her than almost anybody else on the planet. I'm including myself in that statement. He loves her."

"I just feel bad making her stay when Liam's sick. And Holly is helping us. I don't know what I'd have done without her." Then I heard her say to Liam, "Here's your toast, baby.

I heard Liam ask, "Where da raisins?"

"Oh, yeah," I said. "When he asks for toast, he wants the cinnamon raisin bread."

"I know," she said, her voice low, "but I don't think his tummy can handle anything other than plain toast. You don't know what it's been like."

Liam began to cry. My heart broke for him, and I wished I were back in San Antonio, although not enough to give up my last full night of sleep. I'd have made him cinnamon raisin toast and let him drink milk even if it made him puke buckets. Because let's be real; if you've had a stomach virus and finally feel like eating, you're at the tail end of it.

Kevin and I made it back to San Antonio with no anxiety attacks, and with me resisting buying an "I Love New York" T-shirt emblazoned across the front. As clichéd as it sounds, I loved New York. If I'd visited as a teenager or even as a young adult, I'd have moved there in a heartbeat. I'd have been blissfully happy in an apartment smaller than a subway car with three roommates and zero privacy.

When we got back Liam was better, and I sent my relieved parents home. After a couple of weeks in which we sold our house and bought another—crazy, I know—Dr. Roberts finally called.

"In speaking to a few of my colleagues," he said, "they think it would probably be okay to let Colman cry it out. One of the reasons we do these surgeries is so these children can have a normal life. We don't want to turn them into cardiac cripples. So I guess that's the answer."

"You don't sound happy about that," I said.

"I don't like the idea, but I understand the importance of Colman having a good sleep schedule. I just wish there was another way."

"But do you think it's safe? I mean, his heart won't explode or anything, will it?" I was sort of kidding.

"I sure hope not," he said. "You know where to reach me if there are any problems."

This wasn't exactly the blessing I'd been looking for. If anything, it only heightened my anxiety about Colman's fragility. I thought about calling Dr. Callaway, but then I realized he was probably one of the colleagues Dr. Roberts had referred to.

That night I stuck to the same routine we'd had going for months. I gave Colman his bath with the lavender body wash that's supposed to relax babies and make them sleepy. (Bullshit.) I dried him off and carried him upstairs to the nursery. After smearing lotion all over his chubby arms and legs, I put a diaper and some pajamas on him and sat in the rocking chair to give him a bottle.

"I had a little chat with Dr. Roberts, and he says you're going to be fine. Here's the deal. You are welcome to spend the next eight hours however you wish. You can cry, or you can sleep. It's up to you. I, however, am going to spend the next eight hours sleeping. Got it?"

I startled myself, since the next words that almost spilled out of my mouth were "you little fucker."

Colman smiled a huge gummy smile and drooled slobbery milk out of the sides of his mouth. He looked so cherubic snuggled in my arms, with his big blue eyes, impossibly long eyelashes and pink cheeks, that I allowed myself to forget about his heart for a few minutes and pretend I had a healthy baby.

My worst fear was Colman dying on me or finding him dead in his crib. No matter how much pressure I was exerting, I had full confidence in Dr. Roberts. There was no way he'd let me try the cry-it-out method if he thought it was inherently dangerous, but like so many things with Colman, it was an unknown—and that was scary as hell.

For all my tough talk, I fully expected to stand outside Colman's door listening to him scream, and to comfort him in between, which would probably only make him angrier. But none of that happened. He didn't make a peep until he woke up a full twelve hours later.

Even though I had the baby monitor in our room, I woke up every few hours to check on Colman. He was sleeping peacefully. As I watched the rise and fall of his chest, I whispered, "I'm not going to have to leave you at the fire station after all. I think we're going to be okay."

CHAPTER 22

After everything Colman had been through, he hit all of his developmental milestones on time. I'd been told in calculating milestones that I should subtract the number of days he had spent in a NICU or PICU from his actual age. That seemed to be a good formula. Colman crawled at eleven months and walked at fourteen, which was exactly thirty days after Liam did those same things. As far as talking, well, I can't really remember a time when that little guy couldn't talk.

Once Colman was on the move, Kevin and I had to up our game. He was a whirling dervish of destruction, and we nicknamed him "Destructo." We couldn't turn our back for a second without finding him finger-painting the walls with yogurt, grabbing a handful of Liam's hair, eating a roly-poly or playing in the dog's bowls.

Where Liam had been a thoughtful and reasonable child who, at the tender age of three, appeared to consider the consequences of his actions, Colman had a quick temper and insisted on learning everything the hard way. I wished he'd let us show him a little guidance so he didn't have to suffer so many bumps, bruises and smashed fingers.

Colman wanted to be the center of attention, good or bad. Not knowing any other children with complex congenital heart defects at that point, I wasn't sure if his attitude was a by-product of being under constant care and scrutiny for the first several weeks of his life, or if his tough-as-nails, fighting nature was the thing that brought him through those first two surgeries.

Everywhere we went, people were drawn to Colman's rosy cheeks, blond curls and big blue eyes. "What a little angel!" they might say, and I would smile politely but inwardly cringe. "Angel" has a different meaning to mamas in the heart community, and it was a painful reminder of how tenuous Colman's presence with us was.

Also, in South Texas, because of our large Hispanic population, it's customary to touch a person after you compliment them to avoid giving them the *ojo*, or evil eye. The last thing a heart mama needs or wants is random strangers touching the face, hair and hands of her baby, because . . . germs! I thought about making a sign for Colman's stroller that read, "I'm a heart baby. Please don't touch me." I should have done it. Colman was Mr. Irresistible.

Germs were a constant worry. Jack Callaway had said to treat Colman like a normal child, and we succeeded for the most part. If he dropped his pacifier on the floor at home, I'd hand it back citing the three-second rule. I wanted him to have a healthy immune system and tried my best to balance out good germs and bad ones. I'd never been a helicopter mom, and I saw no reason to start with Colman, who already gave me enough to worry about.

With the help of monthly Synagis vaccines during the winter to help ward off RSV—a common cold that is potentially deadly for heart babies—we made it to the ten-month mark before Colman had a fever that wasn't in response to a major surgery. Even though I knew that most of the time fevers are no big deal, Colman's heart was a big underlying condition. I didn't feel like taking any chances, so I loaded him into the car in the middle of the night to go to the emergency room.

Once we were there, they couldn't find anything wrong and wanted to admit Colman. Turns out an HLHS diagnosis makes for a pretty low threshold for admission to a children's hospital. Since Colman wasn't dehydrated and everything else seemed fine, I convinced the ER doctors to let me take him home with a promise to follow up with our pediatrician first thing in the morning. I hoped I was doing the right thing.

The next morning was a Saturday. Frank wasn't on call, so we saw a different doctor in the clinic. He checked Colman over quickly and said in an exasperated voice, "Did the hospital doctor even look in his ears?"

I raised my voice over Colman's shrieking. "I think they did. But now that you mention it, I'm not sure they got a good look in both because he was screaming bloody murder and trying to do an alligator roll. Kind of like right now."

"He has a really bad ear infection," the doctor said. "I'm writing you a prescription for an antibiotic. He should be feeling better in no time."

I took Colman back to the car and strapped him in his car seat. Then I started the car and sat there for a few minutes. A simple ear infection. My face broke into a goofy grin as I looked at the prescription. Since Colman's Glenn, I'd been ready for any little thing to land him back in the hospital. But this was run-of-the-mill normal.

I took Colman home and filled the prescription for the antibiotic. I managed to get the first dose in by implementing the technique I'd come up with for his heart meds. I'd lay Colman down on the floor and sit with his head between my legs. Then I'd pull his arms underneath my thighs to hold him still and slowly trickle the meds between his back teeth and cheek. This involved lots of gagging and spitting on Colman's part, but it was the most effective method I'd found.

My sister, Holly, upon seeing this ritual, said it looked like I was torturing him.

"I am," I said. "You got a better idea?"

"No. I was just thinking maybe he's freaking out because he doesn't want the top of his head smack-dab against your vagina."

"Very funny," I said, wiping sticky medicine from under my eye where Colman had spit it.

This was also how I held Liam and Colman so I could brush their teeth. Liam was probably five or six before he quit lying on the floor in a perfect lowercase T when I said, "Time to brush your teeth." It's just what we did.

When Liam turned three, I put him in preschool three days a week. On his first day I dropped him off—fully expecting tears—and he walked over to one of the play centers, gave a quick wave and said, "Bye, Mama."

That was easy, I thought. As I got ready to walk out, I surveyed the room of children, and my eyes landed on a familiar blond girl in a yellow sundress. My eyes traveled to the telltale scar I knew I'd find on her chest. She was the girl from the PICU when Colman had his Glenn surgery—the one I worried we'd bumped. I had never forgotten her. My eyes threatened to fill with tears of happiness. After four open-heart surgeries, she appeared to be doing well.

With Liam starting school, we made sure to be as careful as possible about germs. Colman still had another winter's worth of Synagis shots, but I made sure to tell Liam's teachers I had a heart baby at home and would be happy to keep Liam out of school if they'd give me a heads-up about any viruses making the rounds.

Colman hardly ever got sick, but not for lack of trying. When he was about eighteen months old we went to Victoria for the weekend to visit my parents. We'd taken the kids to the pond at Riverside Park to feed the ducks. Kevin and I followed the boys around, keeping a close eye on Colman in case he decided to mix it up with the ducks or go for a swim in the murky water.

I reached into my bag to get more bread for Liam and had to take my eyes off Colman for a second. That's when it happened.

"Hey, did you give Colman these Cheerios?" Kevin said.

"No," I said.

I was already panicking. Where had I seen Cheerios? I looked down. They were scattered all over the sidewalk, crunched beneath our feet and mixed with loose feathers, small puddles and duck shit.

I lunged for Colman and struggled to unclench his fists, which were closed tight around the cereal. "No, Colman," I said. "That's yucky! No. No. No. Yucky!"

He screamed as I pried his snack away. Then I did a finger sweep of his mouth to remove as many Cheerios as possible.

We decided the trip to the pond had come to an end and argued about who should have been watching Colman. Once we finally determined that fault couldn't be assigned, except maybe to Colman, Kevin said, "Do you think he's going to get sick?"

"I hope not." I was still disgusted that Colman had eaten a putrid combination of duck shit and bacteria-rich pond water in the form of soggy cereal.

"Avian flu is really big right now. You think he's going to get the flu?"

"I hope not," I said again. What did he want me to do? I didn't have a crystal ball handy.

"If you didn't let him eat stuff off the floor, he probably wouldn't have tried to eat those Cheerios."

Oh, for fuck's sake!

"Really?" I said. "So we're back to this being my fault? This is totally different than letting him eat something he dropped on our clean kitchen floor. You can be too clean, you know? Good germs versus bad germs and that whole bit. We want him to have a healthy immune system."

"I'm just saying it might not have happened if you hadn't set such a bad precedent by letting him eat stuff off the floor."

Kevin had a point, but it still pissed me off.

"You know what? You're right. I quit. You're now in charge of everything that has to do with these kids."

"I think that's taking it a little far," Kevin said. "I'm not saying—"

"What are you saying then?"

"Forget it. Do you think Colman's going to get avian flu?"

"I don't know."

"Can you get it from ducks? They're a type of fowl."

"I don't know."

"But really, do you think he's going to get avian flu?"

"Kevin, I still don't know. Would you like to call Frank or Dr.

Roberts?"

"No. I just want to know what you think."

"I think we have to wait and see. Let's hope he doesn't."

By some miracle, Colman didn't get sick. Then at Halloween, not long after, we went trick-or-treating at the San Antonio Zoo. Liam was walking, and Colman was in the stroller holding onto a huge bag of candy. Colman dropped his lollipop on the ground, and Kevin picked it up and handed it to him.

"Hey, what are you doing?" I asked.

"Three-second rule," Kevin quipped.

"Huh-uh. Three-second rule does not apply at the *zoo*! Are you out of your mind?"

"He was crying."

"So what? He has a whole bag of candy and lots more lollipops. Get him a new one." I snatched the lollipop and tossed it into a trash bin.

Thankfully, Colman didn't get sick from that either.

When Liam was turning four, Kevin and I wanted to throw him a big party. With the Fontan planned for the summer after Colman turned three, we knew we probably wouldn't get the chance to have a party for Liam's fifth birthday. Dr. Roberts had mentioned that their team liked to do Fontans when the child was around three years old and approximately thirteen kilograms in weight. In researching the daylights out of HLHS, I'd come to the conclusion that the timing of the Fontan varied greatly between centers and seemed pretty arbitrary, but Colman was on track for it to take place sometime during the summer of 2007.

We made plans for a swim party at our house and sent out invitations to Liam's friends. Esme wanted to get him a piñata and told me to buy whatever kind of candy I wanted; then she'd have her husband, Alberto, fill it up for us.

The candy was one of the things I'd put off. It was June and hot as hell in Texas, so I was undecided about what kind and how much I should buy. If I got chocolate, it could melt in the sun, but I also didn't want to get hard candy that little kids could choke on.

I called my dad because I figured he'd know how many bags of candy it would take to fill a piñata. Also, I wanted to talk to him, and it had been a while.

"Why are you getting a piñata?" he asked.

"Because Esme offered, it's a birthday party, and piñatas are fun." Duh.

He heaved a sigh of disgust and said, "I hate piñatas."

"You hate piñatas," I said. "What's to hate? They're fun and full of candy. Kids love candy."

"Somebody always gets hurt. And it's never a fair distribution of candy. I don't think you should have one. Think about little Colman. He probably won't get any."

"Okay. Well, we're having one. Esme's already bought it. I didn't call to hear you gripe about how much you dislike piñatas. I wanted your advice on how much candy I needed to fill one."

"I don't just dislike piñatas. I hate them," he said. "Look, who's the biggest kid coming to Liam's party? Why don't you decide how much candy you're comfortable with that little fucker having, and that's how much you should buy."

"Okay. Well, thanks for the help," I said cheerily.

I called Holly. "Hey," I said, "how much candy do you think I need to fill up a piñata?"

"I don't know. Did you call Dad? He'd probably know."

"Uh, yeah. I just got done getting my ass chewed about how much he hates piñatas."

"That's ridiculous. What kind of person hates piñatas?"

"I know. When I asked him, he just said, buy as much as you want the biggest kid at the party to have."

"What'd you say?"

"I got off the phone."

"Who pissed in his Post Toasties this morning?"

"Who knows? But he's in a bad mood. I wouldn't call him anytime soon if I were you."

"No worries."

"I hate piñatas," I said, mimicking Dad.

"I hate a crisp fall day," Holly said.

"I hate freshly spun cotton candy."

"I hate puppy breath," Holly said, and we both dissolved into laughter.

To this day if Holly or I think someone has said something ridiculous, we'll look at each other and say "I hate piñatas" like it's the most normal thing in the world, and we start laughing all over again.

"What is wrong with him?" I asked. "He's so hateful sometimes. I'm just going to grab four giant bags of candy at Sam's. That should be plenty, right?"

"Sounds good," Holly said. "I'll see you Saturday. Love you."

"Love you, too."

On Saturday we had everything ready for Liam's party. After the kids arrived, we all went swimming and then cut the cake. When it was time to do the piñata, Esme asked, "Where are the bags?"

"What bags?"

"For the kids to put their candy in."

"Oh, crap. I forgot," I said, feeling like a failure. "I have plastic grocery sacks we could use."

Esme rolled her eyes. "I'll be right back," she said. "I'm just going to run to the Dollar Store."

As soon as Esme returned with the super-cute candy bags, the kids went to work on the piñata. Unfortunately Dad was right about somebody getting hurt. We weren't two swings in when one of the kids got cracked in the head with the piñata stick. I successfully avoided my father's I-told-ya-so glare. Thank goodness I'd stood firm on not allowing the kids to be blindfolded and spun around, which seemed tantamount to disaster.

When the piñata finally broke apart, there was no shower of candy. Not one piece fell out. A hush of disbelief fell over the children. One child started crying. Esme walked over to Alberto, who was working the piñata rope, and there was a brief discussion.

"Whoops," he announced good-naturedly in his thick Cuban accent. "I put all the candy in the head."

I started to laugh as he pried the piñata head apart and shook the candy onto the ground for the kids to pick up. In the process, he sliced his hand on the wires holding the piñata together. Esme and I took him into the house so he could clean it and wrap it with some bandages.

"Man, Alberto," I teased, "they didn't teach you how to stuff a piñata in Cuba?"

"We didn't have candy in Cuba," he said.

Of course they didn't. I have a real talent for finding new ways of putting my foot in my mouth. Fidel Castro is such a killjoy.

I think it was pretty much the normal disastrous piñata experience. I wouldn't ever want to say my dad was right, but maybe Colman takes after me more than I originally thought when it comes to learning things the hard way.

After I gave Esme the bandages and ointment to wrap Alberto's hand, I went outside to survey the damage. I gingerly picked up the lobotomized, bloody piñata. Somehow it was still in one piece, barely held together with razor sharp wires. As I threw it in the trash I caught myself muttering, "I hate piñatas."

CHAPTER 23

If Liam's gift to me was the realization that I was capable of unconditional love, Colman's gift was perspective. Not a day went by after we learned about Colman's heart that I didn't hug Liam a little tighter and tell him how much I loved him. When Colman came along, he upped the ante. Every second counted, and I didn't want to waste precious time with either of my sons.

On one of my rare visits to the psychologist, I confessed to Dr. Z, "I look at my two boys, one of them healthy and strong, and I think to myself, Liam is going to live a long life and Colman is the child I'll bury. But there are no guarantees. What if I'm sucker-punched and something terrible happens to Liam? I feel like I'd die if that happened. Does that mean I love one more than the other?"

Dr. Z put his hand under his chin and looked at me thoughtfully. "No," he said, "it doesn't. It means you've come to terms with what you know about Colman and his heart. And if something terrible happened to Liam, you'd live. You'd adapt in exactly the same way you did when you learned about Colman. Your grief was a horrible thing. You grieved the healthy child you wouldn't have. You grieved the surgeries you would have to put him through to save his life. You've engaged in an anticipatory type of grief, knowing that Colman will most likely die in your lifetime. You've never had to go there with Liam. You've looked that demon directly in the eye when it comes to Colman."

He was right.

But the funny thing about perspective is not everyone is in possession of the same one, and I found myself making family and friends uneasy when I talked about Colman's health. I've always had a reputation for saying what was on my mind. Some might even say I lack a filter, which is not true. It's just not as tightly woven as some might wish, and some of my honesty escapes.

I didn't relish the thought of making people uncomfortable, but I also realized their distress wasn't my problem. I dealt with one of the worst things imaginable every single day, and I couldn't be the one to reassure everyone that my bouncing baby boy would be okay when I had no prognosis for him. So often people felt the need to fix me in some way—through God, Jesus, prayer, or the untapped resources of medical advances and science. I can't tell you how many times I've heard "You have to think positively," or "You should pray," or "You never know where medicine will be in ten years."

Ten years. We might not have ten years, which showed the vast differences between a normal person's mindset and mine. I didn't have the luxury of thinking in terms of decades. As a heart mom, I thought in terms of heartbeats and moments. Kevin and I often felt as if we were beaten to a pulp at the end of the day, but we were thankful for each day.

I was thinking positively, but no amount of positive thinking would make Colman grow a whole heart. Believe me, if sheer will alone could make Colman whole again, he'd have been healed a hundred times over. Even if he had a transplant down the road, that whole heart would come with a host of other problems most people never even imagine.

I expected a certain amount of understanding from my close friends and family, but I knew I needed to give those same things in return. So I tempered my responses when they asked about Colman. "He's doing great right now," I'd say with a bright smile.

Few people caught the "right now," or they didn't ask. It was an easy way to let us all off the hook. I've found most people don't want to know the painful truth when it comes to children. It's so much easier to pretend it doesn't exist.

On the rare occasions when someone did delve deeper, I felt it was fine to have that frank conversation about the next steps—heart catheterization, Fontan and an uncertain future. And when I mingled with friends at parties and dinners, I placed myself in the shoes of an acquaintance whose biggest problem was her daughter's seasonal allergies. I'd be happy that—thank God—she'd never dealt with anything worse than swollen eyes and a stuffy nose.

During the months leading up to Colman's third heart surgery, my maternal grandmother's health was declining. After her cancer diagnosis, she'd been given six months. She'd lived three years past that time frame, but even so, my mother was having a hard time.

Mom and I had lots of long talks as she struggled to come to terms with her impending loss.

"You know," I said, "nobody expected her to live much past six months. She's been on borrowed time for the last three years. Nana has lived a long good life. Try not to let the worry about her dying eat you up. Try to be in the moment and enjoy the time y'all have left."

"I am," my mother said tearfully. "But it doesn't make it any easier."

Colman's surgeries were palliative, which meant his heart would never be fixed. I was no stranger to borrowed time; that was the business we were in with Colman. I lived every day feeling like a thief, selfishly grabbing another day for myself with him.

"Nana's in her eighties," I went on. "She has children and grandchildren who love her. It's life coming full circle. This is how it's supposed to be."

"Well, I guess y'all won't care much when I die then."

"Of course we'll care when you die," I said, almost laughing at the melodrama.

"No. I don't think you will. Heather, I don't know what's happened, but you're so cold sometimes."

"I'm sorry you think that way. I don't know what you want me to say."

"Nothing," she said dismissively. "You just don't know what it's like to have somebody you love be so sick."

I felt my chest constrict and my cheeks flush. "Yeah, Mom. You're right. I wouldn't have any idea."

I heard her stutter an apology as she realized what she'd said, but I disconnected the call. It was the first time I'd ever hung up on my mom. I didn't feel like I could talk any longer for fear of what I might say.

My mom was the one person, besides Kevin, who really seemed to get what I'd been through with Colman. How could she not see this from my perspective, that eighty-some-odd years was a freaking lifetime that some people never get? When I looked at Colman, I wondered if he'd make it to kindergarten. And if he made it to kindergarten, would he survive to see double digits and graduate from elementary school?

Nana's illness was one of the worst things to ever happen to my mom, and I was having a hell of a time trying to comfort her. I counted her as one of my best friends, but maybe she was right. I'd have traded my life to assure Colman a long life. If push came to shove, I'd have traded the whole lot of Colman's grandparents, too—my parents and Kevin's.

Maybe I was cold.

It wouldn't be the first time I'd heard it. Kevin had accused me of this several times since Colman's diagnosis. My unwillingness, or inability—whatever you want to call it—to cry, coupled with my characteristic directness in discussing Colman and his course of treatment with doctors and nurses had, I guess, earned me the title.

"I know you feel you have to be a certain way with Colman's doctors and nurses," Kevin told me once, "and it's a simple fact that you have to go to war with the insurance company over medications, procedures and tests. And you're great at it. You're a ball-buster. I love that you're such an amazing advocate for Colman. But you don't have to be that way with your family. I'm here for you. I love you."

Yet I didn't know how to regulate the strength I felt. Colman needed me to be strong. Liam needed me to be strong. So did Kevin. It was as if he thought I had a choice in the matter. When there are no other options, all you have left is your strength. My family couldn't afford for me to be anything less.

Mom and I spoke a few days after our phone conversation—the longest we'd ever gone not speaking to one another—and things seemed to be a bit better. I promised myself not to try to counsel her on what she was going through. I would just listen and try to be there for her, as difficult as that was. Mom was living her worst, and I was living my worst. There was no comparing the two because each of us saw things through a different lens of experience.

As we got closer to Colman's third birthday, it became impossible not to notice that he was getting sicker. He appeared bluer because of low oxygen saturations in his blood, and he tired easily when he was playing. At one of Liam's soccer games, Colman said to me, his voice serious, "Mama, I can't run like that."

"I know, baby, but when we get your heart fixed, you will."

Colman nodded. "They fix my ouchy heart?" It was what he called his chest scar.

"Yes. They'll fix it and you'll feel so much better."

In February 2007, Dr. Roberts scheduled Colman for a heart catheterization on March 20, to get a better idea of the timing for the next surgery.

The night before Colman's cath, Holly flew in from Dallas to help us out. Since Colman was the first case that morning, Kevin and I loaded Colman into the car before he'd had a chance to think about breakfast. Holly stayed behind with Liam until Esme arrived at 7:45.

The minutes flew by as we registered Colman at St. John's Children's Hospital and got him checked in. In perfect Colman fashion, he resolutely refused to drink the "goofy medicine" they offered before taking him back to the cath lab, even though I'd made several attempts and even tried bribing him a bit.

I handed the medicine back to the nurse and said, "He's not going to drink this."

"Did you even try?" she asked, rolling her eyes.

"He's not having any of it."

"Here, Colman," she said. "This yummy juice will make you feel better."

"It's not yummy. It's yucky," Colman said, knocking the medicine all over the hospital linens.

I raised my eyebrows at her.

The anesthesiologist came—not our beloved Dr. Stark—and went over the consents. "Why didn't he take the Versed?" she said.

Colman was sitting on a stretcher in pre-op playing with a homely doll he'd found in the playroom. "It's yucky," he said. "I don't like it."

"You haven't even tried it," the anesthesiologist said teasingly. "How do you know?"

Colman squinted, scrunched up his face and growled, "It's yucky!" in a voice several octaves lower than his normal tone.

"It's yucky," I said, and we all laughed.

"It's actually quite yucky," the anesthesiologist agreed. "I'm just wondering how he knows that."

"He hates all medicine. It's a full-on fight every morning."

"It's not a big deal," she said. "Do you guys mind taking him into the cath lab with me?"

"Not at all," I said, relieved. It was one thing to hand Colman over as a tiny baby and quite another to have him dragged from my arms kicking and screaming as a toddler.

In the cath lab Colman was wary of everything that was going on, and I knew he wouldn't go down easy.

"Let's do this," I said to the doctor, not wanting to prolong Colman's anxiety. I grabbed hold of his arms and hugged him tightly, and Kevin grabbed his legs to keep him from kicking. The anesthesiologist covered his nose and mouth with the mask. Colman kicked a foot free from Kevin's hold and knocked the anesthesiologist in the elbow, which caused the mask to come up into my face for a split second.

I felt the edges of my sight go fuzzy and gray, and I leaned my elbows on the table and tried to focus on keeping Colman still.

"Are you okay?" the anesthesiologist said.

"I'm okay," I croaked, surprised that my voice was so hoarse from the blast of anesthesia.

Colman screamed and fought for a few more seconds and finally went under—his face looking not at all peaceful, his brows furrowed together in anger. Kevin and I gave him a brief kiss on the forehead and quickly left the lab.

Kevin said, "I had no idea he was going to fight that hard. Are you okay?"

"Yeah, I think so," I answered, my voice scratchy.

"That was awful," Kevin said, looking a little teary-eyed. "I wish he would just take the medicine."

"I know, baby," I said, hugging him. "Colman never does anything the easy way."

The heart catheterization lasted a couple of hours, which gave Holly a chance to meet up with us. The interventional cardiologist had to use three access points—the right and left groin and Colman's neck—because of his physiology after the Glenn, but the results were good. As far as the hemodynamics of his heart, Colman was exactly where he needed to be going into the Fontan.

The most difficult thing was keeping Colman from moving too much. After a heart catheterization, the patient is supposed to lie flat for at least six hours to reduce the chance of bleeding at the access sites.

Fat chance.

Colman wakes up from anesthesia like a bear interrupted in hibernation—furious. Kevin and I took turns holding and lying across Colman's legs while he screamed over the next six hours. The doctor ordered Versed and Ativan to calm him. One worked, but the other seemed to amplify his discomfort and anxiety. The medications were dispensed in an alternating fashion, so it was impossible to tell which medication he was reacting to.

To my surprise, when the six hours were up they released us to go home. I had an overnight bag in the trunk of my car in anticipation of spending the night.

On the way to the car, I felt like the hospital made a mistake. Colman insisted on walking but was still under the influence of the Ativan and Versed, so he was kind of leading with his head on unsteady feet. Kevin and I each held one of his hands.

"I can't believe they let you guys leave with him like that," Holly said on our way to the car. "He's like a drunk monkey."

"Right?" I said in agreement.

It took several hours for Colman to get back to baseline, even though I pushed the fluids to flush the medication from his system. Holly, Kevin and I took turns sitting next to him. He kept trying to stand on his own, and we didn't want him to fall.

After Esme made sure we were settled for the evening, she left. Holly went into the kitchen to make Liam a peanut butter and jelly sandwich for dinner. Colman was dozing in my arms, so I decided to put him in his bed.

I was dying to pee. With everything going on, the last time I'd peed was when Colman was in the cath lab. I put him in his bed, which was a regular queen-sized bed, and ran down the hall to my bathroom. I'd just finished when I heard a loud thud. I raced toward the sound of Colman's crying with Holly on my heels.

I found Colman on the floor. Once I checked him over to make sure he didn't have any bleeding from the impact, I carried him to one of the recliners in the study.

"What the hell, Heather?" Holly said.

"Sorry. I thought he'd be okay for a few minutes in his bed."

"You can't leave him for a minute when he's like this."

"Yeah, I realize that," I said.

"So much for the whole, 'Send him home. Those parents are perfectly capable.' Whatever."

"Who said that?"

"The nurse and doctor were arguing over whether Colman should go home. The nurse wanted y'all to stay. The doctor said, 'That mom and dad are perfectly capable of taking care of that little boy. He'll be fine.' "

"Famous last words. I wish I'd had a chance to weigh in, because obviously we're not capable," I said, laughing and feeling a little of my stress dissipate as I realized Colman was all right.

"Yeah, y'all suck," Holly deadpanned.

I don't know what I'd been expecting, but after the cath and an entire day of screaming drunkenness, Colman was back to his regular self the next day. He said to me at dinner that night, "You're a stupid-shut-up-boy."

Holly turned her back to laugh so she couldn't be accused of encouraging him.

"That's pretty big talk for somebody going on three," I said, as Colman sidled out of the room before I could place him in time-out. When he was out of earshot, I said, "Shows how much you know, you little dummy, since I'm a girl."

Holly and I settled in and found the movie *Something the Lord Made* on HBO. I'd heard about it from nurses in the PICU during Colman's Norwood, but I'd never watched it, since it was based on the story of the first infant open-heart surgery. I had enough of my own drama in that arena without borrowing from Hollywood.

It was a great movie about the first blue babies—Tetrology of Fallot babies—and Holly was the perfect person to watch it with. There is a scene where Dr. Blalock—a trailblazer in the congenital heart surgery world—is paid a visit by heads of various churches. They try to persuade Dr. Blalock not to perform heart surgery, since they believe opening a child's heart will irreparably damage his soul.

Holly and I looked at Colman, who was playing with his toys, and then at each other. We both had tears in our eyes and, at exactly the same time, said, "It's true!" Then we cracked up because, as much as we loved Colman, he was a hell of a handful.

Later I thanked my lucky stars for Alfred Blalock, Helen Taussig and Vivien Thomas, who pioneered the effort to help children who'd been handed a death sentence at birth, and for all of the talented pediatric cardiothoracic surgeons that followed in their wake.

CHAPTER 24

In preparation for Colman's third surgery, I felt the need to streamline our life. Getting rid of our crazy dog, Lucy, seemed like a great place to start. Lucy was five years old and just as nuts as she'd been as a puppy. Kevin and I took turns running with her, so she got five to ten miles of exercise a day, but it did nothing to alleviate her craziness.

When I mentioned her constant running away and general bad behavior, the vet shrugged and laughed. "That's a Brittany for you," she said. "I had four of these dogs, and that was the running joke in our household. 'When are these dogs supposed to calm down?' From personal experience, I can tell you, with a Brittany, that would be never."

I wanted to have Lucy put down right then, especially when the vet managed to get her to be still for five seconds—the only time I'd ever seen it—by squeezing bacon-flavored processed cheese from a can into her mouth. The vet listened to Lucy's heart and announced that the dog had a heart defect, specifically a prolapsed mitral valve.

I couldn't believe it. It was just too much.

I loaded Lucy into my car to take her home and rolled down the window a bit so she could stick her head out. Once we were on the freeway, she caught sight of something—look, a bird!—and tried to launch herself out. I could end it right now, I thought, with a snap of her neck if I rolled up the electric window.

The day before, we had been playing in the yard when Lucy—look, rustling leaves!—got out again. We could hear cars honking and brakes squealing.

"You better go get her," I said to Kevin.

"Why does she keep running away?" he said.

"Maybe she realized we're not dog people?"

"Not funny," Kevin said.

"Or maybe she's running for her life. She's realized I spend my spare time plotting new ways for her to die that will appear . . . accidental."

"Heather, you don't really want to kill our dog."

"It's like you don't even know me sometimes," I said, rolling my eyes and sighing.

I did want to kill our dog. Lucy was like the dog in the movie *Marley and Me* times ten, but with no love or warm feelings on either end of the relationship. Actually, I wanted my Grandpa Humphrey—God rest his soul—to come back from the grave with his trusty shotgun. He was not a hunter and loathed people who shot big game for fun, but he had no qualms about putting down an animal he'd deemed a menace. Lucy met that definition to a tee.

On one of my mother's many visits to her parents' home in Los Fresnos (if you've ever been to South Padre Island, you'll remember Los Fresnos as the Podunk town where you received your speeding ticket), my mom and grandpa sat on the porch looking out at the orchards that lined the *resaca*, a large body of brackish water. My mom said, "Daddy, what happened to your ducks? Did the alligator get them?"

"Nope," he answered. "I shot them."

Mom paused for a second. "Why'd you shoot them?" she said.

"They're nasty things, coming up here and shitting on my porch." He shuddered. "They make a big mess."

"Because you were feeding them," Mom said, just a little shocked. "You tamed them and then you shot them?"

"Well, yes," he said, with a chuckle.

Since my go-to person for getting rid of animals wasn't around, I came up with the idea of placing Lucy on the Brittany Rescue website. I reasoned she really did need to be rescued.

Within hours of listing her, a family in Houston called. They had three kids and a big ranch and loved to hunt. It was a match made in heaven. Lucy needed a job, and they needed a bird dog. I was worried that her heart defect might squirrel the deal, but they were fine with it. We made a plan to meet that weekend.

If you're going to give your family dog away—and I'm speaking from experience—I recommend doing the exchange in a dark alley in the middle of the night.

I gave Lucy away in front of our kids. I think Colman was too little to realize what was happening, but Liam went in the house and started to cry as the Houston family pulled out of the driveway with our dog. When I walked in the door, Liam said in between hiccupping sobs, "I know Lucy didn't love me, but I loved her."

That statement alone should tell you what a horrible dog Lucy was. She wasn't worth sweet Liam's tears, and I felt a fresh wave of homicidal rage toward her. Colman started crying—probably because Liam was crying—and then Kevin said, "I can't believe you did that in front of the kids."

"You were here, too," I said. "How hard would it have been to take the kids for ice cream?"

Liam settled down as we talked about finding a dog that would love us as much as we loved him after Colman's surgery. I made a mental note to put a little extra money aside for the psychotherapy my kids would need as a result of being parented by me.

Not long after, I received a call from Linda, Dr. Callaway's nurse, scheduling Colman for his Fontan on May 16, 2007, a little sooner than I'd hoped. There's really no good time for heart surgery. You constantly question the timing.

Two weeks before surgery, I received a call from Holly. She'd gotten married a few months before, and she and her husband had just closed on a house. When I answered the phone, she said, "I think Nana is dying."

"Why do you say that?"

"Hunter went by to check on her, and her limbs are cold."

"Okay. Well, we all knew this was coming. Have you talked to Mom?"

"No, but she can't die right now. This isn't a good time for me."

I laughed. "It's never a good time for a funeral."

"I know, but this is, like, the worst time. Seriously. We're moving this weekend, and I want to be able to go to her funeral. Can't you do something?"

"Like what?"

"I don't know. You're her favorite. Can't you send her flowers or something and perk her up a bit?"

"Colman's surgery is in two weeks. If she perks up, that means she's probably going to die the day Colman has his surgery. And that would be seriously fucked up."

"She won't. I promise. I just need her to hold on for a couple days—tops."

"Mom is going to be a disaster. You know that, right?"

"I know." Holly sighed. "Will you send the flowers?"

"I'll send them," I said.

"I owe you—big time! Thank you."

I called the flower shop in Victoria and arranged for a dozen orange roses to be delivered to Nana.

The flowers were a success, or maybe it just wasn't her time yet.

Either way, Nana perked up enough to call and thank me. We visited for a bit. It was one of the last times she was lucid enough to talk, and I was glad I'd sent the flowers. At least she'd have something pretty to look at.

May 16 was bearing down on us, and things were reaching a fever pitch. Nana was hanging on. Esme's husband, Alberto, had accepted a job in Dallas, and they were moving. Her last day would be two days after Colman's surgery.

One night about a week before Colman's surgery, as I was rocking him to sleep, he placed his hand in mine. The sight of his perfect chubby hand, complete with dimples along his knuckles, wrecked me. I felt the tears start to fall. I put him down to sleep and crawled in bed beside him. I watched the rise and fall of his chest as his breathing evened out, the way his long eyelashes brushed the tops of his round cheeks, and I cried until I'd soaked the pillow.

How was I going to do this again? My heart twisted, and my head hurt from crying. I went to our room.

Kevin took one look at my face and pulled me into a hug. "Hey," he said, "have you been crying?"

"Yes," I said. "It's Colman." I blurted out a bunch of nonsensical babble about his hand and his heart and something about freezing time.

"Whatever you need from me, I'm here for you. Got it?" Kevin said, squeezing me to his chest.

I nodded.

"Colman is going to be fine."

"I can't quit crying," I said. "I don't know what's wrong with me."

I washed my face and climbed into bed still feeling weepy and overwhelmed. Kevin put his arms around me again, and we stayed that way. Kevin said, "Do you think Colman's going to hate us later? Do you think he's going to blame us for putting him through this? After everything, he's still going to have limitations."

"Maybe," I said. "The only thing we can do is admit the truth, that we wanted him here with us and we were too selfish to let him die. He can hate us, but really, how can you argue with that?"

CHAPTER 25

The night of my crying jag, I dreamed for the first time since we'd received Colman's diagnosis. In my dream, I'd been diagnosed with an inoperable brain tumor, but Jack Callaway thought he could maybe save me with an experimental surgery. They would detach my head, get the tumor out and then reattach it in, say, six months. If it worked—a big if—I'd only have a little scar that most people wouldn't see because when he made his incision, he would follow one of the wrinkles in my neck. I appreciated his concern for my vanity.

"But you're not a neurosurgeon," I said, the practical side of my brain taking over even during sleep.

Dr. Callaway shrugged and replied with uncharacteristic hubris, "That may be, but what can I do? You don't have any options."

"True, but I'd feel a lot better about you being my doctor if my problem were cardiac-related. I think I'll just make the most of the time I have left."

"It's your choice," he said.

I woke up thinking to myself, Could you be any more stressed out?

I'm not sure whether it added to my stress or helped decrease it, but in the months leading up to Colman's third surgery I researched the daylights out of HLHS. Through reading personal blogs at www.carepages.com and www.caringbridge.com, I felt I was prepared for any eventuality going into and coming out of the Fontan. In a weird turn of events, Kevin didn't want to know anything I found on the Internet, and he couldn't understand my need to gather as much data as possible. Why worry about something that might not happen? But I didn't want any surprises, and I needed to know the right questions to ask.

We took Colman to St. John's Children's Hospital on the afternoon of May 15. As we were loading Colman into the car, I asked Kevin to grab my overnight bag.

"Why do you have this?" he said. "You're not spending the night, are you?"

"Yes," I said, confusion probably evident on both our faces as we tried to figure out what the other was thinking.

"Oh."

"How did you think this was going to go down?"

"I didn't think you'd be spending the night. My parents should be getting into town pretty soon. They're going to wonder where you are."

"You can tell them I'm at the hospital taking care of their grandson. Do you think we can drop our three-year-old at the hospital to spend the night by himself? 'Colman, see the little button with the hat? That's the button to call the nurse. You just push that if you need anything. And here's some medicated soap to use in your bath before you go to bed. See you before your surgery in the morning. Kiss-kiss.' Is that what we're supposed to do?" I was running thin on patience at this point.

"I didn't think it through, I guess. I just don't want my parents to think you're avoiding them."

"Honestly, I don't care what they think. And you shouldn't either. This isn't a social visit. They're coming to support you. They should not need to be entertained. They should not be a pain in your ass. They should not give you any sort of guilt trip whatsoever. If they can't do that, they don't need to be here."

"Yeah," said Kevin. "I agree. Just let me know what you need. I'm here for you. And for Colman."

"Thank you," I said, feeling relieved that we weren't going to have a brouhaha over this.

"Whatever you need," Kevin said. He gave me a hug and kissed my cheek.

I felt that we were so much better prepared going into this surgery. For three years I'd thrown everything I could think of at Kevin to send him running, and he'd stood by me. Our family of four was finally in a rhythm and managing the additional stress of having a chronically ill child. It wasn't easy, but we were both incredibly stubborn when it came to making sure our family came first, and I felt comfortable that our marriage was on solid footing.

"I have everything taken care of," I said. "Mom and Dad are coming today, and they'll be staying at the house to help out with Liam. Holly will be here later tonight, and she and her husband are staying at a hotel. Your parents got a hotel, right?"

"Yeah. I told them to."

That sounded ominous, but I didn't say anything. They could figure it out on their own.

Once we registered at the hospital, we were admitted to the Intensive Moderate Care floor, and Colman had his vitals taken. Then Dr. Callaway stopped by to talk to us about the surgery. He sat in one of the chairs in Colman's room and said, "Well, we made it. This is what we've been working toward."

He brought us up to speed on everything. He'd opted not to have an IV placed in Colman, explaining that they'd do that the following day after he was under anesthesia. "No reason to upset him needlessly," he said.

I was thrilled not to have to worry about Colman pulling an IV out in the night.

"But we are going to need to draw some blood for labs," he continued, "so why don't y'all come on down here and we'll do that real quick."

Being that Colman had always been a pretty tough stick, Dr. Callaway drew the blood himself—one stick and done.

I tried to explain the surgery to Colman in terms a three-year-old would understand. I'd told him the week before surgery that Dr. Callaway was going to operate on his heart and that they would go through his chest.

"You mean my scratch?" Colman asked, which is how he sometimes referred to his chest scar.

"Yeah. They're going to make another scratch on top of that scratch and work on your heart."

"That's fine," he said, shrugging his little shoulders like it was no big deal. Then, as he was walking off, he muttered, "They better not break it."

No, I thought. They better not.

After we signed the papers and finished talking to Dr. Callaway, Kevin left. Our nurse came in to check on us. "Dr. Callaway drew his blood for me, huh?" she asked.

"Yeah," I said with a big smile. "He's awesome."

"I won't argue with you there," she said.

Mom and Dad brought Colman and me dinner before they headed to our house. Kevin and his parents came by soon after.

"Can I see you for a second?" Kevin said.

"Sure," I said, following him out of the room. "What's up?"

"My parents didn't get a hotel. They can't stay at our house?"

"It's up to you. I guess you can sleep on the sofa and give them our bed."

"That's not happening." Kevin rolled his eyes like I'd suggested he spend the night on a bed of broken glass.

"I don't know what you want me to do. I've kind of got my hands full," I said, gesturing to the room Colman was in.

"I guess I should try to find them a hotel."

"If they can't find one themselves, then I guess so."

They'd been in town less than five minutes and had already managed to annoy me. I tried to direct my energy toward making sure Colman had a good night pre-surgery.

Kevin left to take his parents to dinner.

As Colman and I were settling in, they came back. Kevin pulled me aside again.

"I need a doctor's note," he said.

"For what?" I said.

"I found my parents a hotel near here, but they need a note so they can get fifty dollars off the rate."

"You're joking, right?"

Kevin looked at me sheepishly. "I wish I were," he said.

"The doctors' offices are closed. Callaway's gone. Where am I supposed to get a note at this late hour?"

"I don't know. I told them the same thing."

"I'm not doing this. If they had called, say, last week and found the deal with the hotel, I'd have been happy to have Dr. Roberts' office fax me a note. But they rolled into town with no thought about the inconvenience they might cause us. They thought they'd guilt you into staying at our house."

"I know. I'm sorry," Kevin said.

I hated for him to be in this situation, but his parents couldn't be any more insensitive, unhelpful and self-absorbed. Our child was having heart surgery in less than ten hours.

"Here," I said, pulling my Visa from my wallet. "Put their room on this."

"They can pay for it themselves. We're going to have enough expenses from Colman's surgery."

"I'd be happy to talk to them," I said diplomatically.

Kevin laughed. "I can't even imagine how that conversation would go, but somehow I know you'd come out on top."

"I'm not asking for a note," I said, and crossed my arms over my chest. "You want to hunt down a doctor or see if you can find a resident to do it, be my guest. Maybe Callaway can scribble something before he cuts open our son tomorrow morning."

I walked back into the room and sat in the chair beside Colman's bed. I couldn't look at my in-laws. I was seething with anger.

Kevin collected his parents. As they were leaving I heard his mom say, "So did you get the note?"

I'd brought Colman's pillow, blanket, PJs and his favorite DVDs. I was doing my best to make it like a little slumber party. I gave Colman a bath with the medicated soap the nurse left with me, and we climbed into bed early to watch *Air Buddies.*

About halfway through the movie, Colman announced that he was hungry. I headed to the nurses' station to see if I could scrounge up some snacks. Our day nurse was still there, even though it was well past shift change.

"Hey," she said, "are you okay?"

"Yeah," I said. "Why?"

"I don't know. You seem a little stressed out. Are you worried about tomorrow?"

"Yeah," I said, feeling like I was going to cry. "That, and my in-laws are a huge pain in the ass."

She laughed. "Aren't they all?"

"I guess," I said, smiling. "I'm sure my husband feels the same way about my parents."

"Is there anything I can do to help?"

"Is there a resident around? My in-laws are bugging my poor husband about a doctor's note so they can get fifty dollars off their hotel room."

The nurse grabbed a pad of paper and wrote a note. "Here," she said. "It's on hospital letterhead. It should be good enough. If it's not, you can say you tried, right?"

"Thank you," I said, stuffing the note in my pocket. "I really appreciate it."

"Any time," she said with a big smile. "Let me get Mr. Colman his snacks."

Morning came quickly. I changed into a long-sleeved tee and jeans and pulled my hair into a ponytail. The nurses had been in Colman's room several times, and Colman was waking up. I heard his tummy growling and put on one of his DVDs, hoping to distract him from his hunger.

Kevin arrived, and we made our way to the pre-op holding where Colman played with the toys in the waiting area. He was full of energy—a real live wire—and I know Kevin and I were both second-guessing the timing of his Fontan. The two times before when he'd needed surgery, it was emergent. This felt different.

Colman put his pink flamingo plushy in the toy microwave, and Kevin asked, "What are you doing to your flamingo?"

"I'm gonna make that bird hot!" Colman said. He pretended to make us breakfast, and we pretended to eat plastic toy food that many parents pretended to eat before us.

"Hospital food is yucky," I said, making a terrible face. Colman giggled.

As usual Colman refused to take the "goofy" medicine. Kevin and I were both happy to see Dr. Stark come into the waiting room. After we went over the paperwork she asked Colman one more time about the medicine.

"Nope. It's yucky. I don't take that," he said.

"Okay," Dr. Stark said. "Mama, you suit up and come with me." She handed me a sterile white cover-up and mask and helped me into them.

I gathered Colman in my arms and followed her into surgery.

"Mommy, you look funny," Colman said, giggling.

"It's your fault I look like this! If you would take your medicine like a good boy, I wouldn't have to dress up like an alien." I pretended to eat his neck through my mask. He laughed harder.

I followed Dr. Stark into the brightly lit operating room and laid Colman down on the table. I kept my arms wrapped around him. I nodded to let her know I was ready. I didn't want to give Colman a chance to become scared.

"Is this his from home?" Dr. Stark asked, holding up the pink flamingo.

"Yes," I said.

Dr. Stark put the flamingo around the anesthesia mask in order to disguise it and asked Colman, "Is this your birdy?" She then placed the anesthesia directly on Colman's face before he knew what had happened. Even though I had a mask on, I turned my face away to avoid a repeat of what had happened in the cath lab a month earlier. Colman struggled for a second and started to cry. I did my best to soothe him, and then he was out. I gave him a quick kiss on the forehead before I left.

I felt dizzy as I exited the O.R. and worried I might faint. I started to pull down my mask to get some air, but the surgical tech caught me and said, "This area is sterile. Keep your mask on. I'll tell you when you can take it off."

My vision was going blurry from lack of oxygen, but I concentrated on putting one foot in front of the other until I could take the mask off.

I'm not sure how they manage wearing those masks for hours on end in surgery.

The surgical staff promised to call us every hour with an update, and we went to the cafeteria to meet our families.

My mom was on her phone constantly getting updates on Nana. She'd left Nana in the worst shape she'd been in so far to travel to San Antonio. I had serious doubts about whether Nana would make it through the day.

When I asked about her, Mom said, "Don't worry. If the worst happens, we'll wait to have the funeral until Colman is on the mend."

I took comfort in knowing there was a plan if Nana did die before the end of the day or while Colman was in the PICU.

"Okay," I said. "Are your brothers okay with that?"

"Yes," she said. "Funerals are for the living. There's no need to rush it."

We received our first couple of calls from the operating room. Colman was on bypass and doing well. Dr. Callaway had informed us that he would be performing an extracardiac Fontan, and he would probably fenestrate—make a hole—in Colman's Fontan conduit because of the tricuspid valve leak in his heart, even though the heart cath had shown that the hemodynamics of his heart were perfect for moving forward with an unfenestrated Fontan. The fenestration would result in lower oxygen saturations than we'd hoped for, but Colman would feel much better with the Fontan circulation, and his heart would work more efficiently. For whatever reason—call it instinct, experience or some sort of weird Spidey sense—Dr. Callaway felt Colman would do better with a fenestrated Fontan.

The Fontan repair went perfectly. When we received a call from the operating room, it was Dr. Callaway. Colman's tricuspid valve was leaking worse than they'd originally thought. I knew this wasn't good news.

"So what do you want to do?" I said. Kevin was standing right there and made a gesture with his hands, like, What's up?

"It's the valve," I mouthed. "They want to try to fix it now."

Kevin crossed his arms and started pacing.

"Well, the leak looks mild right now, and that's while he's lying perfectly still," Dr. Callaway said. "I called Dr. Moreno to the operating room to take a look at it. Our worry is the leak might be in the moderate category when he's up and running around. I'd like to open his heart and see if I can tighten up that tricuspid valve."

I felt my stomach flop. "What does Dr. Roberts think?"

"I haven't been able to reach him. We're trying to get him on the phone right now."

Even though Dr. Moreno was in the same practice, I didn't know her well. Dr. Roberts had been with us from the beginning, and if he and Dr. Callaway came to a consensus, I knew it would be the best thing for Colman. But we needed to make a decision quickly. I was going to have to go with what we had.

Kevin said, "If Callaway wants to fix it, let him."

I nodded. "Dr. Moreno thinks you should try to fix it?" I said to Dr. Callaway.

"Yes."

There was silence as I tried to weigh our options. I didn't want Colman hanging out on bypass waiting for them to reach Dr. Roberts. Dr. Moreno was in the O.R. with Colman, and she probably had a good handle on what needed to be done. All I could think of was Colman saying, "They better not break it."

"I'd feel better if you talked to Dr. Roberts first," I said, "but go ahead if you can't get a hold of him."

After I hung up, I worried about that decision, even though I trusted them to think through all the angles.

Kevin said, "I forgot about that leaky valve."

"That damn valve is going to put him on track for a heart transplant sooner rather than later," I said, shaking my head.

A couple of hours later, Dr. Callaway came out and told us Colman was doing well. He'd been able to tighten up the valve. It was still leaking, but we were back to a mild leak.

"Were you able to talk to Dr. Roberts?"

"Yes," Dr. Callaway said, laughing and shaking his head.

"What did he say?"

"Jerry called right before we were going to do the repair. He said, 'Go ahead, I guess. Don't you dare mess up that kid's rhythm,' and then he hung up on me."

I could almost hear Dr. Roberts admonishing Dr. Callaway that way. I had a serious doctor crush on Dr. Roberts, and I felt relieved that he'd signed off on the surgery. "You didn't mess up Colman's rhythm, did you?" I said.

"His rhythm is good," Dr. Callaway said. "You should be able to see him in the PICU in the next hour or so."

"Thank you," I said. The two words were completely inadequate to express my gratitude for everything Dr. Callaway had given us.

CHAPTER 26

Colman was as pink as I'd ever seen him. I compared his nail beds on his fingers and toes against my own chewed-up nails; the color was close. I hadn't painted my fingernails in more than three years, just so I could check his nail beds against my own at a moment's notice. If this all worked out well, maybe I'd treat myself to a manicure.

Again, Colman was covered in tubes, IVs, bandages and wires. I sat down beside him and placed my hand on his right foot, one of the only places I could touch him. I was shocked by what I felt. Colman was warm.

His limbs had always been cold to the touch. I swallowed the sob I felt forming. I wondered at how Dr. Callaway had managed to yet again reroute Colman's heart. Colman was paralyzed and sedated, but he didn't feel like a corpse child any longer. He felt alive.

"I can't get over how warm he feels," I said to Shelly, the same nurse who always took care of Colman after surgery. I was happy to see her, but I'd be thrilled when we were handed off to somebody else because that would mean Colman was getting better.

"It's crazy, isn't it?" she said, smiling.

All of Colman's numbers were pretty good, but Dr. Callaway had mentioned that it might take a couple of days for his body to get used to his new plumbing. The plan was to keep him quiet for the remainder of the day with the hope of extubating him the next morning.

When Kevin left to update our families, Holly came in.

"Did Nana die yet?" I asked.

"Would you stop it?" she said. "She's not going to die today."

"Right."

"Why today, Heather?"

"Because that's just my shitty luck."

"Not today."

"Wanna bet?"

"Yeah, I'll take that bet. What are we going to bet?"

"I'll bet you my Louis Vuitton bag you like so much that she dies today."

"Fine. I'll bet you my Rolex that she doesn't."

"Deal," I said.

Now that the Rolex was on the line, Holly went for a status check on Nana. Mom and Dad came to see Colman.

"How's Nana?" I said.

"She's not doing so hot," Mom said. "I just talked to Aunt Robbie, and I don't think it will be much longer."

"What's she doing there?"

"She offered to sit with Nana while I was here with you."

"That's nice." Aunt Robbie is my father's only sibling. It was kind of her to offer to sit with my grandmother on her deathbed—a woman she had no relation to except through marriage.

Mom was teary-eyed. "I don't think it's going to be long now. Especially based on what the chaplain said last week."

"The chaplain?" I said.

"Yeah," she said. "They offered to have a chaplain come by for counseling, and she gave us some signs to look for when someone's life is coming to an end."

Dad rolled his eyes so far up into his head, I'm positive he could've drawn a map of the underside of his brain. I was struggling to not do the same. Science was my safe place. The afterlife? Not so much.

"What kinds of signs?" I listened to beeping monitors and the rhythmic whoosh of the ventilator breathing for my three-year-old in the background.

"Their limbs grow cold. They look to their left and start seeing people waiting for them on . . . the other side."

I wished I'd been at the meeting with the chaplain. Talk about a missed opportunity. Mom was clearly eating this shit up.

"There has to be some physiological reason that people look to the left when they're dying," I said. I was trying not to judge, but it sounded like a bunch of voodoo.

"Well, whatever the reason, Mama's been looking to the left a lot lately."

"Yeah," Dad said, leaning forward and placing his hands on his knees. "Tell Heather what she saw."

"Last week she was looking to the left a lot. I said, 'Mama? Mama?

What do you see?' "

I felt gooseflesh rise on my skin. I didn't want to know this. "Did she answer you?" I said.

"She said, 'A cow.' "

"Damn," Dad said, with a puzzled expression on his face. "I didn't know she was Hindu."

Mom and I burst out laughing. My father's comedic timing was as impeccable as ever.

"A cow," I repeated. "Was she looking out the window?"

"Nope," Mom said. "A brick wall."

"That is such bullshit, you know."

Mom smiled, kissed my cheek and went to call Aunt Robbie for a status check.

With the exception of what seemed to be excessive drainage from his chest tubes, Colman was doing well. I made sure to tell the nurse about the problems we'd had after the heart cath when we alternated the Ativan and Versed. Based on how they'd been stacked after the heart cath, it was impossible to tell which drug was the culprit.

I left Colman with Kevin when he returned and went with Holly to get something to eat in the cafeteria. It was a quick trip, and I was back in less than twenty minutes. When I walked in, the stress level in the room was palpable.

"What happened?" I said.

Kevin looked shell-shocked, and our nurse didn't look much better.

"Colman should not take Ativan," the nurse said, still a little shaken up. "A couple of minutes after I gave him the dose, he stood straight up."

"I can't believe he didn't extubate himself," I said.

"Me either." She shook her head. "I can't believe he didn't fall."

"Thank goodness you were standing right there," Kevin said. Turning to me, he said, "She caught him mid-air."

"He gave us quite a fright," the nurse said. "We're going to try Versed in a minute and see how he does, but my advice is to tell future healthcare providers that he's allergic to Ativan. Actually, what he exhibited was a paradoxical reaction, but that way they'll tag it as an allergy and nobody will give it to him again."

"Okay," I said.

"He's pretty agitated," she said, double-checking to make sure the rails around Colman's crib were secure. Earlier all the rails had been down because nobody was expecting him to move a muscle.

Colman handled the Versed fine, which was odd since that drug is from the same family as Ativan. We were happy, though. Anything to keep him calm while he worked on recovering.

Later that evening Colman was still having significant drainage from his chest tubes. Holly came in to hang with me and said, "Well, Nana didn't die today."

"The day isn't over yet," I said. "It's only 9:30. We still have a couple of hours before midnight."

Holly rolled her eyes. "I'm going to go check with Mom."

The problem was, I'd talked to Aunt Robbie earlier in the day and heard my poor grandmother's moans in the background. It was awful. I didn't know how much longer she could go on like that. I don't know how Aunt Robbie was able to sit with her. I like to think I'd have had the fortitude to pull a Dr. Kevorkian and save a couple of ampules of morphine to give her all at once or maybe smother her with a pillow. It would have been a small kindness. Nobody should have to leave this world in that kind of agony.

I heard a commotion in the hallway—people talking in hushed tones. It was pretty quiet in the PICU with visiting hours over, but my family was still there. When I looked up, Holly was coming through the doorway, her Rolex watch dangling from her fingertips.

"You called it," she said.

"Crap. I was really hoping I'd be wrong," I said, and we both laughed through our tears. "Why are you crying? You didn't even like her. Is this about your watch?"

"Heather!" admonished Holly. "No, I'm sad. I feel bad that I was mean about her and that I didn't like her, and now she's gone."

"Give me a break," I said. "Stop crying. Don't feel bad about all that now. How's Mom?"

"She's a mess."

Right then Mom came into the room and said, "Nana died. I have to go to the Valley. Colman is doing okay. Please—please understand."

I stared at her in disbelief. "Mama, she's dead. There's nothing you can do now."

"I have to go. I need you to understand."

"Do what you feel you have to do," I said. Then I sat in stunned silence feeling abandoned and overwhelmed. It's startling to realize that the only person you can truly count on is yourself.

I had a thousand things running through my mind, the first of which was Colman. Contrary to Mom's belief, he was not doing okay. The bloody drainage from his chest tubes had his team worried. They were working on a plan, talking about taking him back into surgery to see if there was something they'd missed.

The second was Liam. Our beloved nanny was leaving in two days' time, and I'd been depending on my parents to help with him. I had some major logistical shit to figure out to make sure my family was taken care of over the next couple of weeks.

"Heather, please, I need you to understand," my mother said again.

"I don't understand, Mama," I said. "I'm sorry. Nana's dead, and there's nothing you can do to change that fact. I need you."

"I have to go," she said. "You'll be fine." And she left.

Holly and I looked at each other.

"What was all that funerals-are-for-the-living shit?" she said.

"I don't know. I hope she knows, if we're ever similarly situated, that I'm going to put her ass on ice until I'm good and ready to have a funeral."

Holly shook her head. "I can't believe this is happening."

"Are you going to go to the funeral?"

"Hell, no. I roll with you."

I was overcome with emotion. "Thank you," I said.

"No problem. That bitch never even sent me a birthday card."

"Nana was a weird old bird, huh? I wonder if that's why Mom's having such a hard time with all of this. It seems to me like all Mom ever wanted was for Nana to tell her she was a good daughter and that she loved her. How hard would that have been? Maybe we don't understand because we've always had those kinds of assurances from our own mother."

"Mom doesn't like me either," Holly said.

That made me laugh. "She does, too."

"Whatever," she said, giving me a big hug. "I hate everybody right now."

"I don't want your watch."

"Oh, thank goodness. I was wondering if you'd hold me to that."

"Nope. Just as long as you give me credit for calling this debacle."

"Deal," she said.

Since Kevin was home with Liam, Holly stayed with us in the PICU that night. I don't think we slept a wink. We sat up and talked the way sisters do. At about 3 a.m., we had an unexpected visitor. My cousin, Matt, was on his way from Dallas to the Rio Grande Valley and dropped by to check on Colman.

I looked at the helmet under his arm. "You're on your motorcycle?"

"Yeah," he said.

"That's an eleven-hour trip."

He shrugged. "It's no big deal. I wanted to give this to you," he said, handing me a small bottle in the shape of the Virgin Mary.

Great, I thought, more holy water.

"Thank you," I said. "That's really sweet."

"Let's put it on him," he said, rubbing his hands together after hitting the Purell dispenser in the hallway.

"Well, I don't know where it's been."

"Heather, it's *holy* water."

"I know," I said. I didn't want to hurt his feelings, but I was willing to go to the mat before I put the water in that bottle on Colman. "I promise I'll rub some on him as soon as he doesn't have any open wounds."

Matt rolled his eyes at Holly as I shook the bottle and watched small chunks of sediment settle in the bottom.

When I went to give Matt a hug, I slipped the bottle into my purse. I'd deal with it later. And by deal with it, I meant I'd put it in my nightstand along with all the other bottles of holy water I'd received.

Years later, I mentioned my abundance of the blessed stuff to my dad.

"How do you have holy water?" he said.

"People give it to me all the time. It's the weirdest thing. Especially when Colman's going into the hospital or is already in."

"You have a lot of it?"

"Bottles and bottles in all shapes and sizes."

"Really?" he said. "That much, huh?"

"Probably not enough to dunk a Baptist, but I bet I have enough to perform an exorcism or two."

"Why do you keep it?"

"I don't know. It's a sweet gesture. It seems kind of blasphemous to throw it away."

"You could always make Pope-sicles."

"Yeah," I said, giggling. "Because that wouldn't be blasphemous at all."

Although Colman looked the best ever coming out of the Fontan, the first couple of days were rocky. Extubation was tentatively set for five o'clock the morning following surgery, but not long after Matt left Colman became very agitated and had an episode where he dumped ninety milliliters of blood into his chest tubes. They decided to hold off and extubate him around 7:45, but extubation was delayed again when Colman's X-ray came back showing fluid around his right lung. Finally, at 3:20 p.m., he was able to get the breathing tube out. Then he dumped another thirty-nine cc's of blood. It was crazy. I'd never seen actual dark red blood pouring out of his chest before.

Dr. Saldivar—Dr. Callaway's partner—checked on Colman that afternoon and informed me that the X-ray showed a blood clot on the right side that was pressing on his lung.

"Did they tell you about the ninety cc's of blood last night and the thirty-nine cc's this afternoon?" I said.

"Yeah," he said, "they did."

"What do you think?"

"I'm not happy about it," he admitted, his brows knitted together. "We're going to try to keep him quiet. The plan is to see how he does tonight, but we may need to take him back into surgery to irrigate the chest and try to get rid of the clot and stop the bleeding. I'd like to see it stop on its own, though."

"Yeah," I said. "Me, too."

The skin around Colman's incision looked pinched and bruised, and I couldn't imagine the doctors opening him up again. I guess it's probably easier to reopen than open, but I didn't think I could handle them taking him back in to surgery so soon.

Keeping Colman quiet was a real trick. We had to give him enough sedation and pain medicine to keep him calm and resting, but not so much that he wouldn't be able to breathe on his own. When the medicine wore off, he was combative, trying to stand up while pulling at his pacer wires, chest tubes and the central line in his neck.

The bleeding slowed overnight. Then, the following day, the blood draining into the chest tubes thinned out quite a lot. The decision was made that, as long as the blood was no darker than fruit punch Kool-Aid, we were good. No more surgery.

On Friday evening Esme brought her mom with her to the hospital to sit with Colman so Kevin and I could attend Liam's pre-K graduation. I bawled when the graduates from his class sang a song about potentiality, but I wasn't alone. Turns out pre-K graduations are pretty emotional.

Lots of people asked about Colman. One friend who has a son the same age as Colman and another in Liam's pre-K class said, "Oh, I bet he's giving those nurses hell, isn't he?"

"You've got that right. Everybody at the hospital remembers Colman and what a terror he can be."

"I knew it," he said, smiling. "I just love that little fucker."

I laughed. I probably should have been shocked, but there was too much truth in it. "I do, too," I said.

We took Liam out to dinner to celebrate his accomplishment, and then I went back to the hospital. I couldn't believe it was Esme's last day after five years. I'd miss her terribly, and I tried to blink back tears as she and her sweet mom kissed Colman goodbye.

I sat for a long time watching Colman sleep and the fluid collect in the boxes attached to his drains. All of his numbers looked great. His oxygen saturations were 94 percent, the highest I'd ever seen them, and his blood pressure was good. The nurse informed me that his white count had come back a bit high, but he wasn't running a fever, so we were keeping an eye on his temperature and watching for signs of infection.

Holly came by a little after ten o'clock, set her purse down on the bunk, and pulled out bar after bar of chocolate. "I hit the vending machine on the way up."

"I see that," I said, surveying the giant pile of candy. "Did it only take twenties?"

"I thought we needed some chocolate."

"You thought right," I said, unwrapping one of the bars and breaking it in half to share. "This is so good," I said, taking a bite.

"What do we do if that hot surgeon walks in right now and sees all this candy?"

"Who, Javier?" I asked, rolling the "r" with a Spanish accent.

Holly laughed. "Mom said he was ucha magucha."

I laughed. I can't tell you how many times I've heard my mom say that phrase when referring to a good-looking guy. "You haven't met him yet?"

"Not yet," Holly said. "You want to butter his biscuit?"

"God, no!" I hissed. "You are such a pervert."

"Hey, I'm not the one that wants to butter his biscuit," Holly said, waggling her eyebrows.

I smacked her on the arm. "Don't you know I'm dead on the inside?" She burst out laughing. I looked at all the chocolate. "This is pretty bad, isn't it?"

"He'd take one look at that pile and give me a judgmental that's-why-you're-such-a-fat-ass look."

"Doubt it," I said. "He'd probably just think we started our periods."

"Nice," Holly said. "I'm a fat-ass and menstruating. You really know how to make a girl feel special."

Colman started to thrash around. Candy break was over. I jumped up and said, "It's okay, baby. I'm right here."

His face was drawn into a frown. Every muscle in his forehead was bunched together. He opened his eyes to look at me, and I felt the full force of betrayal, anger and sadness in one angry glare. It broke my heart.

"Can I get you anything?" I said.

Colman turned his face away from me—to the left—and I wanted to wring my mother's neck for imparting that little nugget about people who were dying. I walked to the other side of the bed so I could see Colman's face, and he turned back the other way.

It was a relief to realize he was simply avoiding me. I kissed his cheek, and I was still standing beside him when the nurse came in.

"Is Mr. Colman awake?" she asked.

Colman sank deeper into the bed. This was a new tactic. Up until that point, it had been a fight anytime anyone came into his room.

"Yeah, I think he's awake."

Colman opened his eyes to slits and gave me a dirty look, then lay there while the nurse checked him over and stripped his drains—something he absolutely hated.

When she left, Holly said, "I think his give-a-darn is broken."

"I think you're right," I whispered. "I'd rather have him screaming, 'Don't touch me, stupid-head!' than have him try to disappear into the mattress. Do you think he's depressed?"

"Probably," Holly said. "Wouldn't you be? Want a Reese's Peanut Butter Cup?"

"I want five," I said, but my stomach was churning with worry over Colman's about-face in the personality department. I couldn't eat another thing.

CHAPTER 27

The next couple of days consisted of watching *Polar Express*, dodging Methodists and doing everything in my power to make Colman smile. We watched *Polar Express* all day, every day, and I'd never realized what a dark movie it is. It matched Colman's mood perfectly. He shot down all my attempts to switch to something lighter and more fun.

Kevin had made a call to the Methodist church we rarely attended to ask them to put Colman on the prayer list. They asked if he would like for them to visit, and he said, "Yeah, that would be great."

The first time one of the pastors came to our PICU room, Colman was in the middle of a fit that required two nurses, a large dose of Versed and myself to calm him down. I thought the pudgy guy standing with his hands on his hips had stumbled into our room on accident. But he was still there after we'd gotten Colman settled.

"Can I help you?" I said. I needed Colman to drift off to sleep so I could go outside and catch my breath. I needed some sunshine to blast away the smell of hand sanitizer and antiseptic.

"Yeah, you guys called to say you needed a pastor for some spiritual guidance?"

"No," I said, even though I immediately recognized Kevin's handiwork.

"Well, I have here that we were supposed to call on Colman Connelly's parents. Is this Colman?"

"That must have been my husband. He's not here right now," I said, crossing my arms in a display of horrible body language. I felt bad. The poor guy was just carrying out his obligation to provide some eternal assurances to the members of his flock. His brand of comfort was the last thing in the world I needed, but that wasn't his fault. I took a deep breath and felt myself soften. "It's really kind of you, though. I'll let him know you stopped by."

"Do you need anything?"

"Nope. I'm all good," I said, going back to my characteristic brusqueness. Clearly I wasn't, but I was doing everything in my power to cut this visit short. Colman needed some peace and quiet so he could rest.

"One of our church members is an administrator at the hospital. I'm going to have her come by. Her daughter has been in and out of the hospital her entire life. I think you two might have a lot in common."

"You don't have to do that."

"I'm happy to," he said. Of course he was.

About half an hour later Melanie Davis showed up. Since Kevin and I attended church sporadically, it was no surprise that Melanie and I didn't recognize each other. When she asked me what service we usually attended, I wanted to come clean and say, "Look, I'm not sure why my husband contacted the church. We're what I call Bunny Christians. We hop in and out at Easter and Christmas."

I didn't say that, though Melanie probably would have laughed. We did have quite a bit in common. Melanie is smart, tough and funny. But probably the coolest thing I learned about her is that, as an administrator—someone whose top priority, I imagine, is the hospital's bottom line—she's all about doing the right thing when it comes to children's health care. As impatient as I was about the meeting, I'm glad the pastor set it up; Melanie is now someone I count as a friend.

The pastors didn't stop visiting. One of the three pastors came faithfully every day. Their timing was dreadful. They walked smack dab into whatever major crisis we were having that day—and took a seat.

After four days of visits, I remembered to ask Kevin about it.

"I thought it would be nice," he said.

"It's not nice. I mean, I appreciate the sentiment, but they have truly awful timing. Do you think you could tell them to cut the visits for a little bit?"

"What if I want to talk to them?"

"That's fine with me, but you're never here when they come by."

"What's your problem?"

"I have a lot to manage here. I can't deal with people I don't know dropping by to chat."

"You're being ridiculous."

"You're probably right," I said, even though I didn't feel ridiculous.

"Hopefully I'll be there tomorrow when they show up. I'd really like to talk to somebody about the spiritual aspects of all this."

Spiritual aspects? My ass.

Don't get me wrong. It would be one thing if I truly believed Kevin needed spiritual guidance. But we're talking about somebody who systematically lays out all the reasons the Bible story for a particular sermon is not credible. After one service, Kevin was talking about how the concept of Immaculate Conception was thoroughly ridiculous. (It must have been Christmastime.) I was happily ignoring him until he said something like, "Most people think the Virgin Mary was a whore."

What the—what? In all the years I'd been going to Sunday school and church, I'd never heard anybody say that. As I focused on Kevin's words, I realized he thought Mary Magdalen and Mary the Mother of Jesus were the same person.

"There were two Marys, bonehead," I said.

"No," he said. "There was only one Mary."

"No, there were two. One was a prostitute Jesus was kind to, and the other was his mother, the Virgin," I said, using air quotes around the word "Virgin" because of his previously stated problem with Jesus' conception as portrayed in the Bible.

"You're wrong."

"I am not wrong," I said, laughing.

"How would you even know? I went to Sunday school every week."

"As did I, but it seems only one of us paid attention in class."

The Google explanation was not confusing, but Kevin managed to twist the text into what could only be described as a strained interpretation. This is what lawyers do to support their positions. It's incredibly frustrating.

"Call your mom," I said. "She'll know." Surely this level of inattentiveness in church didn't run in the whole family.

Kevin's mom settled the argument quickly, saying, "There were two women both named Mary."

"It looks like there were two," Kevin said, as he hung up the phone.

"And I think you're going to burn in hell for calling Jesus' mother a whore," I said.

"They shouldn't have been named the same thing. It's confusing."

"Nope," I said. "I can't get on board with you there. They always used 'Magdalen' when talking about the prostitute and 'Virgin' before the mother of Jesus. It's not confusing."

I offer this one incident as an explanation for why I saw Kevin needing spiritual guidance as bullshit. There are others.

There was no way I could have articulated to Kevin what I was feeling. I couldn't even understand it myself. All I knew was the daily visits from the pastors felt intrusive and threw things off balance. I couldn't have that.

St. John's Children's Hospital, being a Catholic institution, had nuns who came by to check on patients and their parents. The Sisters never made me feel uncomfortable. They never walked into our room in the middle of a crisis. They came by with a quick question—"You doing okay? Do you need anything?"

If you wanted to talk, they were there, and if not, they were on their way to the next family. They understood sick kids and stressed-out parents. Their concern was not a mask they wore but an integral part of their humanity. I viewed them as part of the same team as the doctors, nurses, X-ray techs and respiratory therapists. I'd grown to love that team. I counted on them.

As the days in the PICU ran one into the next, I began to realize that pleural effusions were the bane of the Fontan's existence. Colman's numbers were good, which made us feel like we were making progress, but the drainage was far worse than I'd anticipated. He had to have an additional pigtail drain placed in his chest because of the extra fluid.

After a couple of days, we were allowed to change to bulbs rather than the giant boxes the fluid drained into. I brought some pajamas from home, and the nurses safety-pinned the bulbs to Colman's pajama bottoms so they wouldn't pull at the sites where the tubes entered his chest. Once Colman was mobile, Kevin and I switched off taking him for wagon rides around the PICU, hoping to cheer him up.

On our last day in the PICU, we were assigned a bubbly nurse named Kelly. After admitting that none of her usual tricks were working, she said, "We've got to get this boy smiling."

"He hasn't smiled since surgery. I've tried everything short of standing on my head. I'm willing to give just about anything a try at this point," I said.

"Colman," Kelly said, "if your mama stands on her head, will that make you happy?"

Colman frowned and turned his head away.

"Okay," she said.

I shrugged and gave her a now-you-know-what-I'm-dealing-with look.

"He's a tough little nut to crack, isn't he?" she said in a low voice as she left the room.

When Kelly came back, she handed Colman several paper plates and a bottle of Heinz ketchup. "I need you to make me some art," she said in a serious tone. "And don't be neat about it. I want a big mess for your mom to clean up." She winked at me.

I'm not sure if it was the look of surprise on my face or the fact that the nurse had just given Colman permission to finger paint with a whole bottle of ketchup, but he smiled in spite of himself and set to work making one of the biggest messes I've ever seen.

Dr. Callaway came by to take out the pigtail drain, which was clogged. He wanted to see how Colman's X-ray looked before he put in another drain. Then he released us to the step-down unit.

The next morning he said Colman's X-ray looked worse. We were sent back to the PICU for a small bedside surgery to have another pigtail drain placed.

After spending most of the day in the PICU, we returned to the step-down unit to continue draining. Apparently drainage after a Fontan could clear up in a matter of a couple of days or last weeks.

All of Colman's medications had to be given by mouth. He hated Motrin, which most kids think tastes like candy, with a passion. When the nurse brought medications, he'd start crying, "No Motrin. No Motrin. No Motrin."

Since Motrin wasn't considered a required medication, we set it aside the first day. No amount of begging, cajoling or bribery would change Colman's mind.

We were still running *Polar Express* nonstop in the DVR, and he hardly slept. The chest tubes caused him quite a bit of discomfort—especially the new pigtail drain—and he still had the pesky blood clot on his right lung. Between the clot and the effusions, he began grunting with every exhalation because he was so uncomfortable.

After my grandmother's funeral was over and Mom had taken a few days to sort out whatever needed her immediate attention, she came to San Antonio. Holly and her husband returned to Dallas, and I was sad to see Holly go.

But I quickly realized I didn't really want Mom with us. She made our room seem heavier. She was obviously still in mourning. And although I've never been the type to hold a grudge—I'd had over a week to get over it—I couldn't help feeling like she had abandoned me when I needed her most. She'd been caught in the middle of a shitty situation, but that did little to dislodge the bitter ache in my chest.

I couldn't control how I felt, so I tried to focus on what I could control. First I wanted to get some Motrin down Colman. Motrin is not only a pain reliever; it's also an anti-inflammatory. I was sure one good dose would make him feel better, and if he was in less pain I'd be able to get him moving around. We needed to mobilize as much fluid as possible, and that wasn't going to happen with him lying in bed watching *Polar Express* for the thousandth time.

We had no luck with the Motrin the first few times. We tried attaching a straw to a syringe and drizzling the medication between his cheek and teeth so he wouldn't taste it. He did taste it and promptly spit it out. We tried hiding it in his food, which resulted in him refusing to eat or drink for twenty-four hours and made him suspicious of food and drink for the rest of our stay.

Around this time Dr. Wright, a pediatrician who'd long been a fixture at St. John's Children's Hospital, popped his head into the room. "Is this Colman?" he said.

Colman shot Dr. Wright a dirty look, probably on account of the white coat.

"Yes," I said.

"Well, I just wanted to say hello. And, Colman, do you have any idea why the nurses would write 'medicine spitter' all in caps next to your name at the nurses' station?"

This question earned Dr. Wright another one of Colman's dirty looks.

"That would be because he is one," I said, laughing.

But Colman's grunting and lack of sleep were no laughing matter. I finally asked his nurse if we could run an NG tube.

"We can do that," she said.

"Heather," Mom said, "I don't think that's a good idea. That's really going to upset him."

"Mom, he can't heal if he can't rest. He's miserable."

The nurse nodded in agreement.

"Let's do it," I said.

The nurse came back with the tubing we needed, but not before one of the pastors showed up. He took a seat next to my mother as we were getting ready to run the tube through Colman's nose and down into his stomach. I could have killed Kevin because he was nowhere to be found, and that's exactly the kind of thing I don't want to do with an audience.

Delivering the Motrin through the NG was a success. Colman gagged and spit and acted like he would throw up, but he managed to keep it down. In less than half an hour he fell asleep for the first time in days. He slept for eight hours straight.

As I was walking down the hall, I saw the nurse who had taken care of Colman the day before the Fontan.

"I heard you let them run an NG down that baby's nose because he wouldn't take his Motrin," she said.

"Yep," I said. "He's been miserable. I couldn't take seeing him like that anymore."

"Call me next time. I can get medicine down the most difficult kiddos."

"You're on," I said.

Despite the name-calling, dirty looks and general bad attitude Colman meted out to everyone we came in contact with, he had the nurses wrapped around his little finger. Cuteness plus dimples plus recent heart surgery will get you anything, any time, in the hospital.

The nurses knew Colman liked his milk warm, so they heated it in the microwave for thirty seconds. After seven nights in the hospital, when he woke at one o'clock in the morning wanting milk, Gabby, our night nurse, brought it warmed up.

Colman took one sip and threw the carton across the room. "Gabby," he yelled at the top of his lungs, "I wanted cold *leche agua!*"

"Leche" is the Spanish word for milk. "Agua" is Spanish for water. For whatever reason, Colman always used those two together when referring to milk.

I was mortified. Up until this point, I'd let his behavior slide some because he'd had a really rough time. A small part of me wondered if Colman just liked seeing me apologize.

"Oh, I'm so sorry, Colman," Gabby said. "I'll be right back with some cold *leche agua* for you."

"No," I said, meeting her at the door. "I've got this. He doesn't act this way at home, and I'm not going to let him treat you guys like this either. He never drinks his milk cold. I don't know why he's acting this way. I'm sorry."

"He just feels bad," Gabby said. "Let me get him some cold milk. I don't mind."

"No," I said, shaking my head. "He'll just do the same thing. I'll take care of it."

I shut the door, and Colman started screaming, "Gabby! Gabby! You get me cold *leche agua!*"

I grabbed some paper towels and mopped milk from the floor and walls. Then I went to Colman. Over his screaming, I said, "Gabby is not bringing you any more milk. You threw the milk she brought and you were very ugly to her. Just because you feel bad doesn't give you the right to treat people in a mean way."

Then I let him pitch a huge-ass fit in the middle of the night while I sent out mental apologies—using telepathy that I don't have—to all the other sick children and parents Colman was disturbing.

His tantrum didn't last long though, because he was so tired. After he calmed down, I fell asleep immediately.

I woke up to Colman crying around three o'clock. My first thought was that he was tantruming again. But something seemed off. He was agitated, hurting. I turned on the small light over the bed, and that's when I noticed dark red blood snaking down his drains and into the bulbs at his waist. I pressed the button for Gabby.

She came on through the intercom right away. "What is it?"

"I need you in here now," I said, surprised I didn't sound as panicked as I felt.

Gabby was by my side in an instant, and I showed her what was draining out of Colman's chest tubes. The look on her face said it all.

"I think we need a doctor," I said.

"You're right. I'll be right back."

She went out to make a call, and when she came in a few minutes later she took Colman's vitals and assessed him. Other than the blood, he seemed okay.

She waited with me for a few minutes. When we didn't hear back, I said, "I think I should talk to one of the residents at least. Dr. Saldivar told me if Colman had any drainage darker than fruit punch, he wanted to know about it."

"Yeah," she said. "It's definitely darker than that."

The resident who stopped by took one look at the drainage and said, "Impressive."

This analysis made perfect sense, since my first thought after seeing the blood was, What the fuck?

"Who's the attending tonight?" I asked.

"It's Dr. Saldivar."

"Are you going to call him?"

"I'm going to let him know about this, yes," he said.

"When?"

"Since the bleeding seems to have subsided, I don't think he's in any danger. Probably on rounds in the morning."

"I'd like you to call him now. Dr. Saldivar said if the drainage was any darker than fruit punch Kool-Aid, he wanted to know right away. Clearly this meets that criteria."

"Yeah, okay. I'll call him."

I doubted that.

Gabby checked on us a little more often than usual, but I didn't hear from the resident or Dr. Saldivar. I sat up the rest of the night watching Colman, wondering if I'd caused the blood dump by being a hard-ass over the milk and letting him get worked up over it.

The X-ray tech came at 4 a.m. for Colman's regular X-ray. I was able to greet him kindly for once, since he wasn't waking me from a dead sleep to help him position a cranky Colman over the freezing cold film cassettes.

It makes sense for surgeons and cardiologists to have a recent X-ray as close to morning rounds as possible. But that doesn't mean I'm a fan of the 4 a.m. X-ray.

During rounds early the next day, I told Dr. Saldivar about the bloody drainage, and he said, "Why didn't you have them call me?"

"I spoke to the resident, and he said he would."

"He didn't."

"I figured as much," I said, rolling my eyes. "It didn't happen again, and Colman's been okay. No harm, no foul. Right?"

Dr. Saldivar gave me a funny look. "Are you okay?"

"That drainage really freaked me out."

"Give me your phone."

I handed it to Dr. Saldivar, and he punched in some numbers.

"That's my cell. This happens again, you call me. Don't run it through a resident."

"It was 3 a.m."

"I don't care," he said, smiling. "Look, I've never seen you rattled. If something happens with Colman that freaks you out, I want to know about it any time of day or night. Got it?"

"Got it. I'm hoping that was the last time, though," I said, as Dr. Callaway came in.

Dr. Saldivar stepped aside, and Dr. Callaway listened to Colman's heart, checked pulses at his hands and feet and then stripped his drains, which still looked pretty bloody. After Dr. Callaway stripped them several more times, a huge hunk of something bloody came through the right tube.

"Wow," I said. "Do you think that was the clot that was pressing on his lung?"

"It probably was," Dr. Callaway said.

Like magic, Colman's grunting stopped.

"Let's x-ray him and see," I said.

Dr. Callaway laughed. "No, we'll wait until tomorrow. We already have an X-ray from this morning."

"So I have to wait until this time tomorrow to see if that was the clot? I want to know right now."

Everybody laughed, but it was clear I wasn't going to get the instant gratification I wanted.

"How are you doing, Colman?" Dr. Callaway asked.

Colman didn't answer. He was usually on his best behavior when Dr. Callaway was around. Dr. Saldivar, not so much.

"He's been kind of grumpy," I said.

"You don't like your breakfast?" Dr. Callaway said, gesturing to the uneaten plate of food.

"I just want macon," Colman said.

"What does he want?" Dr. Callaway asked me.

"He wants bacon."

Dr. Callaway stuck his head into the hall. "Hey!" he shouted toward the nurses' station. "Can somebody bring Colman some bacon?"

Within minutes, four strips of bacon appeared, and Colman greedily gobbled them down. Then he said, "I want French toast sticks."

"If you want French toast sticks, you're going to have to walk down to the nurses' station and ask nicely," I said.

Colman sighed loudly and said, "Okay."

I helped him out of bed, and he held my hand tight as we walked the twenty feet to the station. The nurses were thrilled to see him out of bed, even though it was obvious from the angry look on his face that I'd forced the issue.

"Is there something we can get for you, Mr. Colman?" one of the nurses said.

"French toast sticks," Colman mumbled.

"You have to say 'please,' " I said.

"Please," Colman said, through clenched teeth.

"Of course. We'll order those up and bring them to you right away."

The short walk back to Colman's room exhausted him. I scooped him up and placed him in bed with the promise of a visit to the playroom when he felt like getting up again.

Then I left him with Mom so I could get a hot shower and a fresh change of clothes at home. When I got back to the hospital, I passed the nurse who'd promised she could get Motrin down Colman without an NG tube.

"I did it," she said, with a big smile.

"Way to go!" I said. "That's awesome."

"Your mama wasn't too happy with me."

"Really? Was it bad?"

"Well, yeah. You know how he is—fighting, spitting and using his whole bag of tricks—and your mama was having kittens the whole time."

I laughed. "That sounds like her."

"You'll be glad to know he's sleeping now."

"I appreciate it."

When I stepped into Colman's room, Mom looked like she'd been through the wringer.

"I heard the nurse got the Motrin down him."

"Oh, Heather," Mom said. "It was awful. I think the NG tube was less traumatic."

"Yeah. The nurse said you were having kittens."

"She said that?" Mom said.

"Yep," I said, giggling.

"I was not."

"I know you were. You gasp over every little thing."

"I just don't want them to hurt him. He's been through so much," Mom said, with tears in her eyes.

"I know. I'm glad he's resting. That's all that matters. Hopefully he's getting better."

CHAPTER 28

Colman and I were sitting in the hospital playroom coloring when Dr. Saldivar came in.

"Hi," he said, quickly stepping behind Colman's chair.

"Hi," I said. I reached down to get Colman's attention, but Dr. Saldivar waved me off.

"Don't tell him I'm here," he said quietly. "I don't want to upset him. I'm here to talk to you."

"Okay," I said, feeling relieved. Colman had been a stinker around the doctors and nurses, but he was particularly brutal to Dr. Saldivar, mocking him and calling him "Dr. Salad Bar." I didn't blame the good doctor for wanting to remain invisible.

"X-ray from this morning looks good. The clot that was pressing on his right lung is gone. It looks like that was what came out of his drain yesterday," he said, smiling.

"I knew it!" I felt my face break into a big smile.

Dr. Saldivar smiled. "How do you feel about taking him home?"

"Did you just say the 'h' word?"

"I know Colman's been pretty depressed here at the hospital. In speaking with Dr. Callaway, we think he might get better more quickly at home where he can sleep in his own bed, play with his toys and hang out with his big brother."

"What about the drains?" I asked.

"He'd have to go home with them," Dr. Saldivar said. "How do you feel about that?"

I tried to reconcile my feelings. On the one hand, I thought, Hell, yeah, we're breaking out of this joint. On the other hand, Holy shit! They're sending us home with *drains*. Rollercoaster of emotions couldn't come close to describing how I felt.

"You think sending him home with Blake drains and a pigtail drain is a good idea?" I said.

Dr. Saldivar laughed. "Yes. I wouldn't mention it if I didn't think you were capable of doing it. We've sent a couple of kids home that way. Obviously, most children, we don't. If you don't feel comfortable, you can stay here with him. I just thought I'd give you the option.

"You have my cell. If you decide to take him home, I'm going to need you to call me every morning with a drainage report, and you'd bring him in every other day for an X-ray so we can see how he's doing. If you have any questions at all, you call me day or night."

"I don't feel comfortable," I admitted. "But if you tell me everything that can go wrong with these blasted drains and what to look for, I'll do it. I don't want any surprises."

"I can do that," he said, nodding.

After Dr. Saldivar gave me the rundown on every complication I could possibly encounter, he said, "I'm going to start the process for discharge, and I'll have someone teach you how to care for the drains."

"Sounds good," I said.

Then he slipped out of the room without Colman seeing him and gave me the thumbs-up sign. I knew the feeling all too well. I wished I could avoid Colman's crankiness sometimes too.

I called Kevin to tell him the plan, but I waited to give Colman the news until I was sure we were being discharged.

After I signed the discharge paperwork, I finally said to Colman, "Guess what? We're going home today."

Colman shrugged and looked miserable. Not exactly the response I'd been hoping for.

Kevin met us at the hospital and helped me load our bags into the car. It wasn't until I'd carried Colman through the hospital doors that I saw a small smile settle over his face.

He was happy to be home. Kevin had bought a playscape and had a handyman put it together while Colman was in the hospital. He was excited, but he couldn't play on it until he was six weeks post-op in order to give his chest time to heal.

I called Dr. Saldivar with a drainage report every morning around the same time. A couple of days after we got home, we went back for an X-ray and Dr. Callaway pulled the pigtail drain, so we were left with the two Blake drains.

The drains made me a little queasy. I had to strip them several times a day, which Colman hated. He screamed like I was killing him. Then I had to empty the bulbs with giant sixty-milliliter syringes and make careful notes for my daily report. Even thinking about those drains all these years later makes me feel like gagging.

We'd been home for about five days when Colman's energy seemed to drop and he started grunting when he breathed. Even though we were scheduled for an X-ray the next day, I called Dr. Saldivar. He told me to bring Colman to the hospital for an X-ray, which showed another large pleural effusion positioned below the Blake drains. We were admitted to the step-down unit.

Dr. Callaway came by to check the X-ray and say hello to Colman.

"I guess holding him upside-down isn't an option," I joked.

"No, that probably wouldn't help," Dr. Callaway said, his voice serious. "I think he needs another pigtail drain. Dr. Saldivar will come by later to arrange the surgery."

"Great."

I called my parents to let them know. When I told my dad my comment about holding Colman upside-down, he said, "God, Heather. Don't screw with the surgeons like that. They deal with stupid people all day long."

"You've got a point there," I said. "But I can't resist sometimes."

Dr. Saldivar, Kevin and I discussed the timing for the surgery. We all felt comfortable waiting until the day shift—or A team—came in the next morning. Not much happens on nights and weekends in hospitals unless it's in the E.R. I mean, it looks like a hospital, it smells like one— you get the idea.

The next morning Colman was back in the PICU for bedside surgery. I signed the consents and stayed in the room while they prepped. Dr. Leon was gently turning a vial of milky white substance back and forth.

"What is that?" I said.

"Propofol. It's sometimes called 'milk of amnesia.' It's a fast-acting anesthetic."

"He's a bear after anesthesia."

"I know he is." Dr. Leon smiled. "He won't be after this. The minute it hits his vein, he'll go to sleep. And the minute we stop the medication he'll wake up. You can stay with us until he goes to sleep. It should only take about twenty minutes. If you stay outside his door, I'll bring you back in right before we wake him up."

Just as she indicated, Colman drifted off within seconds, and I went outside to wait.

The pigtail drained a little over 400 milliliters in an hour. Even though Colman was upset about another pokey, he was breathing easier without so much fluid in his chest.

After another overnight stay, Dr. Saldivar came by during rounds to check on Colman. Everything was going according to plan, so he instructed the nurse to switch out Colman's drainage box for another bulb. Then we were on our way home after another quick trip through what I'd dubbed "Thoracic Park."

The pigtail drain clogged within a few days. Dr. Callaway checked on Colman during one of our visits and administered a clot-busting medication through the drain, and that helped for about a day. Then Dr. Saldivar pulled that drain on one of our many X-ray trips. But the fluid in Colman's Blake drains didn't seem to be letting up much.

"Maybe you're giving him too much to drink," Dr. Saldivar said.

"Maybe," I said. "I hadn't realized that was a possibility. How much is he supposed to be drinking?"

"I don't know. I'm not a pediatrician."

I had to keep from yelling into the phone, You're killing me! What kind of doctor are you?

I took a deep breath and said, "I'm going to call our pediatrician. Do you have a suggestion on how much I should cut Colman's normal intake, whatever that may be?"

"I'd think ten to twenty percent. See what your pediatrician says. We want to keep Colman on the drier side without getting dehydrated."

I called Frank, and he figured Colman's normal liquid intake based on kilograms and reduced it by a few ounces.

Now Colman was thirsty on top of being uncomfortable from the Blake drains, and traumatized when we had to go to the hospital for an X-ray. But he was a much happier kid overall staying home. He played with Liam nonstop, the bulbs at his waistband bobbing like tiny hand grenades.

After two more weeks of consistent draining, I called Dr. Saldivar on a Sunday morning to give him the report. One of the drains had tapered off dramatically, and the other hadn't been putting out much at all. I was confident we were finally winning the war.

Dr. Saldivar sighed and said, "They're clogged. Meet me at the PICU about two o'clock, and I'll pull them. We'll probably have to place another one."

I hoped he was wrong. But over the next few hours, Colman began complaining that the chest tube with little to no output was hurting. I put fresh clothes in the overnight bag I kept in my car and threw in my toothbrush and face wash.

At the PICU we gave Colman a dose of Motrin to take the edge off, and then Dr. Saldivar pulled both drains. One was definitely clogged, as evidenced by the liquid that gushed from the hole in his chest where the drain had been. We grabbed some extra gauze, but Colman's clothes were soaked.

"Sorry about that," Dr. Saldivar said.

"It's okay," I said. "It's not like you soaked them on purpose."

Dr. Saldivar smiled. "Yeah, but I knew the drain was clogged. I should've expected this."

We stood there for a few minutes, replacing the gauze as it became sodden with fluid.

"No wonder he complained about it hurting," I said.

"Better out than in, I always say."

I nodded and tried not to laugh. That sounded like something someone would say to try and justify a fart.

"It's still draining pretty heavily," Dr. Saldivar said. "This is—"

"Impressive?"

"Yeah, I'd say so. Now that it's slowing down, I'd like to cover it loosely with gauze so that it can continue to drain. You can change the dressing at home."

"Okay."

"He's been draining for how long?"

"Three and a half weeks."

"If it goes much longer, we may need to bring him in for a pleurodesis."

"What's that?"

"We'd go in and rough up his lungs so they'd stop leaking into the pleural space."

"Through his chest?"

"No, we'd make a thoracotomy incision on both sides and go through the ribs in his back."

Yuck. "How long would he stay in the hospital?" I said.

"He might be in the PICU for a couple of days and in the hospital for maybe a week, but we're getting ahead of ourselves."

I know this is really dumb and probably shouldn't have mattered, but I didn't want Colman to have two more big scars in addition to the ones all over his chest and front torso. I was on the brink of tears.

On our way out, we ran into our nurse, Shelly, who always took care of Colman after surgery. We chatted for a minute while Colman pulled on my hand and pressed the elevator buttons—both up and down.

"I can't believe he's having such a hard time," she said. "You're giving him the Lasix?"

"Yeah," I said. "Although it's really tough to get medicine down him. Dr. Saldivar mentioned something about a pleurodesis."

"Ugh. Those are pretty painful."

"It sounds like something we don't need."

"Not if you can avoid it."

We said goodbye, and Colman and I got on the elevator.

I thought about Colman's meds. The way he spewed his medication, I couldn't be sure he was getting the entire Lasix dose three times a day. It was probably more like two doses. Time to regroup.

At home I changed Colman out of his wet clothes and replaced his bandage, which was soaked through. Then I set him on my lap for a talk.

"Are you happy to have the drains gone?" I said.

Colman nodded, his big blue eyes serious.

"I know you don't like them, but to keep them out for good, you have to take all your medicine and not spit it out."

"I don't like it."

"I know you don't. It's gross. But if you don't start taking it, you're going to have to go back to the hospital for another surgery and stay there for a whole week."

"I don't wanna go."

"Then you have to take your medicine."

"I don't like medicine!" Colman yelled.

"I know. What's worse, though, the hospital for more surgery and medicine or staying home and a little bit of medicine?"

Colman stared into space and didn't answer.

"Colman?"

"Surgery. I don't want surgery."

"Then you'll take your medicine like a big boy?"

Colman shrugged. Not a definite no, but not a yes either.

"I love you, little man. I don't want you to have to go back to the hospital."

"I love you, too," he said, hugging me tightly around my neck.

When it came time for meds that night, I put them out with a handful of chocolate chips. Colman's eyes grew wide at the sight.

"You take all your medicine like a big boy—no spitting—and you can eat this big pile of chocolate chips."

Colman's face screwed up like he was going to cry. "But, Mama, the medicine is too yucky."

"I know it is. But the chocolate chips are super-duper yummy! So you'll have a little bit of yuck and a lot of yummy. Okay?"

Fat tears rolled down Colman's cheeks, and I could tell he was getting ready to pitch a fit.

"Here's the deal, pickle. You have two choices. This is all up to you. I'm just along for the ride. Medicine, home and chocolate chips," I said, holding up my index finger, "or medicine, hospital and surgery." I held up my other index finger. "You decide."

Colman rolled his eyes. "Chocolate chips," he mumbled.

He took the medicine without spitting—although he did make some gagging noises, for my benefit, I'm sure—and ate the chocolate chips.

If only I'd thought of using an incentive before. The chocolate chip chasers made the medicine much more manageable.

I researched pleurodesis procedures in case we ended up going that route. There were two types. In a chemical pleurodesis they sent a substance, commonly talc, through a chest tube. It didn't sound good at all. In a surgical manual pleurodesis, which sounded like what Dr. Saldivar described, they manually roughed up the lungs so they quit draining. Ouch!

Maybe we'd just keep a chest tube forever. I tried to picture Colman in kindergarten with fluid-filled hand grenades safety-pinned to his waistband.

We returned to the hospital on Tuesday for another checkup and X-ray. In the intervening days, a fellow heart mom called to relay her experience with her daughter's pleurodesis. As I expected, it wasn't pleasant. She said if she had to do it all over again, she wouldn't. Not only was it painful, but it also made her daughter's subsequent X-rays difficult to read.

I'd also been researching how long pleural effusions could go on after a Fontan. Words like "risk of infection" and "increased morbidity" showed up in descriptions of patients who drained a really long time. A fenestration in the Fontan conduit via a heart catheterization could help stop the drainage, but Colman already had a fenestrated Fontan, so that wasn't an option.

Dr. Saldivar met us in the PICU to discuss the X-rays, which looked a little worse now that we didn't have the Blake drains.

"What do you think?" I said.

"We need to have a conversation about stopping this drainage."

"You don't think it will stop on its own?"

"Eventually, yes."

"He can't drain forever, right?"

"It's not likely, but once in a while a kid makes us wonder. It's your choice. We could go on like this, or we could do a pleurodesis and you guys will be done in a week."

"What if it doesn't work?"

"Oh, it will," Dr. Saldivar said. "You don't have to decide today, but we're getting to that point. On Thursday we'll x-ray him again. I'm thinking a heart cath on Friday and surgery on Monday."

Ugh.

I brought Colman back on Thursday, and Dr. Saldivar came in to visit.

"Does it look better?" I said.

"No," Dr. Saldivar said.

"Seriously? Because he seems like he's had more energy and I think his color is better."

"It doesn't necessarily look worse either."

"That's good, right?"

"Dr. Callaway and I examined the X-rays together. He wants to give you a chance to work your magic. His words were, 'Give her the weekend. That mama knows how to make that boy well.'"

"But you don't?"

"I think you're prolonging the inevitable."

"You're probably right," I said. "Thank you for your honesty, but I want to take him home."

"Okay," he said. "We'll see you Monday morning." He started out of the room and then stuck his head back in. "Make sure you bring an overnight bag though, because you're going to be staying."

"Gotcha." I nodded.

Colman and I got to the hospital early Monday and went straight to X-ray. The tech was getting Colman ready to take his X-ray when I heard Dr. Callaway outside.

I opened the door. "Hey, this is a surprise," I said. "What are you doing here?"

"I've been looking for you guys," Dr. Callaway said. "I'm curious to see this X-ray, and I didn't want to wait."

The X-ray tech got Colman situated. Then he ushered Dr. Callaway and me behind the wall where we'd be safe from the radiation and told Colman he was ready to take the picture.

"Smile," I said.

Colman smirked as the X-ray was taken.

The tech laughed. "You always do that," he said. "You know he's going to kill you when he finds out you've been messing with him all this time."

"I get my entertainment where I can," I said.

The tech uploaded the X-rays, and Dr. Callaway looked at them. So did I, but I didn't feel confident about what I was seeing, even though I'd probably seen a hundred. Then Dr. Callaway brought up the X-rays from two days prior to compare. He was smiling.

"It's better. He still has a little bit of effusion, as you can see," he said, pointing out some gray areas, "but it's definitely better. Good job, mama!"

"No pleurodesis then?"

"Nope. I need you to go by the clinic and see Dr. Saldivar, but we're going to release you guys."

"Great! We'll head over there now."

"See you later," he said. "Bye, Colman."

"Bye," Colman said with a shy wave.

Darn, I thought. I should've gotten a picture of him with Colman. But he was already out of sight.

At the clinic Colman had an EKG and a blood pressure and pulse ox check. Then Dr. Saldivar listened to Colman's heart and lungs and checked the pulses in his neck, hands, groin and feet.

"I saw his X-ray. It definitely looks better."

"Yeah," I said. "That's great, isn't it?"

He nodded kindly and opened the door to leave. "It looks like you got your miracle."

"Is that what you'd call it?" I asked, a little disturbed by his choice of words.

He shrugged and left. Odd.

I couldn't put my finger on why that statement bothered me. I walked Colman to the car. Then it hit me. The way he said it made it seem like we only got one miracle. And to be honest, that seemed totally unfair. What if we needed a miracle in the future, but we'd already used it up?

I didn't want to start with the "not fair" thoughts. The hole I'd have to pull myself out of was too damn big.

Dr. Roberts gave the okay for Colman to start preschool in July. Colman looked great, sounded great and was full of energy. If you didn't know his story, you'd never guess he had half a heart or that he'd undergone three open-heart surgeries in three short years. The only outward signs were his chest scar, which was fading into a thin white line, and the numerous smaller scars on his torso from the chest tubes.

After spending almost ten weeks with Colman attached at my hip, I was looking forward to going back to work full-time. When I dropped Colman off at preschool on August 1, approximately six weeks after we'd been released from the hospital, I had to stifle the urge to tag the teacher and yell, "You're it!"

All of the time at home had left me feeling a little unhinged.

To make matters worse, the week Colman started preschool Kevin fell ill with a stomach virus. He felt awful the way only men can feel. When I picked up Liam and Colman from school, I stopped by the Central Market H-E-B on Broadway to get Gatorade and chicken noodle soup.

In the checkout line Colman decided to lie down on the floor.

"Get up," I said.

"No," Colman said, giving me his why-don't-you-make-me smile.

"You need to get up. Do you want to go back to the hospital and see Dr. Salad Bar?" I said, using Colman's nickname. "Because that's what's going to happen if you get really sick."

"Nope. I'm not going to the hospital," he said, shaking his head and wallowing on the floor, maximizing his germ exposure—and raising my blood pressure.

"I think you are if you don't get up."

Colman turned onto his stomach and dragged his tongue along the floor. The collective intake of air by the people in line behind us was large enough to deplete the supermarket's oxygen supply.

Liam's eyes were as round as saucers.

"What do you think about that, Mommy?" Colman asked, his blue eyes positively dancing with mischief.

You little shit.

I wanted to snatch him baldheaded. Or shake him until his little white baby teeth rattled clear out of his skull. I wanted to yell, Are you out of your cotton-picking mind?

But I didn't. With as much calm as I could muster, I said, "I don't know what to think about that, Colman."

Colman's face fell when he didn't get the reaction he was looking for, and he quickly stood.

I paid for our items, and we walked to the car. Colman grabbed my hand as we made our way across the parking lot, which was unusual. At that age he would often yell, "I do it myself!" as I chased him down.

He looked perplexed. "I love you, Mommy," he said.

"I love you, too, Colman."

I stifled a smile as I buckled him into his car seat. That's a win for me, I thought. If I keep at it, I might figure out what makes this little guy tick.

I tried not to think about the disgusting germs he could've picked up licking a ten-inch section of grocery store floor. My mind wandered there anyway.

Chewed-up bubblegum, spit and fresh-cut grass laced with fertilizer. Most certainly dog and cat shit. The possibilities were endless.

To be completely honest, I wasn't so sure I'd outlive Colman anymore. He'd chipped away large chunks of my life expectancy with one crazy stunt after another, and I didn't see that changing anytime soon.

All I could do was make the most of everything and enjoy this life while it lasts. One heartbeat at a time.

AUTHOR BIOGRAPHY

Heather Maloy works full-time as a court reporter in district court and writes sporadically on her blog, Crazy Heart Mama. She lives in San Antonio, Texas with her husband, three boys, and their dog Buster, who doesn't seem to mind that none of his people are dog people.

Heather can be found online at crazyheartmama.com.

Acknowledgements

First, I'd like to thank my friends and family who made the you-ought-to-write-a-book suggestion—all seven in total—for not smacking me when I answered with a sarcastic, "About what?"

You guys planted the seed that grew into what has become *I Hate Piñatas.*

I'd also like to thank my good friend, Janene Smith, for encouraging me when I decided to tackle the daunting task of writing this book. Your feedback, instruction and wicked editing skills gave me the confidence I needed to finish this project and turn it over to a professional editor.

I'd like to thank my editor, Sarah Nawrocki, who cut tens of thousands of words and never changed the story or my voice, which technically makes you a magician. I hope we meet in person one day since we live only a few blocks apart.

I'd like to thank all my betas—Karen, Laura, Fred, Sarah, Mac, Mary Beth, Ramona and John—for the valuable feedback. You all caught something completely different.

I'd also like to thank the talented Brook Rosser for my cover art. I wasn't sure what I wanted when we first spoke, but you surpassed all my expectations. I love it.

To Mom, Dad, Holly and Hunter, thank you for making me laugh, even when things seemed bleak. I appreciate all of your support.

To my boys, Liam, Colman and Rowan, I love you more than words can say. You boys are my heart.

A very special thank you to Colman's cardiothoracic surgeons, cardiologists, intensivists, nurses and family pediatrician for always taking the time to answer my many questions and for being honest with me when you knew I wouldn't like your answers. Thank you for simply saying, "I don't know" when there were no answers. It took a long while to wrap my head around this diagnosis and the medical management involved. The kindnesses you've shown us—everything from warming your stethoscopes before placing them on my child to asking me if I was okay—did not go unnoticed. Thank you for loving my little boy and giving me the information and skills I needed in order to take good care of him. You guys touched my heart. (Great. Now, I'm crying.)

Finally, I'd like to thank Kevin for helping me with these crazy kids day in and day out. You're a great husband, father, provider and spider-killer extraordinaire! Thank you for supporting me in telling this story and finding beauty in the imperfect. I love you dearly.